Sport and Gender Identities

This important new book brings together gender studies and sexuality studies to provide original and critical insights into processes of identity formation in a wide range of sport-related contexts. The authors draw on contemporary debates concerning gender and identity, from a range of disciplines including sociology, social and cultural geography, media studies and management studies, to address key issues in masculinity, femininity and sexuality:

- **Part I: Representing masculinities in sport** analyses media representations of men's sports, exploring the variety and complexity of concepts of masculinity.
- **Part II: Transgressing femininities in sport** makes use of case studies to examine the experiences of women in male-dominated sporting arenas.
- **Part III: Performing sexualities in sport** analyses the role of queer theory in sport studies, explores experiences of and responses to homophobia in sport, and examines the significance of the Gay Games.

This book will be of particular interest to students and academics working in sport studies, leisure studies, gender studies, queer and sexuality studies, social and cultural geography, and sociology.

Cara Carmichael Aitchison is Professor in Human Geography at the University of West of England, Bristol, where she specialises in social, cultural and spatial research into leisure, sport and tourism.

D1218237

Sport and Gender Identities

Masculinities, femininities and sexualities

Edited by
Cara Carmichael Aitchison

Routledge
Taylor & Francis Group

LONDON AND NEW YORK

First published 2007
by Routledge
2 Park Square, Milton Park, Abingdon, Oxon OX14 4RN

Simultaneously published in the USA and Canada
by Routledge
270 Madison Ave, New York, NY 10016

Routledge is an imprint of the Taylor & Francis Group, an informa business

© 2007 Selection and editorial matter, Cara Carmichael Aitchison;
individual chapters, the contributors

Typeset in Goudy by
HWA Text and Data Management, Tunbridge Wells

British Library Cataloguing in Publication Data
A catalogue record for this book is available from the British Library

Library of Congress Cataloging-in-Publication Data
Sport and gender identities : masculinities, femininities and sexualities /
edited by Cara Carmichael Aitchison.
     p.   cm.
Includes bibliographical references and index.
1. Gay and sports. 2. Homophobia in sports. 3. Masculinity in sports.
4. Feminism and sports. I. Aitchison, Cara Carmichael, 1965–
GV708.8.S657 2006
796.086'64–dc22   2006021529

ISBN10: 0–415–25956–8 (hbk)
ISBN10: 0–415–25957–6 (pbk)
ISBN10: 0–203–64664–9 (ebk)

ISBN13: 978–0–415–25956–9 (hbk)
ISBN13: 978–0–415–25957–6 (pbk)
ISBN13: 978–0–203–64664–9 (ebk)

Contents

Contributors

Cara Carmichael Aitchison is Professor in Human Geography and Director of the Centre for Leisure, Tourism and Society at the University of the West of England. Cara's teaching and research focus on the integration of social, cultural and spatial theories and policies related to leisure, sport and tourism with a particular emphasis on issues of identity, inclusion and social justice. Her recent publications include *Gender and Leisure: Social and Cultural Perspective* (Routledge, 2003), *Leisure, Space and Visual Culture*, co-edited with Helen Pussard (LSA, 2004), *Geographies of Muslim Identities: Diaspora, Gender and Belonging*, co-edited with Peter Hopkins and Mei-Po Kwan (Ashgate, 2006) and 'Feminist and gender research in sport and leisure management: understanding the social–cultural nexus of gender–power relations' in the *Journal of Sport Management* (2005, 199(4): 222–41). Cara is an appointed member of the 2008 UK Research Assessment Exercise (RAE) sub-panel for Sport-Related Studies, Chair of the Women and Gender Commission of World Leisure (2002–) and was Chair of the UK Leisure Studies Association from 2001–4.

Celia Brackenridge undertook teacher training and degree study at Cambridge and Leeds Universities, and subsequently taught physical education in a Hampshire secondary school. She then moved into higher education for 28 years, first at Sheffield Hallam University and then at the University of Gloucestershire. She ran her own research-based consultancy company for four years before returning to higher education at Brunel University in 2005 as Chair in Sport Sciences (Youth Sport). She is a BASES-accredited interdisciplinary sport science researcher. Her books include: *Spoilsports: Understanding and Preventing Sexual Exploitation in Sport* (Routledge, 2001) and *Sexual Harassment and Abuse in Sport: International and Policy Perspectives* (Whiting and Birch, 2002).

Brendan Gough gained a PhD in psychology from the Queen's University, Belfast (1993) before working as a lecturer at Sheffield Hallam University (1994–2000). He is now a senior lecturer at the Institute of Psychological Sciences, University of Leeds, where he has worked for six years. He is also Deputy Director of the Centre for Interdisciplinary Gender Studies at Leeds. His research interests are in gender issues, especially relating to men and masculinities. He has published in a range of journals on topics such as men's health, sexism and homophobia, and gender and alcohol. He has co-written two books: *Critical Social Psychology: An Introduction* (with Majella McFadden, Palgrave, 2001) and *Doing Reflexivity: Critical Illustrations for Health and Social Science* (co-edited with Linda Finlay, Blackwell, 2003). Brendan is co-founder and co-editor of the journal *Qualitative Research in Psychology*.

Corey W. Johnson is an assistant professor in the Department of Counselling and Human Development Services at the University of Georgia where he uses qualitative research to focus attention on underserved populations in the cultural contexts of leisure, providing important insight into the discriminatory practices and experiences that marginalized people often encounter in mainstream leisure settings. He also uses advocacy, activism, civic-engagement, service-learning and community partnerships to create unique learning opportunities for individuals and institutions.

Amanda Jones is a senior lecturer in the School of Physical Education and Sport Sciences at the University of Bedfordshire, UK. She obtained her PhD from De Montfort University in 2004 for research titled *From Subcultures to Social Worlds: Women in Sport and Women in Triathlon*.

Eileen Kennedy is a senior lecturer in the School of Human and Life Sciences at Roehampton University, where she is Director of the Centre for Scientific and Cultural Research in Sport. Her research has explored the issues of televised sport and the representation of sports celebrities, paying particular attention to the intersections of gender, class, race and national identity in media sport.

Beth Kivel is an associate professor and Chair of the Department of Recreation and Leisure Studies at California State University, Sacramento. Prior to working in California, she was a faculty member at the University of North Carolina at Chapel Hill from 1998–2003. In 2001–2, she was a Leverhulme Research Fellow at Leeds Metropolitan University, England and also taught with the WICE programme in Wageningen, the Netherlands. She is the co-founder and former Director of the Lavender Youth Recreation and Information Centre (LYRIC) in San Francisco which provides social and recreational opportunities to lesbian/gay/bisexual/transgender and questioning youth.

Karen Llewellyn taught physical education for ten years in secondary schools in Hertfordshire and Yorkshire following initial teacher training and degree study at Cambridge and Leeds Universities. She then worked as a marketing manager in sports publishing, as an education development officer for Sports Coach UK and as a lecturer in both further and higher education. Currently, she is a Principal Lecturer at York St John University and Head of Enquiry Based Learning.

Tiffany Muller is a graduate student and teaching assistant in the Department of Geography at the University of Minnesota where she has undertaken doctoral research on the contested spaces of women's basketball drawing on contemporary social, cultural and feminist geographical analyses.

Ian Rivers is Professor and Head of Psychology at Queen Margaret University College, Edinburgh. He is a chartered health psychologist and is the author of over 80 book chapters and journal articles on homophobia and its long-term correlates. In 2001, he received the British Psychological Society's Award for Promoting Equality of Opportunity in the United Kingdom through his work as a researcher and psychologist. Ian currently serves on a number of charitable boards and advisory panels addressing equality and diversity issues for Scotland.

Kate Russell is a senior lecturer in psychology at the University of Coventry. Her PhD, completed in 2002, investigated the development of body satisfaction and identity among women who play rugby, cricket and netball and the role context plays in determining this. She was recently awarded a Fellowship of Social Sciences from the NZ–UK Link Foundation (2003), to undertake research in New Zealand collecting similar data. Her more recent research has focussed on the development of perceptions of physical attractiveness among young children, and the role physical education takes in the development of positive and negative body images. Kate is also an accredited sport and exercise scientist and a chartered psychologist within the British Psychological Society's Division of Sport and Exercise Psychology.

Sally Shaw is a lecturer in the School of Physical Education at the University of Otago, having previously worked in the University of Waikato, and Brock University, Ontario. Sally's research explores gender relations in sport organizations, employing a theoretical perspective that is informed by an intersection of critical management studies and postmodernism. She has conducted research with National Governing Bodies of sport in the United Kingdom and Regional Sports Trusts in New Zealand. In her research, she examines how and why gender is manifested as a power relationship. Sally's research also addresses power relations in other organizational settings such as within sponsorship agreements or between funders and funding recipients in non-profit organizations.

Caroline Symons is a lecturer in the Division of Sport Management and Policy at Victoria University, Melbourne. Her research focuses on gender and diversity in sport, community sport management and participation and social policy in sport. She completed her doctoral thesis titled *Gay Games: The Play of Sexuality Sport and Community*, in 2004 at Victoria University.

Garry Whannel is Professor of Media Cultures at the University of Bedford-shire. Between 1988–99 he was at Roehampton Institute London, where he was a founding Co-Director of the Centre for Sport Development Research. His most recent published work includes *Media Sport Stars, Masculinities and*

Moralities (Routledge, 2001) and (with John Horne and Alan Tomlinson) *Understanding Sport* (E & FN Spon, 1999). Previous books include *Fields in Vision: Television Sport and Cultural Transformation* (Routledge, 1992) and *Blowing the Whistle* (Pluto, 1983). His current research interests include celebrity culture and the vortextuality process, and the growth of commercial sponsorship.

Chapter 1

Gender, sport and identity
Introducing discourses of masculinities, femininities and sexualities

Cara Carmichael Aitchison

Introducing social and cultural critiques of gender, sport and identity

This book explores and explains the complex ways in which both gender and sexuality, as significant aspects of individual identities, identity politics and identity relations, inform and are informed by sport. This dialectic relationship, in which identities are constantly shaped and reshaped, made and remade, presented and represented, engages with sport as a dynamic social and cultural force. The mutable nature of sport, of identity and of the relationship between the two offers possibilities for resistance, contestation and transgression of hegemonic gender and sexual power relations. In this respect, identities that might be marginal in previous sporting times or in contemporary non-sporting spaces might find a place of sanctuary within sport through avenues such as women's football or the Gay Games, for example. But sport is also an ambiguous site of visible and marked embodied identities where the discourses of power that are dominant within wider society can often be exaggerated to construct sporting arenas as veritable prisons for those marginalised as 'Other' in everyday life. Thus sport can be criticised as being the last great bastion of homophobia, racism and nationalism within contemporary western society.

The chapters collected here seek to explore and explain this contradictory nature of sport in relation to the perennially contested, and frequently over-lapping, categories of masculinities, femininities and sexualities. The plurality attached to these terms denotes the sense in which many of the chapters draw on contemporary post-structural critiques to examine sport and identity as mutually informing sites in which dominant power relations are constantly 'in process' and subject to changing patterns of construction, legitimation, reproduction and reworking (Aitchison 2000, 2003, 2005). Indeed, it is this emphasis on 'reworking' that is highlighted in many of the chapters. The contingent nature of identities, as played out in and through sport, is revealed through the mobility in discourses and practices of dominant, residual and emergent cultures within and in relation to sport. Each chapter within the book demonstrates how such discourses and practices serve to inform and, in turn, become informed by the identity relations of sport, in particular sporting arenas and/or in relation to specific identity formations.

The chapters are informed by a range of disciplines and subject fields. Sociology and, more specifically, the maturing sub-discipline of the sociology of sport, undoubtedly forms the major disciplinary underpinning to the text with anthropology, geography and psychology supplementing and complementing social analyses. As such, many of the chapters seek to develop inter-disciplinary analyses of the inter-connected nature of the social, cultural, spatial and individual in forming identities within and in relation to sport. These inter-disciplinary analyses draw on subject fields including gender studies, sexuality studies, cultural studies, media studies, leisure studies, policy studies and management studies to develop comprehensive social and cultural critiques of sport.

Masculinities, femininities and sexualities: structure and outline of the book

The three parts of the book each focus primarily on one aspect of identity formation in sport. Part I, *Representing Masculinities in Sport*, opens this discussion with the deliberate initial focus on masculinities. Here, the two chapters demonstrate the unstable nature of masculinity and the complex ways in which different forms of masculinity co-exist, compete and control one another at different times, in dissimilar spaces and in diverse ways. In Chapter 2, *Mediating masculinities: the production of media representations in sport*, Garry Whannel reveals how masculinity 'has never been especially stable or fixed and has always been subject to unease and internal tensions. Its boundaries have always been policed, and its parameters re-inscribed'. Illustrating his discussion with reference to a wide range of media forms and examples from football (soccer), Whannel discusses the extent to which the representation of masculinity in sport reveals 'a crisis in male power' or 'a crisis in the cultural modes through which masculinity presents itself'. What Whannel does is to render visible those aspects of identity which, until relatively recently, were either invisible within sport studies or presumed to be neutral. In Chapter 3, *Watching the game: theorising masculinities in the context of mediated tennis*, Eileen Kennedy demonstrates how identities related to masculinity not only change over time and space but are represented differently in relation to class, race and nation. Both chapters in this first part, whilst addressing issues of masculinities, demonstrate that masculinity cannot be discussed other than in relation to femininity as each is a relational, if not dualistic, concept defined by its other.

Part II, *Transgressing Femininities in Sport*, then seeks to explore femininities in relation to masculinities through empirically-informed case studies that explore gender and sexuality in women's basketball and triathlon – two sports heavily dominated by men. In Chapter 4, *The contested terrain of the Women's National Basketball Association arena*, Tiffany Muller shifts our disciplinary gaze from sociology, cultural studies and media studies to that of social and cultural geography. Informed by analyses that interweave the social and cultural with the spatial, Muller explores the contested relations of both gender and sexuality in the spaces of women's basketball. In Chapter 5, *Triathlon as a space for women's technologies of the self*, Amanda Jones and Cara Aitchison demonstrate how sport can be experienced as both a dominating force and an empowering experience. Through extensive empirical research of women in triathlon, Jones has found that sport can be both a 'technology of power' and a 'technology of the self'; a concept coined by Foucault (1988) to describe the effect of practices that individuals perform in order to transform their own bodies as a means of transcending technologies of power. These *technologies of the self* embody resistance, transgression and empowerment on the part of the individual, unlike *technologies of power* which signify disempowerment on the part of the individual as a result of oppressive regimes of power effected through dominant discourses. In Chapter 6, *Gender in sport management: a contemporary picture and alternative futures*, Sally Shaw moves our focus from power to praxis as she examines the representation of women in sport management and the meaning of gender equity in relational rather than distributive terms.

Part III, *Performing Sexualities in Sport*, explores the complex ways in which hegemonic masculinities and femininities are intertwined with constructions and contestations of sexuality in sport. This part starts with Chapter 7, *Gender, sexuality and queer theory in sport*, in which Corey W. Johnson and Beth Kivel provide an exploration and explication of theory that has informed recent understandings of gender, sexuality and 'Queer' in relation to sport and leisure. This theoretical underpinning is then developed in Chapter 8 where Kate Russell, in a chapter titled *'Queers, even in netball?' Interpretations of the lesbian label among sportswomen*, examines the ways in which sportswomen are constructed as lesbians and how this labelling is experienced within the specific sports of rugby, cricket and netball. Chapter 9, *Driving down participation: homophobic bullying as a deterrent to doing sport*, by Celia Brackenridge, Ian Rivers, Brendan Gough and Karen Llewellyn, discusses the evidence of homophobia in sport and explores the impact of such power relations on sport participation. Finally, in Chapter 10, *Challenging homophobia and heterosexism in sport: the promise of the Gay Games*, Caroline Symons examines responses to homophobia in sport, the transgressive action of forming the Gay Games, and questions whether such strategies can challenge the conventional hegemonic gender order to allow for alternative ways of experiencing gender, sexuality and sport. The conclusions offered by Symons might also serve as conclusions to the book in that she argues that whilst the Gay Games have provided an alternative sporting space they might simultaneously have created a 'ghettoised space' that makes further barriers between essentialised identity categories all the more real. Thus, the danger is that practices and processes that serve to label and thus essentialise identity categories in relation to sexuality are as likely to result in *marking* a difference as they are in *making* a difference.

In collecting these chapters together the aim is therefore not just to problematise our conceptual thinking relating to gender, sexuality and sport but also to question our policies, practices, rights and responsibilities in relation to developing a more inclusive sport studies within the academy and a more equitable sport management in practice.

References

Aitchison, C.C. (2000) 'Women in leisure services: managing the social–cultural nexus of gender equity', *Managing Leisure*, 5, 4: 181–91.

Aitchison, C.C. (2003) *Gender and Leisure: Social and Cultural Perspectives*, London: Routledge.

Aitchison, C.C. (2005) 'Feminist and gender research in sport and leisure management: understanding the social–cultural nexus of gender–power relations', *Journal of Sport Management*, 19, 4: 222–41.

Foucault, M. (1988) 'Technologies of the self', in L.H. Martin, H. Gutman and P.H. Hutton (eds), *Technologies of the Self: A Seminar with Michel Foucault*, Amherst, MA: University of Massachusetts Press.

Part I

Representing masculinities in sport

Chapter 2

Mediating masculinities

The production of media representations in sport[1]

Garry Whannel

Introduction

In recent years, masculinity has become an intensely researched topic that, in various books, has been discovered, theorised, deconstructed, dislocated, unwrapped, unmasked, and placed in perspective. There is, of course, no single essential trans-historical and trans-cultural masculinity. Investigation of such 'moments' as the Roman circus (Wiedemann 1992; Crowther 1996), the chivalric conventions of the sixteenth century (Brailsford 1969), gentlemanly behaviour in the eighteenth century (Cohen 1996), nineteenth-century muscular Christianity (Mangan 1981) or the Empire adventurers of the late nineteenth century (Dawson 1994), show that masculinity is always shaped in ways that have a social and historical specificity. In analysing these processes, it is therefore necessary to consider discontinuities as well as continuities (Roper and Tosh 1991).

Masculinity cannot be understood separately from its relation to femininity. One dynamic in the post-war growth of feminism was women's perceived need to escape from definition by masculinity and patriarchy.[2] Although 'getting men to change' was a significant feminist goal, many of these texts were addressed primarily to and through the experience of women, and to women's need to act to change their own lives.[3] The impact and influence of feminism, with its emphasis on the socially constructed nature of gender difference, and its insistence that 'the personal is political', constituted a challenge both to the naturalisation of gender roles in mainstream male scholarship and to its characteristic compartmentalisation that served to marginalise both 'women' and the 'domestic' sphere.[4]

Although sexual politics became more prominent in both the public and the academic sphere, men and masculinity did not undergo extensive analysis until the 1980s. Coward drew attention to the continuing invisibility of men's sexuality as 'the true dark continent of this society' and commented that 'controlling the look, men have left themselves out of the picture because a body defined is a body controlled' (Coward 1984: 228–9). The emergence of a 'men's studies' was attacked by many feminists and by some men, for 'me-too-ism', self-indulgence and lack of engagement with feminism or gay politics.[5] Chapman and Rutherford (1988: 11) acknowledged that 'masculinity remains the great unsaid … the cause but still not the site of struggle', and commented on the ways in which 'feminism has pushed men into a defensive huddle' (Chapman and Rutherford 1988: 25). Just as the castle of the self is defended against incursion (Jones 1993), so the fortress of masculinity has been defended, until recently, against the fierce gaze of analysis and deconstruction. In the developing field of sport sociology, masculinity was, occasionally, marked as a concern, but usually, only as a minor one.[6] However, by the second half of the 1980s, sporting masculinities were the focus of greater attention.[7]

The impact of the Thatcher era in the United Kingdom spawned a less optimistic analysis of the possibility of socialist-feminist transformation (Butler and Scott 1992; Rowbotham 1989). Indeed a reaction against feminism could be charted and a new revisionist post-feminist feminism was being elaborated (Falaudi 1991; Walter 1998). Indeed, Coward argued that 'nothing would improve the lot of women unless men themselves changed' (Coward 1992: 6–7). The backlash against feminism, the revisions of it, and the political pessimism, all suggest a form of masculinity, structured in dominance and resistant to change. Yet there is a difference between resistance to change and immunity from it, and examination of the tensions within masculinity can be revealing. This chapter draws on a range of popular media forms including films, novels and newspapers to illustrate the production, disruption, policing and hybridity of dominant and emergent masculinities in sport.

Machines for producing masculinity

The social practices of schooling, the rituals of same-sex peer groups, and the representations of the media all contribute to the ceaseless reconstruction of masculinities; in a sense they are machines for producing masculinity. One of the founding texts of muscular Christianity, *Tom Brown's Schooldays*, makes explicit a link between masculinity and morality. Reduced on his first day to a 'motionless body', Tom is, nonetheless, transformed by the end of the tale into an active and rounded person. Schoolboy fiction is often structured around narratives in which pupils arrive as passive, acted-upon bodies and, through a series of punishing rituals, tests of character and moral challenges, become acting moral subjects; boys are turned into men through the process of schooling. Such narrative structures offer a transformation through which manliness is produced. Consequently, the representations of such processes have much to tell us about dominant notions of manliness and masculinity, their formation in the mid-nineteenth century, and their continued discursive power in the present (Whannel 1999).

By the end of the nineteenth century this new discursive formation, in which public school athleticism, the moral structure of team games, social Darwinism and English Philistinism are linked together, was well established. The split between the sporting philistine and the non-sporting aesthete was highlighted clearly by the contrast between sporting muscularity and the mannered aestheticism of *fin de siècle* figures like Wilde and Beardsley. Noel Coward described the characters of the Greyfriars School stories as 'awfully manly, decent fellows … no suggestion of sex, even in its lighter forms, ever sullied their conversation. Considering their ages, their healthy-mindedness was almost frightening' (quoted in Turner 1976: 232).

The distinction between sporting philistine and non-sporting aesthete continued to be a marked and distinctive feature of English bourgeois culture through the inter-war period, and into the era of the welfare state. In the 1970s, Viv Stanshall of the Bonzo Dog Doo Dah Band alluded to the centrality of sport in this ethos of schooling, and the marginalising of those who rejected it, conjuring up the 'odd boy reading Mallarmé' whilst around him sport rages:

> Sport, sport masculine sport
> equips a young man for society
> Yes sport turns out a jolly good sort,
> its an odd boy who doesn't like sport.

With the rise of television sport, the tabloid press and celebrity culture, major sport stars became the site of intersecting discourses of morality and masculinity, in which they were supposed to be role models and set good examples. Those who failed came in for public castigation in that modern equivalent of the village stocks, the tabloid press (Whannel 1995, 2001a). The careers of sport stars, reconstructed in biography and autobiography, provided narratives of masculinity in which obstacles are overcome, victories won, and enemies vanquished (Whannel 1998).

The growth of fitness chic and body culture during the 1980s, and its connection to the new competitive individualism and philistinism of Thatcherism, reconstructed the discursive formation of muscular Christianity. The concept of sport as a form of character training remains an entrenched one. In the Sports Council (1995) policy document on sport, *Raising the Game*, the then Prime Minister, John Major, referred to sport as a binding force between generations and across borders, and linked it specifically to moral education, declaring that 'Competitive sport teaches valuable lessons which last for life' (Sports Council 1995: 2). The muscular Christianity of Hughes and Kingsley, over one hundred years on, is inscribed into government doctrine in sentiments they would applaud, and in a form of expression that John Major devised but that another Christian, Tony Blair, was happy to endorse: 'If sport is to play a proper role in building a healthy society in general and in the personal, moral and physical development of young people in particular, we must ensure that young people are introduced to it early in life' (Sports Council 1995: 40). Faith, however groundless it may be, is still placed in the ability of team sport to transform the young into acting moral subjects, in the same manner as that celebrated in the narrative structure of *Tom Brown's Schooldays*.

Masculinities: dominant, residual and emergent

Connell (1995: 71) has argued that masculinity cannot be understood outside of its relation to femininity. It is a relational construct, incomprehensible apart from the totality of gender relations (Roper and Tosh 1991: 2). Recent figures such as the 'new man', 'new lad', and 'soft lad', cannot be fully understood apart from their location in a pattern of gender and sexual relations. In analyses in the 1990s there was a growing emphasis on masculinities and on the discontinuities, contradictions and tensions within masculinity.[8] As Connell argues, dominant masculinities also oppress some other masculinities, and some masculinities consequently occupy a subordinate position in relation to masculinity as a whole. Hegemonic masculinity oppresses women, but at any given historical moment there are competing masculinities; some hegemonic, some marginalised and some stigmatised (Connell 1995). Those left marginalised, those who were oppositional, those who sought alternatives, have been relatively voiceless within dominant masculine culture. Sabo and Jansen (1992), for example, draw attention to the socially structured silences that marginalise the physically unfit, those identifying as gay or lesbian, disabled people, and the elderly.

Sport has the appearance of being that which unites men; yet it is also a practice that divides men. Sedgewick (1985) has compared the greater sense of communality amongst women through sisterhood to the 'opposition between the homosocial and the homosexual amongst men'. Sporting practices marginalise and stigmatise gayness and Pronger (1990: 39), in his discussion of sport and homosexuality, comments that despite the growth of a gay gym culture, sport continues to be a place of estrangement for many homosexual men.

Black men, too, are in a particular position in relation to the white heterosexual male sporting culture. The cultural construction of 'blackness' in the European context has roots, according to Paul Hoch, in story-telling and the myth of the 'white hero' who achieves his manhood by winning victory over the 'dark beast' (Hoch 1979: 10). In sport, this struggle is dramatised in diverse forms, such as the search of the boxing establishment, in the early twentieth century, for a 'great white hope': a white man who could win the world heavyweight title. The common mobilisation of stereotypical representations of Latin footballers and African athletes draws on a similar opposition between white (European) and dark (Latin/African) modes of sporting behaviour. English manager Alf Ramsey's castigation of the Argentinians as 'animals' was still being recalled as recently as the England–Argentina match in the 1998 World Cup.

Black prowess in sport has also been the focus of a culture of celebration, validation and approval, but it largely takes place within the frame of reference that Cashmore (1982) referred to as 'the myth of natural ability'; the notion that black sporting prowess is rooted in racial biological difference. In representations of sport, and especially football, non-European worlds are interpreted through contrasts between black tactical naivety and European sophistication, and by the linking of genius and flair to the myth of 'natural' ability. Carrington (1998), for example, has analysed such operation of marginalisation and incorporation in images of black male athletes.

The boundaries of masculinity are always the subject of re-drawing, policing, and contestation. Other versions of manliness also emerged in part as opposition to the conformity of team games. The notion of 'rugged individual self-reliance' can be detected in a lineage that runs through Kipling, Baden Powell, T.E. Lawrence, Kurt Hahn, Edmund Hilary and the Duke of Edinburgh's Award Scheme. If this rugged individualism constituted an alternative masculinity to that of the team game ethos, both grew out of muscular Christianity, which dealt with the feminine by processes of exclusion and marginalisation. A more distinctive alternative in the form of the non-sporting aestheticism epitomised by the bohemian culture of Beardsley and Wilde, was not only defined in opposition to dominant sporting masculinity, but also was typically stigmatised by it as effete and foppish.

If there is not one essential masculinity but, rather, a dominant masculinity and a range of subordinate masculinities, and if the pattern of social relations and gender relations is subject to historical shifts and transformations, then at any one time there are, in Raymond Williams' (1977) use of the terms, residual and emergent cultures of masculinity. That is to say, the process of transformation necessarily requires that some forms of masculinity, such as devout piety, Victorian 'heavy' patriarchs or gentlemanly courtesy, are of declining significance, whilst others, such as new laddism are of emergent importance.

Dominant masculinity is experienced by many men as a strait-jacket; a set of conventions of behaviour, style, ritual and practice that limit and confine, and are subject to surveillance, informal policing and regulation. The film *North Dallas Forty*, for example, counterposes a brutalised world of team sport, in which the men are competitive and acquisitive, the women are objectified, and the male bodies exploited and abused in the training and medication process; the lead character Phil Elliott, who loves the game, becomes distanced from its barbaric rituals (Whannel 1993).

Residual elements of masculinity such as courtesy, modesty, and dignity can sometimes be presented as archaic, whilst in other contexts can be mobilised in the construction of discourses that utilise an imagined past to criticise a despised present day. For example, newspaper obituaries of Stanley Matthews were constructed within a frame of reference that contrasted an idealised past personified by Matthews in which footballers were dedicated, modest and well-behaved, with a present characterised by pampered and overpaid superstars. This frame of reference is part of a discourse in which morality and masculinity are perceived to be in crisis. The image of the sport star has become a significant point of condensation for social unease in which tensions about moral authority and manliness are addressed (Whannel 2002a).

'The past' was a time when footballers had a maximum wage of £20 a week, wore baggy shorts and were watched by men in cloth caps. Football was a hard but fair physical contest, a working-class sport. England then was 'a country in which modesty was respected or worshipped almost as much as popular virtuosity'

(*Guardian*, 4 March 2000). In the present day, by contrast, players are portrayed as overpaid, over-rated, flamboyant, flashy and pampered with their showbiz lifestyles, million-pound homes, Ferraris and celebrity wives. Football has become a 'money driven circus fuelled by dissent and deceit' (*Daily Mail*, 24 February 2000) full of 'bad-tempered stars who regularly drag the game into the mire' (*The Sun*, 24 February 2000). In the modern game, according to these accounts, sportsmanship has gone.

This discursive structure sutures together themes associated with the decline of morality, the crisis of masculinity, the decline of Britain, and the threat to family values. The declining power of authoritarian morality, associated with the supposed declining influence of the Church, the school and the family, provides the structure of a traditional conservative cultural pessimism in which television and conspicuous consumption are threatening stability. One way of understanding this is as a crisis of adaptation, marking the long historical decline of thrift and the work ethic. The coverage, like that accorded to the death of Bobby Moore, reveals the extent to which, in the context of the declining significance of Priest, Father and Teacher in morality, sport stars are constantly looked upon to fill the void, constituting moral exemplars (Williams and Taylor 1994). The images and representations of sport stars are always complex assemblages, referring us, as they inevitably do, to discourses of national identity and of gender and ethnic difference. In particular, in the context of perceived crises in morality and in masculinity, the images of sport stars are likely to be means by which concepts of morality and masculinity are worked through. Emergent elements are also always present, as masculinities reproduce themselves. Studies of the career of David Beckham, for example, reveal the complex processes whereby new emergent elements are, through a process of struggle, incorporated or rejected within hegemonic masculinity. Beckham's image, with its concerns with fashion, appearance and hairstyle, has been part of a reconstruction through which the objectification of masculine bodies and appearance has interacted with more traditional concepts of sporting masculinity (Cashmore 2002; Whannel 2002b, 2002c).

Crisis in masculinity? You're having a laugh

During the 1990s the concept of a 'crisis' in masculinity gained extensive public discussion. The 'crisis' is, variously, linked to work, education and the family, the media and feminism. For some, the decline of the old manufacturing base, the rise of the service sector, the growth in the casualisation of labour, part-time, and flexi-time working, all contributed to both male unemployment and a 'feminisation' of work, whilst, for men in work, greater pressures exacerbated work–family conflicts. The films *Brassed Off* and *The Full Monty* were both rooted in industrial communities hit hard by these changes, in which male self-esteem, wrecked by unemployment, has to be reconstructed.

The education of boys is seen as undermined by the growth of an anti-swot culture, new lad culture and dumbing down. The optimism of girls about the future is contrasted with the pessimism of boys (Wilkinson 1994). Moreover, it is argued that within the family, a breakdown of parental authority with absent fathers and single or working mothers has resulted in a failure to instil moral values. Working women neglect the parental function and absent fathers weaken the disciplinary process whilst, in the media, there is asserted to be a lack of male role models.

Two decades of feminism are portrayed as contributing to male uncertainties, producing both responses, such as the 'new man' and reactions such as the 'new lad'. The new men's movement, triggered by Bly's book, *Iron John* (1990) despite its mytho-poetic pretensions, is also part of a reaction against feminism and a reassertion of 'real manliness', manifest in recent book titles like *Real Men Don't Eat Quiche*, and *The Big Damn Book of Sheer Manliness*.

Masculinity, though, has never been especially stable or fixed and has always been subject to unease and internal tensions. Its boundaries have always been policed, and its parameters re-inscribed. Thus there is not really a crisis in male power, but rather a crisis in the cultural modes through which masculinity presents itself (Roper and Tosh 1991: 18–19).

Reactive masculinity: the new lads

The new laddist discourse is particularly evident in two British television programmes: *Fantasy League Football* and *They Think It's All Over* (Whannel 2000). The *Fantasy League Football* format plunders the archives for clips framed by the irreverent and ironic perspective of the programme. The programme is set in a parodic version of a laddish flat, with echoes of *Men Behaving Badly* and *The Young Ones* (BBC 1982–4) as presenters, Skinner and Baddiel, combine the traditions of variety double acts, the critical irreverence of alternative comedy and the self-conscious vulgarity of new laddism.

There is a masculine unease about women in relation to football culture; it is unsure whether to embrace them or exclude them. It is in the appearance of guests like Birmingham City managing director Karren Brady, or Norwich City director Delia Smith, both figures with a stronger structural link to football than Skinner and Baddiel can claim, that masculine unease with women is most apparent. Even when well armed with the cultural capital of football knowledge, women still are only, at best, admitted as 'honorary' lads. Otherwise, women all too readily become the targets of the humour. The programme offers women the limited options of being a 'babe' or a surrogate lad; any other modes of femininity can only be performed against the grain of the programme's conventions and with resultant unease. Like women, black people, gay people, 'funny' foreigners with funny names, and those with physical peculiarities are all potential targets for jokes. As with much laddish culture this is excused as post-modern irony, and post-modern irony, as Leon Hunt has commented, means never having to say you are sorry.

The humour is also exclusive and exclusionary; it depends upon possession of that alternative form of cultural capital acquired and stored almost exclusively by boys, football knowledge. Girls may be following football in increasing numbers, but few develop that train-spotter fanaticism that permits the squirreling away of information that can be flourished to prove credentials. Football's cultural capital acts as a handy currency expended in the project of defending the castle of masculinity against incursion by the feminine.

Like *Fantasy League Football*, *They Think It's All Over* draws heavily on banter, that form of social cement central to male camaraderie (Easthope 1990), and it is very much a boys' club, with Jo Brand being one of the few women contributors. As with *Fantasy League Football*, the rootedness of the humour in the masculine cultural capital of sporting 'knowledge' functions to marginalise women. The tone is set by banter and laddishness, in which crudeness and vulgarity often tend to be substitutes for real wit rather than an organic component of it. Much of the humour draws on physical peculiarities and the humour of the show is redolent with a giggly embarrassment about sexuality.

New lads are 'men behaving badly', but are also attempting to excuse such behaviour by a degree of distance – putting it in quotation marks as ironic. The misogynistic spin thereby imparted is that if the sexism of the lads is just a joke, those who, unlike the Ulrika Jonssons of the world, choose not to play along, have no sense of humour, and are, in short, a revival of that 1970s figure, the 'humourless feminist'.

Policing masculinity

As surveillance and discipline have become more prominent features of top-level sport, the transgressions of sport stars have encountered greater exposure and less tolerance. New laddism, as a reassertion of elements of traditional young male working-class culture, is clearly both a response to and a reaction against the rise of feminism. It also, in its *Men Behaving Badly* or *Loaded* variety, represents a reassertion of hedonism against the fitness chic gym culture that grew rapidly during the 1980s.

The image of badness as 'fun' – drinking too much, missing training, being generally undisciplined and getting away with it – has been troubled by a more socially reprehensible 'badness' involving violence against women. This is mapped onto a more general discourse about the decline in morality, the crisis of masculinity, and the notion that sport, as a key site for the construction of such masculine behaviour, was itself part of the problem. In the aftermath of the Gascoigne 1998 affair, in which footballer Paul Gascoigne admitted to having being violent towards his wife, 'men behaving badly' were suddenly out of fashion, whilst clean-cut disciplined commitment was in demand: Paul Gascoigne out, Michael Owen in.

The ideology of masculine individualism is a significant part of the sub-text of the mythologised narratives of such stars. The individualism exemplified in the song *My Way* celebrates a masculine fantasy of defying constraint and advice. For sport stars, though, the contradictory tension, of course, is that modern elite sport is a highly disciplined practice subject to intense surveillance, in which maverick masculine individualism is something that coaches and governing bodies are concerned to root out. In a world that is constrained, maverick sport stars appear to offer the power to live a life of masculine individualism, defying constraints and rebelling against regulation whilst still performing. The constraints are associated with authority, the domestic, and the feminine and the well-documented male disregard for health is a rebellion against such constraints and, more precisely, a rebellion against Mother.

Masculine individualism is set against the female, the domestic and the familial and is rooted in the 'naturalness' of aggression and the predatory instinct which mother, wife, and family threaten to tame and civilise. But maverick masculine individualism also conflicts increasingly with the new corporate paternalism, whereby institutions become the moral guardians of their employees by supervising the way they live (Whannel 2001a).

Sport has always involved forms of discipline in its regimes of training but, increasingly, this discipline is being extended to all aspects of a player's lifestyle: diet, daily routine, sex life and sleeping patterns. Brohm's concept of the Taylorisation of the body – the squeezing of maximum productivity from the human frame – seems ever more pertinent here (Brohm 1978). A recomposed masculinity, traditional but disciplined, respectable rather than rough, hard but controlled, firm but fair, is, in ideological terms, placed in dominance.

New lads, new men, New Labour?

The approach of the millennium produced a rash of rebranded newness. With both New Labour and New Man, the debate has been over the issue of substance and spin. The self-reflexive aspect of the writing of figures like Dave Hill, Nick Hornby, Blake Morrison and Tony Parsons are suggestive of a new more self-conscious mode of masculinity. 'New man' is, arguably, something more than a media label but certainly less than a major new social movement or a transformative social force; yet the term does signify forms of unsettling of some mainstream assumptions about gender relations.

If 'new man' was a response to feminism and a reaction against the constraints and limits of mainstream hegemonic masculinity, and 'new lad' was a reaction against feminism, and a magical recovery of aspects of hegemonic masculinity seen as threatened, then the current field of 'masculinities' works across the tension between these two responses.

Nick Hornby's huge success with *Fever Pitch* is, in part, due to the chord his self-reflexivity has struck with women; it was lauded as the first, or the only, book about sport that has been widely read by women. Hornby has subsequently become the paradigm case for new fiction about men and emotions. Yet in narrative terms, in both *Fever Pitch* and *High Fidelity*, there is remarkably little reconstruction of masculinity in the trajectory of the main characters, for whom self-reflexivity is more a substitute for than a route towards change (Whannel 2001b).

Hybridity, diaspora and globalising processes

One could suggest that the discussion so far is too parochial, and Anglo-centric, presenting a picture of masculinities embedded in the development of an English national popular culture with its totemic figures of Stanley Matthews, Bobby Moore, Paul Gascoigne and David Beckham. The cultural field has, it could be argued, been transformed by a set of globalising processes: the growth of internationally circulated mass media, the global mobility of sporting labour, the ubiquity of the promotional culture, and the migration of people. Diasporic communities, hybrid identities and globalised cultures of consumption are the dynamic processes reconfiguring the cultural sphere.

The fame of masculine sporting figures such as Michael Jordan, Michael Schumacher, Andre Aggassi, David Beckham and Thierry Henry works across diverse geographical cultural contexts, in some cases transcending the popularity of their sport. The image of Michael Jordan became a global icon that spoke to audiences who did not participate in or watch basketball. The image of Beckham spoke to audiences in Asia broader than those who followed football. Constructions of Western and oriental, white and black, cool and square, rub up against each other in complex and productive ways. Japanese, Chinese and Indian sport stars who 'make it' in the West acquire a very particular cultural cachet, exploited by advertising in their countries of origin. The production and consumption of such images involve a range of audience expectations and mobilises and speaks to a range of identities.

Take, for example, the film *Bend it Like Beckham*, which succeeded beyond all expectations with diverse audiences. On the face of it, a film about football, featuring a British-Asian girl was not an obvious audience winner even in Britain. Yet, in its clever mobilisation of whole sets of social tensions, it spoke to and called in a range of audience identities. It both celebrated football and criticised its masculine bias. It drew on tensions between masculine and feminine, between femininity and sport, between Britishness and Asian-ness, between parent and child, between practical reality and utopian dream. It alluded in its title to a sporting mythology (David Beckham's great ability to bend the ball in free kicks) without living off that mythology. It was rooted in that strongest of narrative structures, the triumph over obstacles. It reached large audiences in Britain, in India and unexpectedly in the USA. The film points to the contingent and provisional nature of identities, in which nation, class, culture, ethnicity, age and gender all constantly modify each other and produce different hybrid forms in different contexts. Simultaneously, however, it has to be acknowledged that this process is but a bricolage of embedded cultural elements that are forged through historical struggles and written into rituals, practices and institutions. Asian-ness, Britishness, the process of migration and absorption, the institutions of sport, the structure of the media and the conventions of schooling together form the structural elements through which the processes of representation in the film operate.

Indian cinema outstrips Hollywood in numbers of films produced, and is dwarfed by Hollywood in terms of revenues earned. Both are considerably bigger than the frail British film industry. Yet all are caught up here in a complex cultural exchange in which modes of cultural imagery interact. Despite the global dominance of Hollywood, there is also a reciprocal effectivity in which some of the themes, styles, forms and images of Bollywood feed back into Western cinema. It is this process that links such diverse films as *Monsoon Wedding*, *Bend it Like Beckham* and *The Guru*.

Conclusion

In summary, this is a reminder that studying masculinities involves both the contingent and the embedded dimensions; it requires that we recognise both the sedimented traditions and residual cultures, and the dynamic hybridities and diasporic identities that are implicated in the production of masculinities. The male sport stars of the future, whose images will in turn feed into discourses of masculinity may be, like Chinese basketball player Yao Ming who is now a star in the USA, those who bring into collision different cultural contexts, value systems and structures of feeling. The question remains one of assessing the extent to which emergent masculine images challenge and change existing hegemonic masculinities, or are, through processes of tension and adaptation, incorporated.

Notes

1 This chapter is, in part, a reworking of material originally published in *Leisure Studies*, 18, 3: 249–65 (Whannel 1999).

2 Simone de Beauvoir (1953) wrote of women as 'the second sex'. Betty Friedan (1963) said that it was 'easier to live through someone else than to become complete yourself' (Friedan 1963: 294). Germaine Greer (1970) wrote of femininity in terms of a repressed sexuality; a 'female eunuch'. Sheila Rowbotham (1973a) outlined the location of 'women's consciousness' within 'man's world'. The work of Juliet Mitchell (1971), Ann Oakley (1972) and Sheila Rowbotham (1973b) constituted a launch pad for the rapid growth of feminist scholarship in the 1970s.

3 The question of the extent to which 'men', as opposed to patriarchy or capitalism, were the enemy, became the terrain on which distinctions emerged between radical separatism and socialist feminism (see Aitchison 2003; Brownmiller 1975; Delphy 1977; Firestone 1979; Dworkin 1981). Socialist feminism attempted to find alliances for a new politics, 'beyond the fragments' of the disunited left (see Kuhn and Wolpe 1978; Rowbotham et al. 1979; and Barrett 1980).

4 Responses to this challenge (Tolson 1977; Hoch 1979; Humphries and Metcalf 1983) that attempted to deconstruct masculinity paralleled the emergence of men's groups and organisations and publications (such as *Achilles Heel*) that combined, sometimes awkwardly, an anti-sexist intention with a desire to explore maleness from a man's perspective. The privileged power of heterosexual masculinity, and its reluctance to be self-reflexive, meant that gay men played a significant role in these early developments.

5 Some analyses of masculinity, by men, implied or advocated the development of a new academic area of 'men's studies' (Kimmel 1987; Brod 1987; Kaufman 1987). Men's

studies, critics suggested, was focused on 'men' as opposed to patriarchy, neglected issues of male–female relations, marginalised feminism or rendered it invisible, lacked a grounding in feminist research, and did not acknowledge its feminist roots (see Griffin in Hearn and Morgan 1990).

6 Three of the earliest book-length critiques of the social practices of sport all show a concern with sport and sexual repression, and the influence of Freud via the Frankfurt School Marxism can be detected (Brohm 1978; Hoch 1972; Vinnai 1976). The impact of feminism prompted examination of masculinity and sport (see Sheard and Dunning 1973; Kidd 1978; Sabo and Runfola 1980).

7 See Carroll (1986), Dunning (1986) and Hargreaves (1986). Feminist scholarship elaborated the workings of patriarchy in sporting contexts (see for example Vertinsky 1990; McCrone 1988; Hargreaves 1994). The historical formation of sporting masculinity too was being examined more closely (see Mangan and Walvin 1987; Maguire 1986). In Australia, analyses placed issues of gender relations on the agenda (see Lawrence and Rowe 1987; Rowe and Lawrence 1989). Most notably, in North America, Michael Messner and Don Sabo developed an analysis of sport strongly shaped by feminist critiques of sport (Messner 1988, 1992, 1993; Messner and Sabo 1991, 1994). More recently, in the wake of this programmatic field mapping and agenda setting, more precisely focused single-sport studies of masculinity in sport have begun to emerge (Nauright and Chandler 1996; Spracklen 1995, 1996).

8 See Hearn and Morgan (1990), Berger and Watson (1995), Brod and Kaufman (1994), Cornwall and Lindisfarne (1994). Lyn Segal argued that 'looking not at "masculinity" as such, but at certain specific masculinities', and developing an 'understanding of the differences between men' was central to the struggle for change (Segal 1994a: x). The growth of identity politics has produced a heightened visibility not just of gay masculinities but also the complexities and instabilities of sexual identities (Weeks and Holland 1996; Garber 1992; Simpson 1994; Ekins and King 1995).

References

Aitchison, C.C. (2003) *Gender and Leisure: Social and Cultural Perspectives*, London: Routledge.

Barrett, M. (1980) *Women's Oppression Today*, London: Verso.

Berger, M. and Watson, B. (eds) (1995) *Constructing Masculinity*, London: Routledge.

Bly, R. (1990) *Iron John: A Book About Men*, Reading, MA: Addison-Wesley.

Brailsford, D. (1969) *Sport and Society: Elizabeth to Anne*, London: Routledge and Kegan Paul.

Brod, H. (1987) *The Making of Masculinities: The New Men's Studies*, Boston, MA and London: Allen and Unwin.

Brod, H. and Kaufman, M. (eds) (1994) *Theorising Masculinities*, London: Sage.

Brohm, J. (1978) *Sport – A Prison of Measured Time*, London: Ink Links.

Brownmiller, S. (1975) *Against our Will: Men, Women and Rape*, New York: Simon and Schuster.

Butler, J. and Scott, J.W. (1992) *Feminists Theorise the Political*, London: Routledge.

Carrington, B. (1998) 'Sport, masculinity and black cultural resistance', *Journal of Sport and Social Issues*, 22, 3: 275–98.

Carroll, J.B. (1986) 'Sport: virtue and grace', *Theory Culture and Society*, 3, 1: 91–8.

Cashmore, E. (1982) *Black Sportsmen*, London: Routledge and Kegan Paul.

Cashmore, E. (2002) *Beckham*, Cambridge: Polity Press.

Chapman, R. and Rutherford, J. (1988) *Male Order, Unwrapping Masculinity*, London: Lawrence and Wishart.

Cohen, M. (1996) *Fashioning Masculinity: National Identity and Language in the Eighteenth Century*, London: Routledge.

Connell, B. (1995) *Masculinities*, Cambridge: Polity Press.

Cornwall, A. and Lindisfarne, N. (1994) *Dislocating Masculinity*, London: Routledge.

Coward, R. (1984) *Female Desire: Women's Sexuality Today*, London: Paladin.

Coward, R. (1992) *Our Treacherous Hearts*, London: Faber and Faber.

Crowther, N.B. (1996) 'Sports violence in the Roman and Byzantine Empires: a modern legacy?', *International Journal of the History of Sport*, 13, 3: 445–87.

Dawson, G. (1994) *Soldier Heroes: British Adventure, Empire and the Imagining of Masculinities*, London: Routledge.

de Beauvoir, S. (1953) *The Second Sex*, London: Cape.

Delphy, C. (1977) *The Main Enemy: A Materialist Analysis of Women's Oppression*, London: WRRC.

Dunning, E. (1986) 'Sport as a male preserve: social sources of masculine identity', *Theory Culture and Society*, 3, 1: 79–90.

Dworkin, A. (1981) *Pornography: Men Possessing Women*, London: The Women's Press.

Easthope, A. (1990) *What a Man's Gotta Do: The Masculine Myth in Popular Culture*, London: Unwin Hyman.

Ekins, R. and King, D. (eds) (1995) *Blending Genders: Social Aspects of Cross-Dressing and Sex*, London: Routledge.

Falaudi, S. (1991) *Backlash: The Undeclared War Against Women*, London: Chatto and Windus.

Firestone, S. (1979) *The Dialectic of Sex*, London: The Women's Press.

Friedan, B. (1963) *The Feminine Mystique*, New York: Dell.

Garber, M. (1992) *Vested Interests*, London: Routledge.

Greer, G. (1970) *The Female Eunuch*, London: Paladin.

Hargreaves, J. (1986) 'Where's the virtue? where's the grace? social production of gender', *Theory Culture and Society*, 3, 1: 109–21.

Hargreaves, J. (1994) *Sporting Females*, London: Routledge.

Hearn, J. and Morgan, D.H. (eds) (1990) *Men, Masculinities and Social Theory*, London: Unwin Hyman.

Hoch, P. (1972) *Rip Off The Big Game*, New York: Anchor.

Hoch, P. (1979) *White Hero, Black Beast*, London: Pluto Press.

Humphries, M. and Metcalf, A. (eds) (1983) *The Sexuality of Men*, London: Pluto Press.

Jones, A. (1993) 'Defending the border: men's bodies and vulnerability', *Cultural Studies*, 2, Birmingham: Dept. of Cultural Studies, University of Birmingham.

Kaufman, M. (ed.) (1987) *Beyond Patriarchy: Essays by Men on Pleasure, Power and Change*, New York: Oxford University Press.

Kidd, B. (1987) 'Sports and masculinity', in M. Kaufman (ed.) *Beyond Patriarchy: Essays by Men on Pleasure, Power and Change*, New York: Oxford University Press.

Kimmel, M.S. (1987) *Changing Men: New Directions in Research on Men and Masculinity*, Newbury Park, CA and London: Sage.

Kuhn, A. and Wolpe, A. (eds) (1978) *Feminism and Materialism*, London: RKP.

Lawrence, G. and Rowe, D. (eds) (1987) *Power Play: The Commercialisation of Australian Sport*, Sydney, Australia: Hale and Iremonger.

Maguire, J. (1986) 'Images of manliness (late Victorian and Edwardian Britain)', *British Journal of Sports History*, 3, 3: 265–87.

Mangan, J.A. (1981) *Athleticism in the Victorian and Edwardian Public School*, London: Cambridge University Press.

Mangan, J.A. and Walvin, J. (1987) *Manliness and Morality: Middle Class Masculinity in Britain and America*, Manchester: Manchester University Press.

McCrone, K. (1988) *Sport and the Physical Emancipation of English Women 1870–1914*, London: Routledge.

Messner, M (1988) 'Sports and male domination: the female athlete as contested ideological terrain', *Sociology of Sport Journal*, 5: 197–211.

Messner, M. (1992) 'White men misbehaving: feminism, Afrocentrism and the promise of a critical standpoint', *Journal of Sport and Social Issues*, 16, 2: 136–44.

Messner, M. (1993) *Power at Play: Sports and the Problem of Masculinity*, Boston, MA: Beacon.

Messner, M. and Sabo, D. (eds) (1991) *Sport, Men and the Gender Order*, Champaign Il: Human Kinetics.

Messner, M. and Sabo, D. (1994) *Sex, Violence and Power in Sports*, Freedom, CA: The Crossing Press.

Mitchell, J. (1971) *Woman's Estate*, London: Penguin.

Nauright, J. and Timothy, C. (eds) (1995) *Making Men: Rugby and Masculine Identity*, London: Frank Cass.

Oakley, A. (1972) *Sex, Gender and Society*, London: Temple Smith.

Pronger, B. (1990) *The Arena of Masculinity: Sports, Homosexuality and the Meaning of Sex*, London: Gay Men's Press.

Roper, M. and Tosh, J. (eds) (1991) *Manful Assertions: Masculinity in Britain Since 1800*, London: Routledge.

Rowbotham, S. (1973a) *Woman's Consciousness, Man's World*, Harmondsworth: Penguin.

Rowbotham, S. (1973b) *Hidden From History*, London: Pluto.

Rowbotham, S. (1989) *The Past Before Us: Feminism in Action Since the 1960s*, London: Pandora.

Rowbotham, S., Segal, L. and Wainwright, H. (1979) *Beyond the Fragments: Feminism and the Making of Socialism*, London: Merlin.

Sabo, D. and Jansen, S.C. (1992) 'Images of men in sports media: the social reproduction of gender order', in S. Craig (ed.) *Men, Masculinity and the Media*, London: Sage.

Sabo, D. and Runfola, R. (eds) (1980) *Jock: Sports and Male Identity*, Englewood Cliffs, NJ: Prentice Hall.

Sedgewick, E.K. (1985) *Between Men: English Literature and Male Homosocial Desire*, New York: Columbia University Press.

Segal, L. (1994) *Straight Sex: The Politics of Pleasure*, London: Virago.

Sheard, K. and Dunning, E. (1973) 'The rugby football club as a type of male preserve', *International Review of Sociology of Sport*, 8, 1: 5–24.

Simpson, M. (1994) *Male Impersonators*, London: Cassell.

Sports Council (1995) *Sport: Raising the Game*, London: Sports Council.

Spracklen, K. (1995) 'Playing the ball or the uses of league: class, masculinity and rugby – a case study of Sudthorpe', in G. McFee, W. Murphy and G. Whannel (eds) *Leisure Cultures: Values, Genders, Lifestyles*, Eastbourne: Leisure Studies Association.

Spracklen, K. (1996) '"When you're putting yer body on t'line fer beer tokens you've go'a wonder why": expressions of masculinity and identity in Rugby communities', in

Scottish Centre Research Papers in Sport Leisure and Society, 1, Edinburgh: Moray House Institute of Education.

Tolson, A. (1977) *The Limits of Masculinity*, London: Tavistock.

Turner, E.S. (1976) *Boys will be Boys*, Harmondsworth: Penguin.

Vertinsky, P. (1990) *The Eternally Wounded Woman*, Manchester: Manchester University Press.

Vinnai, G. (1976) *Football Mania*, London: Ocean.

Walter, N. (1998) *The New Feminism*, London: Little, Brown.

Weeks, J. and Holland, J. (eds) (1996) *Sexual Cultures: Communities, Values and Intimacy*, Basingstoke: Macmillan.

Whannel, G. (1993) 'No room for uncertainty: gridiron masculinity in North Dallas Forty', in P. Kirkham and J. Thumin (eds) *You Tarzan: Masculinity, Movies and Men*, London: Lawrence and Wishart.

Whannel, G. (1995) 'Sport stars, youth and morality in the print media', in G. McFee, G. Whannel and W. Murphy (eds) *Leisure Cultures: Values, Genders, Lifestyles*, Eastbourne: Leisure Studies Association.

Whannel, G. (1998) 'Biography as narrative in the representation of sport stars', paper presented to Annual Conference of the North American Association for Sport Sociology, 4–7 November, Las Vegas.

Whannel, G. (1999) 'From "motionless bodies" to acting moral subjects: Tom Brown, a transformative romance for the production of manliness', *Diegesis: Journal for the Association for Research in Popular Fictions*, 4, Liverpool: Association for Research in Popular Fictions.

Whannel, G. (2000) 'The lads and the gladiators: traditional masculinities in a postmodern televisual landscape', in E. Buscombe (ed.) *British Television: A Reader*, Oxford: Oxford University Press.

Whannel, G. (2001a) 'Punishment, redemption and celebration in the popular press: the case of David Beckham', in D. Andrews and S. Jackson (eds) *Sport Stars: The Cultural Politics of Sporting Celebrity*, London: Routledge.

Whannel, G. (2001b) 'Working up a high fever: notes on the sociology of leisure, and "work" and " leisure" in the writing of Nick Hornby', paper presented to the Association for Research on Popular Fiction Annual Conference, 4–6 November, Liverpool John Moores University, Liverpool.

Whannel, G. (2002a) 'From pig's bladders to Ferraris: media discourses of masculinity and morality in obituaries of Stanley Matthews', *Culture, Society, Sport*, 5, 3: 73–94.

Whannel, G. (2002b) *Media Sport Stars, Masculinities and Moralities*, London: Routledge.

Whannel, G. (2002c) 'David Beckham, identity and masculinity', *Sociology Review*, 11, 3: 2–4

Wiedemann, T. (1992) *Emperors and Gladiators*, London: Routledge.

Wilkinson, H. (1994) *No Turning Back: Generations and the Genderquake*, London: Demos.

Williams, J. and Taylor, R. (1994) 'Boys keep swinging: masculinity and football culture in England', in T. Newburn and B. Stanko (eds) *Just Boys Doing Business: Men, Masculinities and Crime*, London: Routledge.

Williams, R. (1977) *Marxism and Literature*, London: Oxford University Press.

Chapter 3

Watching the game

Theorising masculinities in the context of mediated tennis

Eileen Kennedy

Introduction

Gender has long been an important concept for feminism. Yet only recently has gender begun to be considered as relevant to both men and women. Not until 1991 did Van Zoonen ask why 'we really think gender is constructed only in "women's media"?' suggesting that the investigation of media such as 'sports programmes, war movies, *Playboy* and *Penthouse*' (1991: 48–9) might be as revealing of constructions of masculinity as the investigation of soap opera and romance novels has been about femininity. Since then, throughout the 1990s and into the twenty-first century, as Beynon (2002: 3) observes, 'masculinity is being placed under the microscope as never before'. No longer can masculinity retain its cloak of invisibility enabling it to masquerade as neutral, beyond analysis and above inspection. Instead, the masculine position has been seen to be as culturally located as that of femininity, and with it, all those aspects of sport not previously considered as gendered, because they were not associated with women, have revealed themselves to be subliminally marked as masculine.

Yet, despite this sea change in gender theory, much discussion of masculinity in sport remains at the level of description. Within sport sociology masculinity still largely falls short of being theorised as gender. For example, Free and Hughson (2003: 139) present a critique of ethnographic accounts of football supporter subcultures, which, despite 'highlighting masculinity as an analytical category', suffer from 'a blindness to gender issues in [the] data ... missing the performative dimensions of [the supporters'] professed working-class masculinity'. Petersen warns of the dangers of producing definitions of masculinity which

> ... entail little more than the compilation of lists of what are seen to be characteristic masculine qualities or attributes such as aggressiveness, competitiveness, and emotional detachment which, it is implied, distinguish it from its counterpart, femininity ... despite scholars' rejection of essentialism, masculinity is often referred to as though it had a definable, distinctive essence.

(Petersen 2003: 58)

Free and Hughson (2003: 140) similarly point to the reproduction in ethnographic accounts of football supporters of a view of masculinity related to 'club allegiance, propensity to violence, and related activities as virtually naturally given attributes'. At the heart of feminist theorising of gender has been the undermining of such essentialist 'biology is destiny' versions of gender identity. Nevertheless, the relationship between the material and the symbolic in relation to gender has been seen to be a complex one. While culture is considered to interpolate us as gendered subjects in a myriad of ways, there often remains a notion of an internal essence or presence preceding 'social and linguistic coding' (Poovey, cited in Lloyd 1999: 196).

The work of Judith Butler has become hugely influential in current gender scholarship because it enables theorists to step away from the need to assume the existence of 'a something which is regarded as fundamental to female [and male] identity prior to engendering' (Lloyd 1999: 196). Butler's (1990) theory of gender performativity allows for gender to be understood 'not as an expression of what one is, but ... as something one does: "the stylised repetition of acts through time"' (Lloyd 1999: 196). Adapting the work of Austin and Derrida, Butler (1993: 23) proposes that the performative 'enacts or produces that which it names' and, as such, there is no gendered self separate from, or prior to, its constitution as a series of bodily gestures, movements and styles.

Masculinity, then, is far from being a stable entity. In fact, within masculinity research, the term 'masculinity' has become replaced by its plural, 'masculinities', referencing the multiple ways in which, as the subtitle of this volume emphasises, masculinity can manifest itself. However, as Connell (1998: 5) observes, these plural masculinities 'exist in definite social relations, often relations of hierarchy and exclusion'. A hegemonic form of masculinity exists in most contexts, but, importantly, 'this need not be the most common form of masculinity' (Connell 1998: 5). In fact, as Connell goes on to assert, 'many men live in a state of some tension with, or distance from, hegemonic masculinity' (Connell 1998: 5).

As patterns of gender practice, masculinities 'are sustained and enacted not only by individuals but also by groups and institutions' including sport (Connell 1998: 5). Sport can construct multiple masculinities and hierarchies between them. The male body presents itself as the site for the enactment of gender, 'addressed, defined and disciplined ... and given outlets and pleasures' (Connell 1998: 5). Far from being the result of passive disciplining, however, sports bodies are actively produced through a sustained engagement with the demands of the institution. This need not, however, produce a coherent response. Masculinities are complex, often contradictory, always in process and never finished.

The sport media provides an opportunity to study the performance of masculinity and to understand the performativity of that performance; that is, to observe the 'reiteration of norms which precede, constrain, and exceed the performer' (Butler, cited in Lloyd 1999: 201). In so doing, it is possible to de-naturalise what is constructed as given and obvious, revealing the fluidity and multiplicity of gender. Thus, analysis of masculinity in the sport media can be understood as part of a political project to destabilise the categories of gender. In order to facilitate such a project, it may be helpful to borrow from the analytical approach termed by Saco (1992) 'masculinity-as-signs'.

Saco's approach to analysing masculinity in the media understands gender differences as symbolic categories and sees the media as not simply reflecting or representing gender difference, but also as helping to construct that difference. Rather than analysing the media as offering representations of *real* gender differences that might exist separate from the text, Saco suggests a move towards the analysis of gender differences as (re)presentations, using the parentheses to call into question the possibility of any direct knowledge of masculinity outside of representation. Saco's theoretical position is to shift 'from the *signs of masculinity* to *masculinity as signs*' (1992: 26, original emphasis).

A media text such as a televised broadcast of live sport, the sports pages of a newspaper, a fitness magazine or an advertisement featuring athletes, is a system of signs. Saco (1992) refers to the work of Roland Barthes and Stuart Hall to think about the ways in which these signs are combined to form cultural codes, which need then to be 'read' or interpreted by the consumer of that text:

> Readers have a number of options for reading texts: They may adopt conventional or dominant codes, negotiated codes or oppositional codes ... in the process of reading, thereby producing a multiplicity of possible meanings. Reading, therefore, is a 'writerly' process ... because it can involve the production of plural texts, with different meanings. In this sense, then, shared meanings are possible only because of conventionalized ways of reading.
>
> (Saco 1992: 31)

The consumer of a sport media text is therefore involved in a kind of conversation with it. The text talks to, or addresses, the consumer in a particular way. In order to be able to 'hear' the meaning and to make sense of the text, consumers must adopt an appropriate relation to the text by placing themselves in the right position. Because of the complexity of the sign combinations, texts only make sense from particular positions or perspectives. In this sense, the sport media text can be said to offer 'subject positions' for the audience to step into, from which they are able to make sense of the text.

It is necessary, therefore, not simply to analyse the texts of media sport, but also to think about the positions from which these texts can be read. In other words, it is important to look not only at the images of sport in the media, but also at the ways these images ask to be looked at. We need to analyse the process of engagement with the text and to consider the ways in which masculinities are subject positions constructed in relation to the media representations.

It is impossible, however, to think about gender separate from its inflection by the interplay of class, race and nation. Different sport forms manifest these combinations in different ways, culminating in the particular 'flavour' of each sport. The mediation of sport adds another layer of meaning as the complex significations are sifted, selected and interrogated. The analysis of different forms of sport media can therefore reveal the plurality of masculinities constructed in sport and allow us to consider how these masculinities are presented for consumption, often in conflicting ways.

Wimbledon and the myth of the great, white, athletic Englishman

For two weeks each year, the tennis championships at Wimbledon construct an imagined Englishness of the past, located in a leafy South London suburb. While Wimbledon seemingly allows class hierarchies to be re-signified and celebrated, its aura of exclusivity is simultaneously offered for consumption by the masses. The live event is inseparable from its mediation. When the International Management Group chose to resist title sponsorship, competition sponsorship and arena ads in favour of marketing and licensing Wimbledon's name and logo (Whannel 1992: 179), they successfully commodified class and Englishness through the green, white and purple of the Wimbledon brand to reap global television revenues. The version of Englishness at play in the mediation of Wimbledon constructs a mythical land where spectators dine on strawberries and cream, often, forbearingly, beneath umbrellas, and politely applaud every good shot. This is a nostalgic England signified within the careful product placement of Robinsons and Rolex: cosy, privileged and of unquestionable worth.

The Englishness of Wimbledon eschews crass commercialism (while still raking in profits) and reinscribes class and gender distinctions: the privileged are allocated tickets, the less so queue; the men's match has top billing while the *ladies* are compensated with flowers. Wimbledon thus invigorates the legacy of the Victorian amateur gentlemen for whom sport was a means of displaying the inherent superiority of the white, middle-class, English male over the rest of the world. Yet, it does so in the context of a twenty-first-century global sports spectacle, and the anachronism of Wimbledon and its cast of characters can result in there being a range of competing masculinities at play simultaneously. The mediation of the event attempts to narrate these conflicts in a way that preserves 'gentlemanliness' as a key characteristic of the hegemonic version of masculinity, but it does not always succeed.

Given this nostalgic reinvention of Englishness, the victory of a suitably gentlemanly English tennis player in the championship could offer coherence to the narrative of sport, nation and gender that surrounds the event. In the past, the British media have embraced Greg Rusedski as a likely candidate for this role. Rusedski certainly looks the part – tall, slim, benignly grinning, he embodies the good-humoured athletic manliness of the nineteenth century. However, aside from the unevenness of his career, Rusedski displays too many complex significations to sustain this dominant narrative. Rusedski's un-English sounding name and origins in ex-colonial Canada do not in themselves make him atypically English. As Young (1995: 3) observes, using a phrase from Kipling, 'monstrous hybridism' can be considered a longstanding feature of English cultural identity, as evidenced by the uncertain crossing and invasion of identities, whether of class, gender, culture or race, which has been the dominant motif of much English fiction. It is, he says, a lack of core identity that has 'enabled it to be variously and counteractively constructed' (Young 1995: 3). Yet Wimbledon's mythical version of Englishness constructs it as timeless and fixed, and when Rusedski opens his mouth he threatens to puncture this fantasy.

Rusedski has become known for arguing with the umpire. Stearns (1987), in an article tracing the historical relationship between masculinity and anger in American society, highlights the very different traditions of expressing anger in America and Europe. While the eighteenth and nineteenth centuries saw common trends towards the need to control anger in the West, Stearns maintains that in the late nineteenth century an American ambivalence concerning anger arose which could still be discerned in the 1950s. Personal displays of temper were still disapproved of, but for men, anger, properly channelled, could be a useful spur to achievement. The new approach to anger paralleled, and was fed by, two movements: 'growing interest in competitive sports and the progressive esteem for moral indignation in the cause of reform as part of masculine culture' (Stearns 1987: 84), hence the tradition of giving a symbolic pair of boxing gloves as growing-up presents to American middle-class boys, a practice which persisted until the 1940s.

In recreating a mythical past, Wimbledon simultaneously recreates different traditions in emotional control. The English 'stiff upper lip' is contrasted with American indignation at perceived official ineptitude which, in turn, is frequently constructed in the British media as American temper tantrums. The most prominent example of this representation is John MacEnroe who, demonstrating the lack of fixity of such media representations, is now a stalwart of BBC Wimbledon commentary. Similarly, Rusedski, with his rather ambiguous national identity, sometimes leaves it unclear as to which side of this Atlantic emotional divide he represents.

Washington at Wimbledon: a different kind of player

Another Anglo-American split is reconstructed in Wimbledon in relation to its purported hostility to commercialism, associated with the classless naked capitalism of Americanised sport. When, in 1996, the black American player, Mal Washington made it to the Wimbledon Men's Singles Final, this unseemly relationship with money became the abiding feature of the BBC's representation of Washington in the short film which they showed as a prologue to his Finals match against Richard Krajcek (BBC1, 7 July 1996). An analysis of this film demonstrates the conflation of race, class and nation in the construction of heroic masculinity in Wimbledon, and the potential threat to this hegemony that Washington represented.

The feature on Mal Washington thus began with some action from his semi-final match against Tod Martin, at a point where Washington was trailing five games to one. This focus on Washington snatching victory from the jaws of defeat, facilitated his positioning within the narrative as an underdog, a characterisation underscored by the accompanying music from Kate Bush, 'Don't give up … '. Washington's unrestrained displays of emotion at winning were replayed (he sank to his knees, fists clenched, as the lyrics to the music asserted 'I know you can make it', and the commentator exclaimed 'He's done it!'), adding further to the impression of the unlikelihood of his presence in the final. Washington was then shown being interviewed against a backdrop of green leaves supported by a trellis. In contrast to the nature/purity connotations of the green and white Wimbledon colour scheme reflected in everything from the court designs, score-board and on-screen graphics, however, the commentary, graphics and musical soundtrack to Washington's film emphasised financial considerations. First, the commentator expressed disappointment that Washington had not placed a bet on his chances in the tournament as the odds against him were so high. Then a complex narrative emerged which culminated in an image of Washington's head being superimposed on a dollar bill. This is the kind of subtle everyday practice by which the success or failure of African-Americans is attributed to 'their ability or inability to take advantage of the "American Dream"' (Wilson 1997: 177), a phenomenon sometimes termed 'enlightened' racism.

Evocations of England past all but disappeared during the televisual retelling of Washington's path through the championship, but the vestiges of green-tinged nostalgia which remained contrast sharply with the image of Washington presented in the film. While the fast-paced theme tune from the movie *Pulp Fiction* was heard, a sequence of camera shots of the scoreboard, interspersed with play, charted Washington's various successes in the championship. The camera shots became increasingly dramatic, with a shot of the scoreboard so close that the writing was illegible, then zooming out at a speed that caused the letters to blur. The explosive pace of the music and camerawork, however, stood in stark relief to the 'low-tech' character of the courtside scoreboard used in the sequence in preference to computerised, on-screen graphics. Washington was similarly constructed in contrast to an imagined white English hero as the film focused on both his American-ness and his blackness. The music used inevitably evoked the film, *Pulp Fiction*, a contemporary tale of US gangsters, in which black characters feature in central positions. If the musical soundtrack indicated one context in which to consider a black player, another was presented in the sequence comparing Washington's achievements to those of Arthur Ashe over twenty years previously. Ashe was shown holding the Wimbledon trophy, and Washington is heard saying 'that was a great victory for him', constructing a connection between them, yet the reference served to underline the exceptional nature of the appearance of a black player in the final. Library shots of Washington playing against tennis celebrities such as Edberg and Lendl were replayed, creating a tournament history for Washington, but one in which his status as the unknown became his most remarkable feature: 'Well, everyone says Mal because they can't pronounce his name – that's how unknown he is'. Shots of his brother in interview constructed him in a particular family context, which, while stopping short of the family narrative that casts female players as daughters (Kennedy 2000), was an infantilising gesture nonetheless as other male tennis players are regularly seen in relation to wives or girlfriends, signifying the maturity of their heterosexual masculinity.

While a belief in hard work reaping reward was alluded to during the film, first by Washington, then by his brother, 'Work hard. Work hard. That's the only way you'll get him', the work narrative was somewhat undermined by the references to gambling, criminality and, finally, by the graphic image of a dollar bill unfurling and the accompanying assertion that 'Win or lose he'll go home with lots of these. For victory, nearly six hundred thousand dollars. Even as runner-up, he'll collect nearly three hundred thousand'; words that gave a very material interpretation to the lyrics of the Phil Collins song which played simultaneously: 'I'm on my way I'm making it'. This sequence culminated with an effect that banished any residual thoughts of amateur gentlemanliness as Washington's head was placed over George Washington's at the centre of the dollar bill. Finally, the film ended with a series of shots that gave the effect of Washington competing against himself, suggesting an interpretation of sport as an internal battle and the existence of a personal flaw that needed to be overcome. As the music died, a last image of Washington's head superimposed on the Wimbledon trophy faded into a long shot of an empty court.

Several themes are interwoven within this feature – tradition, family, work and money, resulting in ambiguity and contradiction. The attempts to create a black tradition for Washington to exist within places him firmly outside the nostalgic English gentleman tradition into which Rusedski, for instance, finds himself co-opted. Vestigial elements of that tradition which do emerge only serve to highlight Washington's distinctness from it. The constant reference, visually, musically and verbally, to Washington's prospective financial rewards make impossible any association with a tradition of amateurism, and even the honesty of his labour is undermined by associations with gambling and gangster culture. The televisual image of Washington constructs him as outside, and contrasting with, the nostalgia of Wimbledon. Washington becomes tinged with dangerous glamour (gangsters) and aspirations for social mobility ('I'm moving up', as Phil Collins sings). Even the battle against the self, a visual sequence regularly invoked for Wimbledon finalists, here contributes further to the sense of Washington having a personal agenda, fighting his own battle, embodying a different – Black American – set of cultural values, separate from the history of Wimbledon.

Thus, more than one form of masculinity is constructed here. The nostalgic masculinity of the Wimbledon hero conflicts with the masculinity of the contemporary sportsman, and the signifiers of glamour, determination and hard work are at odds with the poise, easiness and generosity of an idealised victor.

This is the context, then, that Tim Henman also exists within, and the media narratives surrounding Henman make multiple references to these conflicts.

Dreams on hold: Henman as a failed hero

For many, 2004 looked like it could have been Tim Henman's year at Wimbledon. Ultimately, however, it was not. Having reached the quarter-finals Henman, England's No. 1 men's tennis player, once again lost; this time to the Croatian player, Mario Ancic. The following day, British newspaper coverage was explicit in its appraisal of his campaign, albeit in divergent ways.

On 1 July 2004, the morning following his defeat, *The Times* newspaper (a right of centre, former broadsheet, recently re-launched in tabloid size) announced on the front page, quite quietly in a smallish headline 'Henman's title dream on hold again'. Underneath, a large close-up photograph featured Henman's wife, Lucy, looking romantic and thoughtful in side profile, wearing dark glasses, her finger pressed enigmatically against her lips. The caption accompanying the image read 'Lucy Henman watches anxiously as her husband, Tim, slides to defeat against Mario Ancic of Croatia. But the British No.1 has outperformed bigger names at Wimbledon over the years'. Beneath the image and under the lead-in, 'Better than Becker?', Henman's name appeared, ranked second to Bjorn Borg, in a table showing the number of quarter-finals reached in relation to number of Wimbledons played. In a bizarre manipulation of statistics, Henman, according to this formula, managed to outperform such champions as Becker, McEnroe, Sampras and Laver. Next to the table, in large print, against a background of a faded Wimbledon logo, a quote from an article inside the paper read, 'There was a time when people said Henman was due a bad Wimbledon. But he doesn't do bad Wimbledons'.

Images of Henman himself were absent from the front page of *The Times*, and the back page showed him only from behind as he walked off court. Instead we were asked to consider Henman in the context of other people: his supportive wife, former champions and loyal autograph hunters at the side of the court. *The Times* constructed a narrative around Henman's defeat that asked for him to be considered a hero despite his defeat, a 'King without a crown'. The tone of the match reports themselves was one of high drama, retelling a tragedy of epic proportion: 'A pall of gloom descended, the heavens duly wept and the brollies came out, and once again the nation paid the terrible price of hoping too much'. *The Times* focused on his advancing years as a reason for his defeat: 'The last 30-year-old champion of Wimbledon was Rod Laver in 1969 and he was regarded by many as the greatest player who unsheathed a racket'. Henman is cast as a mature, romantic hero for whom the 'title dream dies'.

Yet, despite the romantic spin, *The Times* struggled with conflicting signifiers to create a coherent narrative. Henman was also considered as 'ripe for plucking', being 'disappointing', 'like someone who wasn't really trying' – even if that amounted to 'the exact antithesis of Henman'. In spite of itself, *The Times* found Henman to be lacking the signifiers of the contemporary sports champion. For *The*

Times, Henman would have been an ideal sporting hero – public school educated (with a vocabulary matching their own literary style), uncomplicatedly white and English with a gentleman's physique, appropriately heterosexual and with an English rose for a wife. Thus *The Times* appeared to mourn not just the loss of the Wimbledon title, but the loss of the kind of champion they wanted Henman to represent.

However, a different kind of picture emerged from elsewhere in the British press. For example, on the same day, the front page of *The Sun*, a daily populist right-of-centre tabloid, carried the headline 'Wimpledon' on a green background amidst other stories and beneath which was a small head-shot of Henman biting his bottom lip accompanied by the words, 'Timid Tim lets us down again' and an indication of more on pages 6 and 7. Inside the paper, an image of a dejected Henman walking off court with his head down, was accompanied by an invitation to 'Extreme ironing anyone?', with the suggestion that the 'sport' of extreme ironing (which entails transporting an ironing board across inhospitable terrain) was the only one that England is any good at. Inserts of 'aghast' female fans and Henman's wife Lucy, 'putting her hand to her brow' added to the image of failed masculinity constructed by the paper, as did the other more sizeable insert featuring pictures of the 'British actor Jude Law [playing] tonsil tennis with his girlfriend Sienna Miller yesterday – at least *he's* offering the fans some action' (photographs show Law kissing and laughing with his partner in the crowd).

The representation in *The Sun* of Henman's defeat, asks the reader to judge Henman against a criterion of masculinity which is at odds with the Victorian gentleman image of Wimbledon. While *The Times* attempted to rescue an aspect of the heroic from Henman's stated objective of 'fulfilling your potential', *The Sun* preferred Hollywood glamour and actual victory irrespective of whether Henman had fulfilled his potential. *The Sun* berated Henman for being a wimp, constructing a different impression of the characteristics of the public school boy. The unflattering photographs of Lucy Henman accompanying the article undermined her function of signifying his successful heterosexual masculinity, as did the images of female spectators averting their gaze at the prospect of Henman's defeat. Even Henman's physicality is signified differently in *The Sun* where he is presented as bowed and ungainly, affecting the child-like habit of biting his lip, his height and build making him look like a lanky schoolboy rather than a gentleman hero.

On the back page of the same edition of *The Sun* another unflattering photograph of Henman appeared, this time next to shots of David Beckham, Michael Vaughan and Lawrence Dallaglio, creating a link between Henman's lack of success in tennis and recent national defeats in the sports of football, cricket and rugby. Against a background of horizontal lines (reminiscent of the police height chart used in *The Usual Suspects*), a head-and-shoulders 'mug shot' of each of the sportsmen had been digitally supplied with a tag around his neck detailing name and crime: HENMAN CRIME: Crashing out of Wimbledon to world No 63; BECKHAM CRIME: Blowing England's Euro 2004 chances; VAUGHAN

CRIME: Leading us to two disasters in 3 days; DALLAGLIO CRIME: Getting stuffed 3 times in a fortnight. The disciplinary gaze that is exerted by *The Sun* is interestingly aimed at all four men who might be said to conform to hegemonic masculinity. Henman and the three captains of the national teams in football, rugby and cricket all exhibit white, English middle-classness (Beckham perhaps not so obviously, but his style of masculinity is regularly associated with that of the 'new man' which enables the press to co-opt him into the middle class and contrast him to more old-fashioned working-class men of football like Manchester United manager, Alex Ferguson; Kennedy 2004). In addition, the men display the characteristics of leadership and have the physical capital associated with playing sport at international level. Yet, in enormous red capitals, 'GUILTY' has been written above their heads, and underneath: '… of crimes against English sports fans', the voice of *The Sun* having been personified into 'SunSport' which 'speaks its mind' commanding the men to 'RAISE YOUR GAME'. Without a win, 'SunSport' displayed intolerance at Henman's performance of restrained, athletic, middle-class masculinity: 'gutless Henman carried the hopes of the nation with all the strength of a knock-kneed gnat'.

Multiple masculinities of mediated tennis

There is not one, stable code for masculinity observable in mediated tennis. Rather, there are multiple, competing codes at play. Yet, at any given point it is possible to elicit a hierarchy among these codes. In one context, that of the broadcast of Wimbledon by the BBC for a British audience, middle-class, white English masculinity is preferred, excluding more troublesome masculinities from the possibility of occupying the narrative position of hero. Yet these other masculinities do exist within the text, like spectres set to threaten the narrative coherence, and the complex ways they are incorporated into the story is testimony to their potential to disrupt this (re)presentation of masculinity. The narratives and media conventions surrounding these sporting masculinities exist prior to the enactment of masculinity by any given sportsman. There is a narrative opening for a middle-class, white, English champion in the mediation of Wimbledon that both constrains and exceeds the individual contenders for the role. As a result, it is necessary to understand the media as not simply reflecting gender differences in the 'real' word, but also helping to construct those differences. This is the sense in which we need to understand 'masculinity-as-signs' (Saco 1992: 26), as the congruence of complex, often competing, codes of gender, class, race and nation in specific formations whose repetition enables them to achieve the effect of naturalisation. To unthread the connections, then, is to expose the fluidity of gender and the lack of obviousness of its performance and representation.

Sporting masculinities are brought into being through their representation. The media constructs a way of seeing masculinities, a way of appraising and ranking masculinities. The perspectives from which the audience is asked to view masculinities and the subject positions they are asked to occupy are equally complex and multiple. In order to understand the way the sport media makes sense of masculinity, then, it is vital to consider not simply what is represented, but the ways in which the representations address the audience. In considering mediated tennis, a panoply of signs is identifiable: Englishness competes with Americanness, blackness with whiteness, middle-class Victorian gentlemanliness with capitalism, glamour and celebrity. So many signs are there, that it might be argued that a hegemonic masculinity is absent. Yet, different media construct different ways of viewing these signs and thus serve to (re)produce different masculinities. Characteristics of white, middle-class masculinity may not be observable in the representation of Mal Washington, but they are identifiable in the gaze that the BBC constructs. Similarly, Henman's Wimbledon defeat is narrated by *The Times* in such a way as to encourage its readers to continue to view him as heroic in the face of tragedy. The subject position offered to its readers to identify with is characterised by hegemonic masculinity even if Henman falls short of its successful performance.

In conclusion, to discuss hegemonic masculinity in any homogenising way may be to oversimplify the media construction of masculinity-as-signs. The subject position offered by *The Sun* might be said to challenge the hegemony of the masculinity constructed in Wimbledon. Drawing on a competing discourse of masculinity, *The Sun* invites its readers to discipline Henman for failing to display passion and aggression at odds with the image of the Victorian gentleman beloved by *The Times* and the BBC. The masculinity inscribed into the address of *The Sun* has characteristics more commonly associated with mediated sports less dominated by nostalgia than Wimbledon. It is not a subjugated masculinity, but simply a competing one. Wimbledon's nostalgia is for a world of fixed hierarchies, including those of class, gender, race and nation. With Henman's defeat, however, the bubble has burst for *The Sun*. As a populist tabloid, the interests of its readers are not so readily represented in such a fantasy as those of *The Times*. The different viewing positions made available by the media thus indicate the instability of gender, demonstrating that sporting masculinity is in process and constantly subject to reinvention.

Rather than document and describe masculinities as if they were the natural correlates of being a man, a consideration of masculinity-as-signs presents a means to de-naturalise sporting masculinity. The multiplicity and flexibility observable within the sport media's construction of masculinity, both in terms of image and subject position, allows sporting masculinity to be theorised as performative, being brought into being as it is performed, neither timeless nor essential.

References

Beynon, J. (2002) *Masculinities and Culture*, Buckingham: Open University Press.
Butler, J. (1990) *Gender Trouble: Feminism and the Subversion of Identity*, London: Routledge.
Butler, J. (1993) *Bodies that Matter: On the Discursive Limits of 'Sex'*, London: Routledge.

Connell, R. (1998) 'Masculinities and globalization', *Men and Masculinities*, 1, 1: 3–23.

Free, M. and Hughson, J. (2003) 'Settling accounts with hooligans: gender blindness in football supporter subculture research', *Men and Masculinities*, 6, 2: 136–55.

Kennedy, E. (2000) 'She wants to be a sledgehammer? Tennis femininities on British television', *Journal of Sport and Social Issues*, 25, 1: 56–72.

Kennedy, E. (2004) 'Bodies laid bare: sport and the spectacle of masculinity', in E. Kennedy and A. Thornton (eds) *Leisure, Media and Visual Culture: Representations and Contestations*, Eastbourne: Leisure Studies Association.

Lloyd, M. (1999) 'Performativity, parody, politics', *Theory, Culture and Society*, 16, 2: 195–213.

Petersen, A. (2003) 'Research on men and masculinities: some implications of recent theory for future work', *Men and Masculinities*, 6, 1: 54–69.

Saco, D. (1992) 'Masculinity as signs: poststructuralist feminist approaches to the study of gender', in S. Craig (ed.) *Men, Masculinity and the Media*, London: Sage.

Stearns, P. (1987) 'Men, boys and anger in American society', in J. Mangan and J. Walvin (eds) *Manliness and Morality: Middle-Class Masculinity in Britain and America 1800–1940*, Manchester: Manchester University Press.

Van Zoonen, L. (1991) 'Feminist perspectives on the media', in J. Curran, D. Morley and V. Walkerdine (eds) *Cultural Studies and Communications*, London: Edward Arnold.

Whannel, G. (1992) *Fields in Vision: Television Sport and Cultural Transformation*, London: Routledge.

Wilson, B. (1997) '"Good Blacks" and "Bad Blacks": media constructions of African-American athletes in Canadian basketball', *International Review for the Sociology of Sport*, 32, 2: 177–89.

Young, R. (1995) *Colonial Desire: Hybridity in Theory, Culture and Race*, London: Routledge.

Part II

Transgressing
femininities in sport

The contested terrain of the Women's National Basketball Association arena

Tiffany K. Muller

Introduction

On Sunday, August 2, 2002, during a New York Liberty Women's National Basketball Association (WNBA) game, a group of New York Liberty women's basketball fans, 'Lesbians for Liberty', staged a kiss-in. In a planned protest of Liberty management policy, specifically aimed at the lack of support for Gay Pride Month, Lesbians for Liberty drew attention to the WNBA's perceived disregard for its large lesbian fan base. Participants did this by, most notably, standing and kissing during breaks in play, and by waving banners stating, 'Liberty: Lesbian fans fill your stands. Liberty for All?'

This protest signifies the space of the New York Liberty basketball arena as a site of cultural importance. WNBA game space, which includes the sports arena and the urban centre in which it is located, is a public venue through which hegemonic cultural norms are simultaneously constructed and challenged. In this chapter, I explore the spaces of two U.S. women's professional basketball teams generally, and the transgressive act of one politically motivated group specifically, to argue that WNBA spaces are sites laden with social and cultural significance. Practices within this space offer insight into both the changes in and reification of historic norms of femininity. Moreover, the spatialized politics of lesbian participation in WNBA spaces depict a complex illustration of identity politics in which lesbians both accept and resist the prevailing (hetero)norms that define these spaces. Yet a closer look at lesbian participation also suggests that an overt protest like the Liberty kiss-in masks the complexities of lesbian identities.

This chapter, then, seeks to develop one reading of one type of leisure landscape, as well as exploring an act of resistance within this terrain. To begin, I provide a theoretical overview in which I outline major concepts informing this chapter, highlighting in particular the socio-spatiality of sport venues. Next, I use ethnographic research to describe one venue of women's sport space, the arena of U.S. women's professional basketball. Through this illustration, I suggest that a nuanced understanding of WNBA spaces must highlight how practices within these spaces challenge and reinscribe historic notions of heteronormative femininity. As such, this analysis grapples with how WNBA spaces serve to maintain *and* disrupt the current masculine-centred system of sport. In so doing, I argue that female basketball fans compose a type of counter-public, or group of marginalized identities that, through participation in WNBA venues, tries to contest the hegemonic masculine norm. Finally, I turn to lesbian participation in WNBA spaces. Arguably the largest and most dedicated group of WNBA fans, lesbians are rendered nearly invisible through heteronormative inscriptions including WNBA marketing strategies and practices within game spaces, which lesbians both resist and accept. Still, the complexities of lesbian identities are similarly obscured by protests like the Liberty kiss-in that reify certain identity categories. By way of conclusion, then, I examine the Lesbians for Liberty kiss-in as a disruptive performance within WNBA space, both in terms of its function in situating lesbians as an opposition counter-public, and as it conceals the nuance of lesbian identities. To analyze the former, I place lesbian identity politics in conversation with a theory about counter-publics in order to demonstrate how accepted strategies to access and expand public space and discourse, such as the Liberty kiss-in, cannot be interpreted simply as an act of resistance. Indeed, the Liberty kiss-in was a protest to claim recognition within a heteronormative space whose efficacy was challenged because two counter-publics, women Liberty fans generally and one active group of lesbian fans specifically, both grappled for the right to be recognized and to claim public space in a historically undisputed male arena. Yet the consequences of that conflict resulted in a diffused attempt to challenge the hegemonic masculine norm that dominates sport space. To analyze the latter, then, I situate the kiss-in within scholarship that complicates lesbian identity. Various reactions to and interpretations of the kiss-in demonstrate that this political strategy obfuscates the richness of lesbian identities.

This chapter is based on doctoral research that began in June 2003 at three WNBA sites: Minneapolis, MN; Seattle, WA; and New York, NY. The research is qualitative in focus; it includes discourse analysis, participant observation, in-depth interviews and focus groups with self-identified lesbian participants. While this analysis is admittedly partial, a close look at the portion of the WNBA fan base comprised of lesbian identities is fruitful for highlighting what I perceive as a series of contradictions between lesbian use of and experience in WNBA spaces on the one hand, and the heteronormative mapping of WNBA spaces on the other. By focusing on lesbian participants only, I want to call attention to the heterosexual–lesbian binary that is at play in WNBA spaces, and attempt to make sense of how 'otherness' is constructed, organized, ignored, and contested in and through the use of this binary in these leisure sites. The ethnographic content of the chapter, then, is drawn from more than fifty hours of participant observation in two venues, Minneapolis and New York. The analysis of the Liberty protest relies both on ethnography and analysis of the media discourse from event coverage.

Theorizing sport space

The spaces of U.S. women's professional basketball are examples of women's sport spaces more broadly, which are socially produced. Following Lefebvre (1974, 1991), I understand social space as produced in and through the context of social life. Space as a social construct is imbued with social structures and relations and, as a constitutive location, it 'is integral to the production of social relations' (Massey 1994: 4). In other words, as Morin and Berg (1999: 374) contend, 'the relationship between the spatial and the social is invariably recursive ... space is socially produced, but at the same time, space itself is productive of the social'. Sport space, then, is the space produced by athletes, fans, and many other stakeholders in the system of sport. Sport space is influenced by numerous factors including the event location, participant make-up and involvement, politics of sport and the policies that are an outgrowth of those politics. Moreover, sport space influences those who consume it. As Vertinsky and Bale (2004: 9) argue, '[D]ifferent sporting places can be distinguished from each other through the operation of the relations of power that construct boundaries around them, creating spaces with certain meanings in which some relationships are facilitated, others discouraged'. In the context of contemporary United States culture, the production of sport space and the productive qualities inherent within sport space are significant because of sport's influence as a cultural institution, as is evidenced by its location as a multi-billion dollar industry and as a focal point for millions of spectators.

Despite this influence, sport spaces have not received due attention: sport scholars have only recently considered the importance of space, while cultural geographers have been slow to take sport spaces seriously. Sport scholars, for example, have examined the constitution of dominant gender roles in sports through textual and media analyses (Disch and Kane 1996; Kane and Lenskyj 1998; Pirinen 1997). However, the spatiality of sport landscapes, or how these landscapes are both produced by and productive of social relations, has largely been ignored. If the social spaces of sport are acknowledged they are depicted as unproblematic containers for athletics. One recent exception to this trend is an edited volume by Vertinsky and Bale (2004: 10), *Sites of Sport: Space, Place, Experience*, which highlights the impact of the 'spatial turn' for sport scholars: '[N]ew historical analyses of space and place have encouraged scholars of sport and physical culture to look much more closely at how forms of popular culture such as sport have been worked out in particular places through the production and maintenance of social relations and the distribution of power'. Few chapters within the collection, however, develop a spatial analysis that extends beyond description.

Similarly, whereas Aitchison *et al.* (2000) point to the ways in which geographical literature on leisure landscapes reflects a sensitivity to spatiality, little geographical literature on sport contends with sport spaces as they are implicated in social relations. Rather, geographical scholarship has been largely limited to descriptive accounts of the relationship between sport facilities and urban environments (Bale 1994; Edensor 2002); analyses of sport landscapes as reflective and productive of national identity (Crouch 1999); and examinations of sport landscapes as spectacles through which national identity is performed (Tervo 2001). Raitz's (1995) introduction to the text *The Theatre of Sport* is one minor exception: his analysis briefly explores how the built environment for sport is related to the social context that sport occurs within. Still, this examination does not interrogate the events that occur *within* the stadium. Cumulatively, this lack of attention to spatiality has the effect of maintaining an assumption that sport landscapes are insignificant.

By examining the arena spaces of U.S. women's professional basketball through a spatial lens, it becomes possible to observe how social relations are played out: how certain norms are adopted and/or contested by those who participate in and create these spaces.[1] As demonstrated through the empirical evidence discussed below, I argue that WNBA spaces are contested terrains that are implicated in both the elimination and reification of traditional heterosexual norms of femininity. As Messner (1988) and Hartmann (2002) show, a sport landscape becomes a metaphorically contested terrain when the athletic achievements earned by historically marginalized groups, and the subsequent messages that those accomplishments send, are constricted by broader social forces and historic norms. WNBA spaces, then, are material illustrations of this concept: they are spaces in which the performance of strong female athletes is both celebrated and constrained by social forces, like game day practices within WNBA spaces, and historic norms, such as traditional expectations about femininity.

A spatial analysis of the WNBA also offers material evidence to illustrate how U.S. sport is defined through embedded dominant heteronormative, gendered relations of power that privilege the male body and notions of masculinity. Messner (2002) describes these power relations metaphorically, exposing sport's masculinist theoretical centre and many contiguous margins, including women and other groups who have traditionally been marginalized in sport:

> ... the centre of sport ... [includes] the most highly celebrated, rewarded, and institutionalized bodily practices that are defined largely by physical power, aggression, and violence. The centre of sport is where it all starts, a place that serves as symbolic and economic reference point for alternative images and practices ... And sport's centre is still, by and large, a space that is actively constructed by and for men.
>
> (Messner 2002: xviii)

Further, the centre of sport is a hegemonic norm in that it gains its privileged position through consent instead of force and through 'seemingly apolitical' cultural institutions, such as professional sport leagues (Grant and Darley 1993; MacNeill 1994). In a women's professional basketball league, these relations of power show up in the very structure of the league, and they are (re)produced through specific social and spatial practices discussed below. By situating sport generally, and women's professional basketball specifically, within a spatial framework, then, power relations and social norms that are implicated in non-spatialized analyses take on a material form.

WNBA spaces

Seen through a spatial lens, the contradictions within WNBA spaces become less natural. An examination of spatial practices, for instance, highlights not only relations of power as they play out in WNBA arena spaces, but the ambiguous ways that both the WNBA organization and lesbian participants actively position themselves in relation to a sport space that is traditionally constructed as masculine. To illustrate these points, I start by giving a brief background of the WNBA, and then discuss the practices that commonly occur in WNBA spaces. Though each WNBA game, space has some unique elements, a profile of game day experiences at the Lynx and Liberty arenas offer a general portrayal for WNBA spaces on the whole.

In the summer of 2005, the WNBA began its ninth season; the league currently consists of thirteen teams, with a fourteenth to be added in 2006. The league began with a direct connection to the National Basketball Association (NBA), its men's professional counterpart. WNBA teams sprang up in cities where NBA teams already existed; WNBA teams played in the same facilities as their NBA counterparts and the NBA was partly responsible for the financial underwriting of the fledgling women's league. Though this connection has dissipated in some respects in that not all WNBA teams are owned by NBA counterparts now and the league has also become more financially independent from the NBA, WNBA teams are generally located in urban centres and play their games in stadia that, during the WNBA season (which occurs during the summer months), are vacated by men's professional sports. The Minnesota Lynx, for instance, play in Minneapolis, Minnesota at the Target Centre, an 18,000-plus-seat arena that is home to the NBA team Minnesota Timberwolves and hosts a variety of concerts and other events. Likewise, the New York Liberty play at Madison Square Garden in midtown Manhattan; it seats over 19,000 people for basketball games and is also home to the NBA Knicks and hosts the National Hockey League's New York Rangers in addition to concerts and other events. The scale of the physical setting in which WNBA events occur is obviously huge; for many WNBA franchises that are situated in minor urban markets, small WNBA audiences are swallowed up by the size of the arena spaces. A comparison between the average attendance figures for the Minnesota and New York teams illustrates the difference in audience size: in 2003, average attendance for Minnesota was 7,074 per game, whereas New York attracted an audience of 12,491 per game.[2] Still, the WNBA generates a fan base that sets it apart from other (men's) professional sports. For instance, the audience often consists of many little girls, parents with young children, and groups of teenage girls; there is also a sizable lesbian presence, which I will discuss in detail below. There is a noticeable increase in the number of women in WNBA audiences as compared with NBA games, and in many cities, a more racially diverse fan population.[3] It is feasible that this distinct audience make-up is due to the price structure of WNBA games. Compared with many professional sporting events, and men's basketball specifically, admission prices are low cost; the average New York Liberty ticket is significantly lower than the average New York Knicks ticket.[4]

In addition to the basketball event that fans come to enjoy, there are several other features of WNBA games that make them less like sporting events and more like spectacles. Though there is some variation of the game day experience at each venue, it tends to follow a general pattern. During pre-game (the thirty minutes prior to the start of the game), while teams warm up, ushers hand out game guides that introduce players and the team is contextualized in relation to the local community. This takes the form of announcers advertising the team's involvement in a fundraising campaign for a community programme, for example, or team spokespeople recognizing community members such as coaches who have been nominated as role models for young athletes. The official start of the game comes with the announcement of the home team line-up: the lights go down, there is a short video with loud music intended to get fans riled up, and the players run through an organized crowd of little girls, aged 8–12, slapping hands. Then both teams go to tip-off.

During (and sometimes after) the game there is a variety of spectacular events designed, presumably, to keep the crowd entertained. The most obvious is the 'cheer squad' who perform one or two dance numbers during time-outs and otherwise spend time in the audience encouraging, in particular, little girls to emulate their cheering. Another notable game activity that attracts fan attention involves the giant scoreboard that hangs in the centre of the arena; in addition to displaying the score and game statistics, the scoreboard has a video monitor facing each section of the audience and it plays both pre-programmed videos and 'live' audience clips. During each game, for example, one WNBA player is highlighted in a pre-programmed movie: she is videotaped sharing answers to personal questions, like 'My favourite NBA player is … Michael Jordan' and 'My role model is … my mother'. Following the format of reality television, clip art and video clips are used to make these short movies funny and personable, even silly. Similarly, video cameras throughout the arena create live audience clips by highlighting fans throughout the game. Often, cheering or dancing fans, especially children, are caught on camera as a way to keep audience attention during breaks in game play. Sometimes, however, catching fans at play is part of a contest: the audience is instructed to applaud at, for instance, the best banner or fan dressed in team paraphernalia. Finally, some WNBA teams also sponsor post-game events, like concerts.

Many of the elements mentioned above could occur at any professional sporting event. At the WNBA game, however, the spectator's experience is also defined by the portrayal of strong female athletes. Unlike representation of women at men's sporting events, where hyper-feminine (hetero)sexualized models are the norm for cheerleaders and dancers (NBA dance teams are examples which demonstrate how athletic cheering is trivialized as a sexualized object of consumption), the sport space of WNBA games is imbued with images of women as powerful and as world-class athletes. There, female athletes perform aggressively and show muscular prowess, and there is little mediation from sport announcers who inflict interpretation upon performance. WNBA game spaces are therefore sites in which female athletes 'represent challenges to hegemonic definitions of women as the "weaker sex", and the reproduction of traditional gendered power hierarchies is challenged through the very presence of the female athletes' bodies' (Sabo and Messner 1993).

Yet this analysis is too simplistic. Indeed, it misses many components of WNBA spaces that contradict the representation of 'woman as powerful athlete'. Just as Hartmann (2002) has pointed to the presence of racist practices, WNBA spaces also contain elements that reinscribe depictions and concepts about women and practices involving women that are sexualized, if not simply sexist. For example, WNBA athletes themselves often reinforce ideals of heterosexual femininity, whether consciously or unconsciously. It is not uncommon, for instance in post-game celebrations shown on screens inside the arena and to television audiences, to see WNBA players and female coaches with their children, which serves as a reminder of a woman's 'primary' role as a mother, and it is equally significant that this type of celebration is rarely seen or expected from male basketball players. This depiction of female athletes as markedly different to their male counterparts and therefore as 'feminized and sexualized others' belittles their athletic accomplishments and reifies gender hierarchies (Kane and Greendorfer 1994). As such, it is difficult to identify this space straightforwardly as one of cultural transformation.

Countless similar examples abound in WNBA spaces. WNBA players are regularly represented out of uniform and wearing make-up and jewellery (Dolance 2004; McDonald 2002). These feminized representations occur in video clips played in game spaces, in web-based and other marketing venues like the WNBA website, and in 'game guides' that are occasionally offered to audience members. These guides, often handed out free as a way for fans to get to know athletes, regularly contain player profiles and ads that depict WNBA athletes as fashion models. Consequently, in the spaces of women's professional basketball, representations of powerful athletes are largely limited to images that are traditionally heterosexual and feminine. Though representations of strong athletes and representations of femininity should not be mutually exclusive categories, the effect of this specific set of practices is to render WNBA spaces simultaneously resistant to and complicit with the traditionally masculine system of sport which categorizes women athletes as 'other'. In so doing, WNBA spaces allow little room for participants who do not conform to a specific set of heterosexual, feminine norms (Caudwell 2003; Griffin 1998; Ingham and Dewar 1999; Pirinen 1997; Sabo and Messner 1993). Homophobia and heterosexism reinforce this norm and, as I will explicate below, the ways in which the WNBA and its lesbian participants position themselves in these spaces demonstrate how these sites give rise to both complicity and contestation.

WNBA spaces and lesbian identities

A consideration of the spatiality of sport landscapes must go hand in hand with an examination of those who participate in these spaces and whose practices have a hand in constituting the spaces under examination (de Certeau 1984). As I suggested at the outset, sport spaces involve myriad participants, from fans and athletes to administrators who make the event happen and media personnel who publicize the event. For the purpose of this analysis, I focus narrowly on the relationship between WNBA spaces and one (albeit large) component of the WNBA fan base: lesbian WNBA fans. After briefly contending with theoretical questions about identity, I argue that WNBA spaces, already full of multiple, ambiguous readings about gender norms, are contested terrains for yet another reason: lesbian participants are rendered (in)visible in ways that foreclose recognition of the complexity of lesbian identities. An examination of the Lesbians for Liberty protest in 2002 highlights how the WNBA and lesbian fans position themselves in relation to one another through spatial claims, and how the complex nature of lesbian identities loses visibility as lesbians themselves are rendered simultaneously incoherent and absent.

As is the case for any space, the social norms and spatial practices in WNBA game spaces are informed by the identity positions embodied and/or performed by WNBA participants. Yet identity, as many have noted, is a slippery concept. It is dependent on the conditions of its existence (Laclau 1990), and is best considered a process in motion rather than a static and contained object (Keith and Pile 1993). Indeed, as Pile and Thrift (1995: 49) contend, identity should be understood neither as object nor as fact; it is rather 'a fiction which must be continually established as truth'. Lesbian identities are similarly fluid (Bell and Valentine 1995a, 1995b; Jenness 1992; Valentine 1995) and, as Valentine (1993a) has noted, lesbians may perform certain identities in certain spaces, and maintain or perform multiple spatialized identities across different times. In as much as lesbian participants inform WNBA spaces, however, lesbian identities disappear into heteronormative spatial practices, as well as media and marketing strategies that play a role in structuring WNBA spaces. This phenomenon has been widely covered in the gay press; the following is one example from *The Advocate*, a national publication:

> [G]etting the WNBA to acknowledge the support of [lesbians] seems tougher than a shot from the three-point line ... observers say the presence of lesbian fans at women's basketball games is obvious. Viewers at home would never know that, however, because television coverage ignores the cheering lesbians in the stands in favour of pom-pom-waving kids.
>
> (Kort 1997: 59)

McDonald (2002) and Dolance (2004) are among the few scholars to have examined the WNBA fan base and marketing techniques, and they confirm these observations; in spite of a large lesbian audience which embodies a wide range of identity categories like age, race, and class, these participants are hardly acknowledged as taking part in WNBA spaces.[5]

A closer look still at the lesbian identities which do inhabit and experience WNBA spaces illustrates the diversity one would expect from a group numbering in the thousands. In addition to the range of identity categories listed above, lesbian participants have divergent views about the WNBA's policy of mapping the league in a heteronormative fashion. Although a lesbian kiss-in protest, like the one to be examined, could momentarily lead onlookers to think that lesbians actively resist such mapping, Dolance (2004) has shown that some lesbians in fact closet themselves for the sake of the WNBA. Her empirical data reveal that because lesbianism is the threat 'masked' by heteronormative practices and marketing:

> ... the solution to this threat for some fans is to play down the lesbian presence at games, [and] for players and coaches to remain 'in the closet' ... For these fans, the problem is not institutional homophobia but a league on the verge of folding that might be saved if only the lesbian issue might be effectively avoided.
>
> (Dolance 2004: 141)

There remains an attraction, however, to using identity politics 'as a way of establishing the legitimacy of alternative bodied subjects' (Pile and Thrift 1995: 49), in spite of the potential to foreclose the diversity of the identity group itself. One way to understand this tendency is to consider how identity politics are used to establish legitimacy through inclusion in public spaces (Fraser 1997; Marston 1990; Mitchell 1995; Staeheli 1996). Feminist critiques of Habermasian conceptualizations of the bourgeois democratic public sphere, for example, demand a more nuanced understanding of political agency within public spaces, including a focus on both the materiality of location and on the content of political claims (Staeheli 1996: 602). One such revision to the Habermas model is Fraser's (1997) theory that there are publics as well as subaltern counter-publics, or groups whose membership stems from marginalized communities and whose participation in democratic societies also enables the expansion of discursive space through contestation. Identity politics clearly fits within this framework and lesbians can be recognized as one of many counter-publics. Understanding lesbian resistance to hegemonic discourse requires paying attention to multiple counter-discourses and to how certain actions destabilize normative geographies and identities by being 'out of place' (Cresswell 1996). Taking a closer look at the content of protest action, then, a kiss-in, which locates a seemingly private action in the public domain, demands attention and calls for social change by challenging dominant, heteronormatively defined space through competing discourses of sexuality and public action (Valentine 1993b). The kiss-in, as an act of 'resistance', equally politically intentioned and reliant on outcome, demands that attention be paid to the expectations that inform both consumption and production of practices in this venue. Yet for the lesbian counter-public that participates, launching a kiss-in protest risks demonstrating a false unity on behalf of the entire identity group. This is just one of the many limitations to identity politics and strategic essentialism, as previous research has noted (Brah 1996; Butler 1991; de Lauretis 1986; Fuss 1989). Claims to voice and space, and therefore legitimacy, often occur only by essentializing lesbians as an identity group, which forecloses the complexity and fluidity of lesbian identities (Butler 1991).

The Liberty kiss-in

The New York Liberty WNBA team claims to be for all fans; the management rhetoric is inclusive, claiming that the team is for everyone and does not reach out to any groups specifically. Yet their community outreach efforts and team-sponsored events in game spaces show a different picture, as Overstreet (2002) details. Pointing out a scheduled Father's Day game, Kid's Game theme, and observation of Black History Month, Overstreet says, '[E]ven a quick glance of the schedule of games raises questions about that assertion' (Overstreet 2002). In spite of annual requests by lesbian fans to acknowledge Gay and Lesbian Pride month (June) during one game, or the Gay and Lesbian Pride March, which often occurs on the same day as a home game, and regardless of the fact that New York claims one of the largest urban gay populations, the Liberty organization has never overtly recognized Gay Pride celebrations.

Lesbians for Liberty, a politically motivated but fairly disjointed group of lesbian fans and activists, was born out of frustration around this issue. The group contends that the Liberty organization should lend its weight to the lesbian community as it does for other fan communities, most importantly because, they argue: 'to refuse to acknowledge the presence of lesbians is to further promote intolerance, homophobia and violence against lesbian, gay, bisexual, and transgendered people' (http://www.lesbiannyc.com/liberty). Before the August 2002 kiss-in, they pursued various tactics, including contacting the Liberty General Manager, herself an 'out' lesbian, conducting letter-writing campaigns, and handing out literature at Liberty games, in order to 'challenge the notion that lesbian lives must be lived in a more private manner than heterosexual lives' (Overstreet 2002: 3). The kiss-in was the last in a series of unsuccessful acts but, unlike the letter-writing campaigns, this confrontation included several components: Lesbians for Liberty fans attracted attention to themselves during time-outs by kissing and by displaying critical banners; they carried critical banners around the perimeter of the arena during half-time and one Lesbians for Liberty fan staged a performance of the 'invisible fan,' by dressing in a trench coat and hat: her face was covered with gauze to look like Ralph Ellison's character, *The Invisible Man*. She also wore a sandwich-board sign; written on the front and back of this sign was 'The Invisible Fan' along with a pink triangle, a common symbol of gay and lesbian communities.

By situating themselves as the voice of lesbian fans, Lesbians for Liberty claimed legitimacy as a counter-public and, as such, the right to participate and be recognized in WNBA spaces. This group used their marginal location as a space to move a counter-public into the normative, and presumably more inclusive and redefined, public sphere by making visible the inequality that lesbians persistently face as part of contemporary U.S. society (Hooks 1990; Pratt and Hanson 1994; Valentine 1996; Wilson 1995). By staging a kiss-in and redirecting the audience gaze at lesbian bodies, Lesbians for Liberty resisted the norms and limits ascribed to lesbians as sexual citizens, and therefore the challenge that lesbian lives and actions need to occur outside of the public gaze (Bell 1995; Kitchin and Lysaght 2004; Valentine 1996). Still, their claims to legitimacy centred on the assumption that they acted as a cohesive and unified counter-public against heteronormative WNBA practices and policies.

Yet there were many lesbian fans who were not involved in the kiss-in. According to personal accounts of fans in attendance at the late summer game, most of those contributing to the protest were white women, and this was reflected in the press coverage that recorded the event. Moreover, there was a diverse response to the kiss-in within the gay press. In addition to supportive articles and editorials, there was dissension among lesbian fans about the kiss-in as a necessary or effective strategy. In 'Spare me the outrage: I go to Liberty games for the basketball', for example, Kathleen Warnock (2002) discusses her disappointment with the protest tactics, considering them to be wasted political effort in the wrong venue, as well as her disgust with the idea of more specialized niche marketing for the WNBA. She interprets marketing tactics that reach out to explicit (lesbian) communities as making the support and consumerism for the WNBA different from support for its male counterpart and argues that this distinction further marginalizes women's basketball (Creedon et al. 1994). Warnock also comments on her irritation that the kiss-in generated publicity that took more attention away from women's basketball; she states:

> Newsday can't even run the damned standings every day or send a reporter to the away games, but they had a bylined piece in the 'entertainment' section about kissing lesbians ... Congratulations, girls! You've titillated a nation and drawn attention away from professional athletes doing their job.
>
> (Warnock 2002)

Among lesbian fans, then, competing discourses emerged in response to spatial claims made on behalf of a 'united' counter-public. Competition among counter-discourses is useful to broaden public dialogue and, according to Fraser (1997: 82), to promote 'participatory parity'. Moreover, conflict within the counter-public reduces the potential to read lesbian fans as an unproblematically singular identity group. Lacking a cohesive response from a lesbian audience, however, the end result of the kiss-in protest was not a lasting resistance to the heteronormative discourse it tried to displace. Despite Lesbians for Liberty claims for recognition, little has changed in Liberty's spatial practices or marketing strategies to suggest that the individual team, or the WNBA as an organization, acknowledges lesbian fans as a significant component of their organizational identity. Consequently, although the visibility of the kiss-in may have opened an important, if short-lived, fissure in the dominant spatial narrative, long-term political gains that may have been achieved if a conscientiously diverse lesbian counter-public staged a campaign were thwarted. In effect, the visibility gained by the Lesbians for Liberty kiss-in rendered the diversity of lesbian identities invisible and, through the clamour that ensued within the counter-public, rendered lesbians invisible entirely by allowing the WNBA to not take seriously the antagonisms that caused the protest.

There is yet one more reason to question the effectiveness of the Liberty kiss-in, which is that the protest took place in a WNBA space where contentious readings about gender norms already exist. As specific forms of femininity and heteronormativity are spatialized through structural elements of WNBA spaces, especially game-day practices and media and marketing discourses, the right to claim public space in a historically male arena is constrained for female participants more generally. As a result, women in WNBA spaces themselves constitute a counter-public as they resist and comply with the confines of appropriate femininity set forth in WNBA spaces. Lesbian protestors, who demanded recognition in the face of overwhelming heteronorms, therefore competed with another, albeit unorganized, counter-public that challenged spatialized femininity. By performing the kiss-in within a WNBA space, where women still must actively situate themselves in relation to the traditional norm that male equals athlete, competition between two counter-publics, women participants generally and one group of lesbian fans specifically, promoted a type of disparity wherein the parties talked *past*, not *to* each other. Consequently, the openings to contest oppressive heteronormativity momentarily facilitated by the kiss-in were rendered less effective by competition with another marginalized group.

Though theories about counter-publics suggest that competition is beneficial for the expansion of inclusive discursive space as a whole, this case suggests the opposite: on the one hand, competition within a counter-public may undermine the group's efforts, and competition between counter-publics may detract from the strength of the individual group. Worse still, either type of competition may benefit the exclusionary gendered and heteronormative discourses and practices that dominate WNBA spaces.

Conclusion

Examining WNBA spaces highlights the necessity to appreciate 'politics in particular places and at particular spatial scales' as culturally relevant (Brown 1997). As landscapes that are highly structured through gendered and heteronormative discursive and spatial practices, WNBA spaces are politically contentious, asking that those who participate in these spaces conform to and/or ignore feminized and heterosexualized discourses and practices in order to support women's basketball. Unless the WNBA undergoes a drastic change in organizational policy, it is likely that some participants will find active opposition necessary; political organizing may be the obvious strategy to claim space and recognition, and therefore legitimacy, and simultaneously counteract hegemonic norms. This case study therefore demonstrates at least two potential pitfalls of techniques that centre on representing an identity group as a cohesive counter-public. On the one hand, Lesbians for Liberty professed to speak for all lesbian fans, and made a political claim on behalf of a marginalized and presumably unified identity group. The kiss-in, then, claimed legitimacy through its portrayal of lesbian fans as a singular counter-public; in so doing, the protest masked the diversity within the identity group, which became decidedly apparent through contestation within the lesbian fan base over reaction to the kiss-in. On the other hand, the efficacy of the protest was jeopardized by competition between counter-publics. Because conflict over normative gender assumptions already exists in WNBA spaces, which situate women fans generally within a counter-public, Lesbians for Liberty was not the only group to make claims for space and recognition. Competition, however, did not seem to promote a widening of discursive space or a reconsideration of heteronormative spatial practices. Rather, competition between counter-publics may have diluted the claims of both groups, leaving the WNBA to continue to enact gendered and heteronormative policies and practices.

Acknowledgements

I would like to thank the University of Minnesota Geography Department and the Woodrow Wilson Fellowship in Women's Studies for assistance in funding this research.

Notes

1 In this chapter, I am using 'arena spaces' to refer strictly to the material environments in which WNBA games are played: the courtside area of large sport stadia. It should be noted, however, that I am conducting a more thorough spatial analysis of the sport landscape for my dissertation, including the sport stadia and other aspects of the built environment used by WNBA teams.
2 These figures are approximate totals. New York's attendance decreased during the 2004 season, but figures may have been adversely affected by two unrelated factors: the month-long break during August for the 2004 Summer Olympic Games, and the temporary (6-game) relocation of the team to Radio City Music Hall. See http://www.womensbasketballonline.com/wnba/wnbattendance.html for more complete attendance statistics.
3 Whereas the average WNBA crowd is 78 per cent female (Potkey, R. (29 June 2003) 'Fashionably proud', Ventura County Star).
4 New York Liberty ticket prices vary, but $30 U.S. covers a wide range of seats in the arena. For a comparable seating location at a New York Knicks game, the price

increases to $110 U.S. Val Ackerman, WNBA President until 2005, explicitly notes the difference in the WNBA fan base as compared with the male counterpart NBA; she states that it is 'very different than what you would see at an NBA game'. Ackerman, V. (2002) *WNBA.com: Val Ackerman News Conference*. WNBA. Retrieved December 8, 2002, from http://www.wnba.com/allstar2002/ackerman_020715.html, p. 3.
5 The Los Angeles Sparks demonstrate the exception to this policy by partnering with a lesbian bar in order to garner support for the team. See Smith, M. (14 June 2001) 'WNBA team partners with lesbian club, to promote games', *Orange County Register*.

References

Aitchison, C.C., MacLeod, N.E. and Shaw, S.J. (2000) *Leisure and Tourism Landscapes: Social and Cultural Geographies*, London and New York: Routledge.

Armstrong, K. (2001) 'Self and product image congruency among male and female minor league ice hockey spectators: implications for women's consumption of professional men's sports', *Women in Sport and Physical Activity Journal*, 10, 2: 1–27.

Bale, J. (1994) *Landscapes of Modern Sport*, Leicester: Leicester University Press.

Bell, D. (1995) 'Pleasure and danger: the paradoxical spaces of sexual citizenship', *Political Geography*, 14, 2: 139–53.

Bell, D. and Valentine, G. (1995a) *Mapping Desire: Geographies of Sexualities*, London and New York: Routledge.

Bell, D. and Valentine, G. (1995b) 'The sexed self: strategies of performance, sites of resistance', in S. Pile and N. Thrift (eds) *Mapping the Subject*, London and New York: Routledge.

Brah, A. (1996) *Cartographies of Diaspora: Contesting Identities*, London: Routledge.

Brown, M. (1997) 'The cultural saliency of radical democracy: moments from the AIDS quilt', *Ecumene*, 4, 1: 27–45.

Butler, J. (1991) 'Imitation and gender subordination', in D. Fuss (ed.) *Inside/Out: Lesbian Theories/Gay Theories*, New York: Routledge.

Caudwell, J. (2003) 'Sporting gender: women's footballing bodies as sites/sights for the (re)articulation of sex, gender, and desire', *Sociology of Sport Journal*, 20, 4: 371–86.

Creedon, P.J., Cramer, J.A. and Granitz, E.H. (1994) 'Pandering or empowering? Economics and promotion of women's sports', in P.J. Creedon (ed.) *Women, Media and Sport*, Thousand Oaks, CA: Sage.

Cresswell, T. (1996) *In Place/Out of Place: Geography, Ideology and Transgression*, Minneapolis, MN: University of Minnesota Press.

Crouch, D. (ed.) (1999) *Leisure/Tourism Geographies: Practices and Geographical Knowledge*, London and New York: Routledge.

de Certeau, M. (1984) *The Practice of Everyday Life*, London: University of California Press.

de Lauretis, T. (1986) *Feminist Studies/Critical Studies*, Bloomington, IN: Indiana University Press.

Disch, L. and Kane, M.J. (1996) 'When a looker is really a bitch: Lisa Olson, sport, and the heterosexual matrix', *Signs: Journal of Women in Culture and Society*, 21, 3: 278–308.

Dolance, S. (2004) *We Are Family? The WNBA's Appropriation of Lesbian Community and Culture*. Doctoral dissertation. UMI: 3138140, available on ProQuest.

Edensor, T. (2002) *National Identity, Popular Culture, and Everyday Life*, Oxford: Berg.

Fraser, N. (1997) *Rethinking the Public Sphere: A Contribution to the Critique of Actually Existing Democracy: Justice Interruptus*, New York: Routledge.

Fuss, D. (1989) *Essentially Speaking: Feminism, Nature and Difference*, London: Routledge.

Grant, C. and Darley, C. (1993) 'Equity: what price equality?', in G. Cohen (ed.) *Women in Sport: Issues and Controversies*, Newbury Park, CA: Sage Publications.

Griffin, P. (1998) *Strong Women, Deep Closets*, Champaign, IL: Human Kinetics.

Hartmann, D. (2002) 'Sport as contested terrain', in D.T. Goldberg and J. Solomos (eds) *A Companion to Racial and Ethnic Studies*, Malden, MA: Blackwell.

Hooks, B. (1990) 'Marginality as a site of resistance', in R. Ferguson, M. Gever, M. Trini and C. West (eds) *Out There: Marginalization and Contemporary Culture*, New York and Cambridge, MA: New Museum of Contemporary Art and MIT Press.

Ingham, A.G. and Dewar, A. (1999) 'Through the eyes of youth: "deep play" in Pee-Wee Ice Hockey', in J. Coakley and P. Donnelly (eds) *Inside Sports*, London: Routledge.

Jenness, V. (1992) 'Coming out: lesbian identities and the categorization problem', in K. Plummer (ed.) *Modern Homosexualities: Fragments of the Lesbian and Gay Experience*, London: Routledge.

Kane, M.J. and Greendorfer, S.L. (1994) 'The media's role in accommodating and resisting stereotypical images of women in sport', in P.J. Creedon (ed.) *Women, Media and Sport*, Thousand Oaks, CA: Sage.

Kane, M.J. and Lenskyj, H.J. (1998) 'Media treatment of female athletes: issues of gender and sexualities', in L. Wenner (ed.) *MediaSport*, London and New York: Routledge.

Keith, M. and Pile, S. (eds) (1993) *Place and the Politics of Identity*, London and New York: Routledge.

Kitchin, R. and Lysaght, K. (2004) 'Sexual citizenship in Belfast, Northern Ireland', *Gender, Place and Culture*, 11, 1: 83–103.

Kort, M. (9 December 1997) 'The girls in the bleachers', *The Advocate*, 748: 59.

Laclau, E. (1990) *New Reflections on the Revolutions of our Time*, London: Verso.

Lefebvre, H. (1974, 1991) *The Production of Space* (trans. D. Nicholson-Smith), Oxford: Blackwell Publishing.

MacNeill, M. (1994) 'Active women, media representations, and ideology', in S. Birrell and C. Cole (eds) *Women, Sport, and Culture*, Champaign, IL: Human Kinetics.

Marston, S. (1990) 'Who are "the people"?: gender, citizenship, and the making of the American nation', *Environment and Planning D: Society and Space*, 8, 4: 449–58.

Massey, D. (1994) *Space, Place, and Gender*, Minneapolis, MN: University of Minnesota Press.

McDonald, M. (2002) 'Queering whiteness: the peculiar case of Women's National Basketball Association', *Sociological Perspectives*, 45, 4: 379–96.

Messner, M. (1988) 'Sports and male domination: the female athlete as contested ideological terrain', *Sociology of Sport Journal*, 5: 197–211.

Messner, M. (2002) *Taking the Field: Women, Men, and Sports*, Minneapolis, MN: University of Minnesota Press.

Mitchell, D. (1995) 'The end of public space? People's Park, definitions of the public and democracy', *Annals of the Association of American Geographers*, 85, 1: 108–33.

Morin, K.M. and Berg, L.D. (1999) 'Emplacing current trends in feminist historical geography', *Gender, Place and Culture*, 6, 4: 311–30.

Overstreet, R. (2002) Liberty for all: lesbians matter to women's basketball, *Gay City News*. http://www.gaycitynews.com/GCN11/basketball.html. Accessed 1 December 2002.

Pile, S. and Thrift, N. (eds) (1995) *Mapping the Subject*, London and New York: Routledge.

Pirinen, R.M. (1997) 'The construction of women's position in sport: a textual analysis of articles on female athletes in Finnish women's magazines', *Sociology of Sport Journal*, 14, 3: 290–301.

Pratt, G. and Hanson, S. (1994) 'Geography and the construction of difference', *Gender, Place and Culture*, 1, 1: 5–29.

Raitz, K. (ed.) (1995) *The Theatre of Sport*, Baltimore, MD: Johns Hopkins University Press.

Sabo, D. and Messner, M. (1993) 'Whose body is this? Women's sports and sexual politics', in G. Cohen (ed.) *Women in Sport: Issues and Controversies*, Newbury Park, CA: Sage Publications.

Staeheli, L. (1996) 'Publicity, privacy, and women's political action', *Environment and Planning D: Society and Space*, 14, 5: 601–19.

Tervo, M. (2001) 'Nationalism, sports and gender in Finnish sports journalism in the early twentieth century', *Gender, Place and Culture*, 8, 4: 357–73.

Valentine, G. (1993a) 'Negotiating and managing multiple sexual identities: lesbian time–space strategies', *Transactions of Institute of British Geographers*, 18: 237–48.

Valentine, G. (1993b) '(Hetero)sexing space: lesbian perceptions and experiences of everyday spaces', *Environment and Planning D: Society and Space*, 11, 4: 395–413.

Valentine, G. (1995) 'Out and about: geographies of lesbian landscapes', *International Journal of Urban and Regional Research*, 19, 1: 96–111.

Valentine, G. (1996) '(Re)negotiating the "heterosexual street": lesbian productions of space', in N. Duncan (ed.) *Body Space*, London: Routledge.

Vertinsky, P. and Bale, J. (eds) (2004) *Sites of Sport: Space, Place, Experience*, London and New York: Routledge.

Warnock, K. (2002). 'Spare me the outrage: I go to Liberty games for the basketball', *Gay City News*. http://www.gaycitynews.com/GCN11/opinionbasket.html. Accessed 1 December 2002.

Wilson, E. (1995) 'Rhetoric of urban space', *New Left Review*, 209: 146–60.

Chapter 5

Triathlon as a space for women's technologies of the self

Amanda Jones and
Cara Carmichael Aitchison

Introduction

Informed by the theoretical work of Foucault (1978, 1979, 1988), the feminist writings of Bordo (1993) and the sport feminist work of Markula (2003), this chapter examines triathlon as both a cultural site and practice in which 'technologies of the self' are performed (Foucault 1988). Technologies of the self can be described as practices that permit individuals to effect, by their own means or with the help of others, a certain number of transformations to their own bodies, thoughts, conduct, and ways of being in order to develop or attain new states of happiness, purity, wisdom, perfection or empowerment (Foucault 1988: 18). *Technologies of the self* embody resistance, transgression and empowerment on the part of the individual, unlike *technologies of power* which signify disempowerment on the part of the individual as a result of oppressive regimes of power effected through dominant discourses.

Through these technologies of the self the woman begins to recognise herself as an active subject or individual with agency and, in this sense, she can be understood to counter dominant discourses of power. Rail and Harvey (1995) argue that technologies of the self release the individual from the control of disciplinary practices and consequently lead to self-transformation. Although sport feminists such as Markula (1995) have analysed how sport acts as a technology of power and domination, few researchers have analysed how sport acts as a technology of the self, particularly from a sport feminist perspective (Ashton-Shaeffer *et al.* 2001; Guthrie and Castelnuovo 2001; Markula 2003). Chapman (1997), however, has identified such technologies as coping mechanisms within discourses of power, and Wesely (2001) has identified technologies of the self in athletes' changing body shapes. These findings suggest that sport and, in this case, triathlon can function both as a technology of power and as a technology of the self. It is this contradiction between technologies of the self as empowering and technologies of power as oppressive that this chapter seeks to explore. Such an exploration takes place within the research context of the sport of triathlon.

Defining technologies of the self

Diet and exercise can form technologies of power for women as they subject themselves to the feminine discourses and feminising practices of dieting and compulsive exercise (Garner *et al.* 1998). However, such practices can also form women's technologies of the self when women aim consciously to transform themselves in ways that will serve to counter dominant discourses of power. What a woman wears, what she eats and how she trains in triathlon may be constructed by dominant discourses of femininity thus constituting technologies of domination or power (Nasser 1997). In contrast, feeling free to choose what she wears, how she trains and what she eats can be viewed as contributing to discourses of resistance and empowerment (Foucault 1979). When such cultural practices of resistance and empowerment are combined with critical awareness, they can be defined as transgressive practices or technologies of the self in that they consciously challenge the dominant discourses of power (Foucault 1988; Lloyd 1996; Markula 2003).

Technologies of the self is a complex concept. Wesely (2001) and Chapman (1997), for example, debate the difference between coping mechanisms and developments of the self. A coping mechanism is a reaction to the effect of power relations. For example, one of the interviews informing this chapter revealed how, in Jackie's case, sport is used as a release valve for pressures she experienced at home. She would play squash, feel momentarily empowered, but then return home and experience what she deemed to be abuse within what could be identified as a patriarchal regime of power. The difference between a coping strategy and a technology of the self is the presence of an embodied conscious self. Betty, for example, consciously immersed herself in triathlon practices as a way of developing her sense of self or subjectivities. She described how, through triathlon, there were times when she was empowered by training; she broadened her social circle through the people she met in triathlon, she travelled a lot with her job and was a powerful figure in the organisation of major triathlon events. Betty reformed her sense of self through triathlon and, more importantly, she consciously used triathlon as a tool for removing herself (physically at first and then through embodied power) from the patriarchal power relations that once constricted her.

A woman can be seen as operating simultaneously in two terrains: 'the inside' and 'the outside' (Markula 2003: 98). Feminist interpretations of Foucault's earlier works focus on dimensions located outside of the woman: dimensions of truth (how women are subjected to knowledge) and power (how women as subjects act upon each other). In contrast, feminist interpretations of Foucault's later work (1988, 1997) centre on the woman's relationship with herself and particularly the 'insider' dimension and how the inside (the relation to herself or subjectivity) is derived from power and knowledge without being dependent on them (Deleuze 1988). Foucault conceptualises this relationship as, 'the double'. 'The double is a type of interiorisation of the outside: the doubling of one's own relationship with others: a relationship that is never a projection of the interior, on the contrary it is an interiorisation of the outside' (Deleuze 1988: 98). Doubling requires a 'folding' of the outside force that relates it back to the self. This is subjectivation: 'a dimension of subjectivity derived from power and knowledge without being dependent on them' (Deleuze 1988: 101). Thus, recuperated by power-relations and relations of knowledge, the relation to oneself is continually reborn (Markula 2003: 98).

This chapter explores, through dialogue with women triathletes, the extent to which they experience technologies of power and/or technologies of the self within triathlon. This exploration engages with narratives of 'consciously planned, critical resistance' to dominant discourses (Markula 2003: 103), and what Lloyd (1996: 250) refers to as, 'particular practices of femininity [that] have the potential to operate transgressively'. In exploring these narratives we seek to understand the extent to which women triathletes embody technologies of the self to operate transgressively.

Researching triathletes' life stories

This chapter is derived from research inspired by the life stories of two triathletes, both of whom had developed osteoporosis. One of these triathletes (Karen), although under 30, had low bone density equivalent to that of a 90-year-old woman. Karen said:

> I am frightened that I have ruined my life ... It was good at the time and it seemed harmless. No one is to blame, because nobody knew of the consequences ... I want to stop it happening to other young women ... If ritualistic behaviour patterns are learned and not innate then it would be possible to prevent them ... but how?

Both women clearly wanted explanations for their osteoporosis which, they believed, had resulted largely from various ritualistic patterns of behaviour within their sport. They were determined that their voices be heard in order to alert fellow sportswomen to the dangers of ritualistic behaviour in sport, particularly behaviour that can result in what has come to be known as the 'female athlete triad' of osteoporosis, anorexia and amenorrhoea (Drinkwater *et al.* 1990; MacSween 1993; Otis *et al.* 1997). Their stories inspired Jones to examine the discourses related to the political and cultural practices embodied in the triathlon, an event that requires the triathlete to swim, then cycle and then run over various distances.

This chapter draws upon evidence from a three-year feminist ethnography in which Jones undertook participant observation within a triathlon club in the south of England. Through a feminist ethnographic lens Jones recorded, via interviews, diaries and drawings the women made of their social worlds, the culture that women triathletes inhabit so that an understanding of the everyday social construction and impact of sporting experience on the participants' lives and subjectivities could be developed. To provide a comprehensive study all 13 women who were members of the case study triathlon club at the start of the research were interviewed. To contextualise the research it is useful to offer a brief biography of each participant using their adopted pseudonym:

JACKIE: I am 41 years old and I suppose I'd classify myself as an able bodied, Caucasian woman from a working class background ... I am definitely a novice!

MARTHA: ... a 35-year-old Irish lass from a working class, strict Catholic background ... I am married to Rod and we never want children ... I am a novice triathlete.

PAULA: I am 34 years old ... white middle class ... I live with my partner Sandy ... I joined the club a year ago and am definitely a novice at triathlon.

SANDY: I only started triathlon last year. I am 34 years old, and a white, middle class, lesbian woman. I work full time in teaching ... I am able bodied ... We do not have children.

I'M LOUISE! ... 28 years old. I'd say I am middle class, and very much a novice to all sport! I live with my boyfriend, no children.

BETTY: I am a 30-year-old, white, Welsh, heterosexual woman. I'm able bodied and currently a novice at triathlon.

TRISH: I would say that I am an intermediate veteran triathlete. I only took up triathlon a few years ago and I am now 38. I am married but have no children and I work full time.

TINA: I suppose you could say that I am white, middle class and married (no children). I am 34 years old and a full time nurse. I have belonged to the club for 3 years and to my horror I am now classified as a veteran triathlete!

COACH: I am 35 years old ... a white, middle class, married woman with no children. I work full time ... and coach triathlon part time. I am an intermediate triathlete myself.

DEIRDRE: I am an intermediate triathlete. I am 30 years old and work full time in a professional job. I am white, middle class ... single with no children.

HARRIET: I am 21 years old. I am an elite triathlete and I have competed in two World Championships in triathlon ... white, middle class background.

CLAIRE: I am 15 years old and still at school. I am an elite junior triathlete ... white ... middle class background.

Hi, I am SHARON: I am 31 years old and a full time triathlete. I am an elite triathlete
… I was part of the Great Britain team and participated in the 2000 Olympic
Games in Sydney … white, middle class and able bodied.

The discussion within this chapter is divided into two sections with both
sections examining different forms of technologies of power and/or technologies
of the self. The first section explores the cultural appropriation of the materialities
of equipment, clothing and fashion as technologies of power, in that they
perpetuate discourses of femininity, and as technologies of the self in that they
are used to transgress dominant discourses of power. The second section explores
discourses of performance and attainment embodied within training regimes as
both technologies of power and technologies of the self. Here, issues of eating and
anorexia, exercise addiction, amenorrhoea and osteoporosis are explored. In both
discussions the women's stories reveal how the cultural practices within triathlon
can be viewed as both technologies of power and technologies of the self.

Cultural practices informed by equipment, clothing and fashion in triathlon

Equipment and clothing in triathlon, although primarily functional, also construct
(symbolic) identities that are based on a system of codes and rules including
those relating to ability, knowledge and cultural capital (Bourdieu 1984). Such
knowledge and experience, in both the use of specialist equipment and the
wearing of sport-specific clothing, become important benchmarks against which a
woman is judged in triathlon.

Because triathlon has three disciplines it affords more variety of clothing and
equipment than single sports. Clothing and equipment play a functional purpose
in swimming, biking and running as they facilitate the activities. Clothing provides
some protection from adverse conditions (for example, triathlon wet suits for
cold water) and equipment contributes in the context of safety (helmets) and
technological efficiency (for example, carbon fibre bike frames and quick release
pedals). Triathlon is thus an expensive sport with much in the way of equipment
and clothing to buy. The starting price of a carbon fibre bike frame, for example, is
about £1,000 thus indicating that economic as well as cultural capital is required
to perform in the sport. The women also described triathlon as a 'gadget sport'
and this discourse of technology in triathlon is frequently aligned with a discourse
of masculinity. Moreover, triathletes have to learn key 'transition skills' which
involve the art of changing clothing and equipment on the move during the race
and in a limited zone. Because both transitions are timed, triathlons have been won
and lost in transition. Individuals may gauge the effectiveness of a performance
through comparisons that will draw heavily upon the gadgets or props provided
by clothing and equipment. In triathlon this functional component sits alongside
the symbolic discourse of fashion. In addition to practical considerations, much

of triathlon equipment and clothing is also now considered to be fashionable and attracts prominent designer names such as Oakley.

The tight-fitting clothing and fashion of triathlon can be seen to perpetuate discourses of femininity and, specifically, the discourse of the sexualised body. For example, the skin-tight clothing is very revealing and puts emphasis on the Western idealised notion of beauty as toned, slim and bulgeless. These discourses of femininity have changed over time such that contemporary culture values physical activity and aligns the toned slim athletic female body with the sexy woman. Thus triathlon clothing serves as a technology of power in that women are encouraged to wear skimpy figure-hugging lycra that accentuates the body. However, the data illustrate ways in which clothing can be seen both as a function of power and as a technology of the self. For example, Sandy, Paula, Martha, Jackie and Trish are conscious of their bodies and think triathlon clothing only looks good on slim, toned and bulgeless figures. These discourses of attractiveness, femininity and sexuality have synchronicity in triathlon culture (Bordo 1993). In contrast, Sandy, Martha and Paula show how they use clothes to resist such discourses and, at every opportunity, throw on a baggy T-shirt to hide their skimpily clad triathlon bodies.

Although the women showed that their decision to take on the identity and subjectivity of a triathlete was individually managed, their narratives also indicated that to be accepted as a triathlete by others was not entirely within their own control. Donnelly (1993) argues that there are two distinct audiences involved in confirming and accepting an individual's identity. These are identified as the larger culture (for example, friends, family, the stranger in the street) and, more importantly in this context, the established members of the triathlon community itself. The extent to which an individual refers and defers to the wider culture or the more proximate community is likely to depend on how long they have been a 'member' of the community. Novices to triathlon, for example, may bring equipment and fashion items (like mountain bikes) which, although perfectly acceptable within the larger culture, are seen to be outside the dominant triathlon culture. Other newcomers, however, often try to buy respect by arriving at the club with the latest, most expensive, triathlon gear: a new lightweight carbon bike, tri-bars and designer sunglasses. Paradoxically, however, although this type of initial modelling may be good enough to be accepted by the larger culture, acceptance by established triathletes in the club requires far more. Donnelly (1993), for example, found that new members of a sport 'subculture' began to adopt mannerisms and attitudes, styles of dress, language and behaviour that they perceived through a variety of means.

This guided Jones, as the empirical researcher, to ask to what extent are equipment, clothes and fashion used as technologies of power or technologies of the self within triathlon. The discourses that the women linked to clothing were the discourses of femininity and, specifically, the discourses of the sexualised body, body image, attractiveness and 'the gaze' (with both men and women as voyeurs). The discourses that the women linked to equipment were the discourse of money, which they aligned with class and capitalism, and the discourse of masculinity which featured strongly when the women were engaged in technical talk or talking 'techy'.

The following evidence from the interview data and field notes can be used to explore ways in which the women in the triathlon club interpreted the symbolic value of triathlon clothing and equipment within what they all perceived to be an 'image sport'. When asked what was meant by an 'image sport', Betty replied, 'because it is all about the right sunglasses, the right shoes you wear, the latest swimsuit, the best bike, so I think it very much an image sport!' Betty admits that she loves living the image of triathlon which has become ingrained into her social world. Not only did she train as a triathlete but her job was also to promote triathlon events and to help host large triathlon events like the Ironman. Betty even admitted that she preferred to date triathletes. Similarly, Sandy stated:

> An image sport? God yes! Definitely! Posing, you know the shades, and the, oh so nice kit, the Oakley this and the £3,000 bike (not quite sure why because most of them are 'weekend warriors') and do not do it for a living; yeah, I think that it is very, um, 'image conscious', very image conscious. I have been to races where I have seen both sexes posing equally, so I think that it is 'an equal opportunity image' definitely! (laughs) Definitely, definitely ... Maybe it just attracts people that are posy!

However, another triathlete, Martha, was more critical when she described her negative feelings about the image of triathlon:

> ... that aspect actually turns me off. The races, with all the people with all their top-notch gear, their top-notch bikes and all geared up, that aspect of it does not interest me at all. That is the wealthy aspect of triathlons. 'I've bought a new bike for £1,000, let's put it on the web so everyone can see it!' That aspect of triathlon probably pisses me off ... some of these people I find quite sad, that all their money seems to go on triathlon goods – the best bike, the newest bike, the newest shoes, the best helmet, the best clothing, the best watch, the best everything! Maybe it's because they have nothing else in their lives but triathlons! Whereas I have a lot else to spend my money on! You go to races, like, and you have people like myself who, for the race, just throw on a T-shirt and who wear ordinary running shoes on the bike, and then you have people like Jackie who have shoes, but that is because she got her husband's bike and has not got to invest much money herself, because her husband invests all the money initially. And then you have got the likes of Sharon, who doesn't show off about it, but has a bike worth thousands of pounds. And for me it seems to be the difference between the elite and the winners of the age categories as opposed to people who are doing it for fun ... The men are worse, the men are more 'poserish'. It is a two-tier image, yes you know very quickly who the potential winners of the races are, you know by

who they are hanging out with, who they are talking to, how they are talking, you know the people who are new generally by the gear that they have got, but there are always the anomalies, there are always those who have loads of gear but are not particularly good.

All of the women identified how equipment and clothing were both very important to the image of triathlon. There were also many examples of what can be described as 'bricolage' (Levis-Strauss 1966). Bricolage is the process by which styles are created through the appropriation of objects from other cultural realms and fitted into a form of collage that generates new meaning for the objects (Hebdige 1979). During our dialogue Sandy identified the example of the tattoo when she spoke about how ten people in the club suddenly:

> ... all developed these rather amazing tattoos around their upper arms about two years ago, the Celtic wedding bands thing – and it was a triathlon thing, and I notice now when I go to the races just how many people have actually got them.

It seemed that the beginners had constructed a frame of reference from the equipment and clothing that other more experienced triathletes were using and wearing at races. Martha, Louise, Sandy and Paula all realise that they do not meet the fashion standards demanded by the triathlon image. Martha uses clothing to differentiate herself from others and is clearly comfortable with her own choice of consumer goods (she even did her first triathlon on a 'shopper' bike with a basket and a bell!). This discussion suggests, therefore, that there is a connection between experience and fashion-related confidence in triathlon. Martha is an experienced sportswoman who feels she does not need expensive clothing and equipment as a form of status, whereas a beginner like Jackie, who is already very self-conscious about her body, feels very sensitive to the fashion display around her.

Consumer goods for triathlon show two contrasting tendencies: adherence to and absorption in the club and triathlon culture (Jackie, Coach, Betty, Tina, Trish, Deirdre, Claire and eventually Sandy and Paula) and individual differentiation and distinction from other club members (Sharon, Martha, Louise, Harriet). Martha and Louise's stories told how they resisted the dominant discourses surrounding equipment and clothing whereas Sharon and Harriet used equipment to stand out from the rest of the club. Moreover, both Sharon and Harriet were sponsored and often received personalised clothing and equipment that no one else could buy.

Many of the women, however, were highly critical of those (men and women) who had all the gear but could not deliver an equally high-quality performance with their bodies. In the culture of triathlon these people were nicknamed 'weekend warriors' (Martha). Sandy also informed me that these types of participants were often called 'wannabe triathletes; all the gear, no idea'. Martha elaborated:

Jackie is probably a prime example of that ... I actually felt quite sorry for Jackie, the fact that she went off and she bought two bikes worth about £2,000 each, shoes – another £70, with all the triathlon training gear, with her helmet, with her sunglasses, with her heart monitor and her bike monitor, what she didn't do was then invest any time or effort or money into learning about the sport. And for me it is the exact opposite. I would prefer to spend the money in learning how to do the sport better, rather than going and buying the equipment, and yes, a brand new bike might take a minute off your time but a training day on how to train better, might take 10 minutes off your time.

This section of dialogue shows a number of elements related to the materialisation of bodies and the construction of subjectivities. Martha illustrates a disparity between the symbolic statement of equipment and clothing and the discourse of performance in the culture of triathlon. Martha clearly feels that beginners like Jackie too often try to 'buy their triathlete status'. Jackie's perception however was that she just wanted 'to fit in more'. Ultimately, however, the right to the identity of an active triathlete has to be earned through the body and triathlon training. To gain respect from established triathletes who are dominant within the club, a person needs to produce a physical curriculum vitae to support their material claims. Sandy and Paula (partners) started out with equipment that was functional and, at first, Sandy relished overtaking better bikes on her mountain bike. As their performances got better, however, so did their will to belong to the culture of triathlon and, therefore, to its dominant image. Sandy therefore bought goods that would gain symbolic approval, and Sandy and Paula's house and shed are now littered with the latest triathlon gadgets, clothes and equipment that they perceive as symbolic of *real* triathletes.

Thus equipment, clothing and fashion provide evidence of both technologies of power and technologies of the self in triathlon. The cultural appropriation or bricolage of such materialities within triathlon is dynamic and constantly undergoing revision and change due to a variety of processes both within and outside the women's social worlds. Moreover, it is clear from the data that the display of equipment, clothing and fashion played an important part in constructing gender-power relations between men and women in addition to power relations *between women*.

The discourses of performance and attainment: 'train, eat, work, train, eat, sleep'

It has been suggested that sport is socially constructed to celebrate the attributes of power, speed and strength; all symbols of sporting prowess historically aligned with masculinity (Hargreaves 1994). Triathlon is a sport that is standardised in distances and times. Races are timed overall with various split times (for example, the swim leg, the bike leg, the run leg) and change-over times (for example, how long it takes to get out of the pool, go though the transition area and start the bike leg). An obsession with time was evident in all of the women's stories. On the poolside, in the changing rooms and at social events there is a constant masculinised banter of athletes asking each other 'what time did you do?' Martha told a story of a time in her social world when she had to put triathlon 'on the back burner'. She mentioned her lack of time to train to Harriet and five men who were horrified that she had not given up the *other* things to make time for training, rather than the other way around. Martha said: 'the club wouldn't understand that … if you can't train, you haven't got time to train, well then give up everything else – and train!'

This shows how the dominant discourse of the club, which Martha suggests centres on performance, only sees the isolated functional or dysfunctional woman's body, ignoring the social, gendered, holistic individual. Such dominant discourses normalise women members to believe that a *real* triathlete puts triathlon and training as the pinnacle of their lives and frowns on those (like Martha) that do not or will not centralise the sport within their lives. For the dedicated, often obsessive triathlete, triathlon participation is a way of life. It dictates their leisure time, their work time, their choice of career, and even where they live. For example, during the research Betty spent 10 months in Australia opting to live in Cronula because that part of Sydney is known as the centre of triathlon culture. She lived with her new partner (an elite triathlete) whom she met whilst working on an Ironman competition. She spoke of how, in Australia, she 'lived triathlon' adopting the ritualistic regime of 'train, eat, work, train, eat, sleep' in a repetitive cycle:

> I'll give you a time when I was actually training in Cronula … a standard day: go out on your bike for a two maybe three hour ride, come back, you'd eat, rest a couple of hours, go for a run and then go squad (swim) training. The bike distance would be anything between 50 and 80 km, your running would be three different distances, you would do a speed run, a middle distance and a long distance; a long distance being anything up to an hour's running. And the swimming – you would normally do all that in swim squad, five maybe six times a week. Swimming is something that you need to keep up, as you know, and that would be between 2.5 and 3 km per day. So your total distances over a week would be 250–300 km training on a bike, 20–30 km running, and 12–15 km in the pool. That is training full time.

Betty's story tells how she is motivated 'just for the fact I love training'. Betty's extreme training was a practice that allowed her to maintain her subjectivities of a triathlete and to be accepted in the triathlon culture. But Lloyd (1996) argues that technologies of the self can only turn into feminist alternate politics under two conditions: they have to involve a critical attitude, and an act of self-stylisation (Markula 2003). Betty tells how, at 18, she made a conscious decision to escape from Wales and the dominant discourses of her childhood (discourses of femininity and specifically discourses of domesticity and reproduction through the asymmetrical power relations of the patriarchal family). She was driven by her determination not to 'end up like my mother' who had 'married young, had four children, never worked, and never been abroad'. It could be argued that triathlon is Betty's technology of the self. She immersed herself in the triathlon culture and was conscious that, by adopting its practices, she could transform herself into what she now describes as an 'independent, professional ... free to do what I want ... strong, powerful sportswoman'.

Deirdre described the competitive environment that she encountered when she first went to the club swim session: 'they all looked so fit! I had to totally redefine what I thought was swimming!' Deirdre admitted that she made a pact with herself the first night to do 'whatever it takes to be just like them'. In her personal diary she tells how she is not happy if she is not maintaining a subjectivity in triathlon as 'one of the boys'. Hargreaves (1994) argues that women who play alongside men in sport constantly have to negotiate their status in traditional cultural contexts of men's power and privilege and also within general discourses of femininity, patriarchy and compulsory heterosexuality. Within the club, evidence of such discourses of language and performance can be seen in the use of the term 'honorary boy', devised by the women for women. Women position themselves, and refer to other women, as honorary boys if they perceive they, or another triathlete are good enough to train with the men. It could be argued that being an honorary boy is perpetuating a masculinised standard in triathlon based on the discourse of performance which is itself based on the performance of the fastest men. The term implies that it is an honour for the women to be performing at the same level as the men. It could also be deconstructed as a term that implies that by being an honorary *boy* as opposed to an honorary *man*, the women are still not quite there in terms of physicality. An alternative reading, however, sees an *honorary boy* as a woman who is empowered through triathlon and one who has agency to transform herself to a new level. Thus, it can be argued that these women use language differently in order to challenge conventional gender-power relations and discourses of femininity, patriarchy and compulsory heterosexuality.

The attainment and performance discourses that drive many of the women to maintain a masculinised standard are too strong for them to ignore. Only when Deirdre is doing over and above the expected norm does she feel she is doing her best and able to enjoy the respect of her peers and family. Performance discourses become dangerous when they are so dominant that women engage in training practices that can be physically, psychologically and socially harmful (Sharon, Harriet, Betty, Deirdre, Tina, Trish). Deirdre, for example, emphasises the extent of her investment in triathlon by stating that she puts in 'time, dedication, hard work, commitment, a degree of effort and energy that I know is more than "the norm" ... working hard, training hard'. Deirdre identifies herself as a perfectionist whereby everything she engages in must be performed to such a high standard that there is no room for criticism. So is Deirdre's perfectionism a coping strategy, or a conscious practice that she employs to counter her residual feeling of being 'out of control' at home within some patriarchal discourse of power? Such perfectionism or obsessive levels of training are not bizarre or anomalous but, rather, are the 'logical (if extreme) manifestations of anxieties and fantasies fostered by our culture' (Bordo 1993: 15). At work or out training Deirdre feels that she constantly has to prove to herself and to others that she is the best. She is, however, also critically aware of how her extreme behaviour can help her transgress her childhood feelings of inadequacy and insecurity. Transforming her body and controlling her eating are two areas where Deirdre feels she alone 'wields total control' (Bordo 1993). This illustrates Bordo's (1993) second axis of continuity: the control axis, where the woman feels 'hooked on the intoxicating feeling of accomplishment and control' (Bordo 1993: 148).

Harriet and Sharon both describe similar arduous training regimes involved in maintaining the subjectivity of an elite triathlete. The difference in theirs and Deirdre's stories, however, is that Deirdre is an intermediate triathlete who has no coach writing her programmes or pushing her to these extremes; she is self-driven. Harriet described a typical training week in 1995 at a time when she was solely focused on competition:

> **A:** So when you were at university you said that you trained three times a day, was that every day?
>
> **H:** Yes, I got a rest day on Saturday when I only had to go for a run!
>
> **A:** So how many hours would that take?
>
> **H:** It was approximately an hour session in each, so three hours a day.

In the interview dialogue Jones asked what motivated her to train so hard and, unhesitatingly, she said 'the winning, there is no point in taking part if you are not going to win'. Harriet thus set herself even higher goals than Deirdre. Whereas Deirdre was striving for faster personal bests, Harriet was not happy unless she had won the race. Sharon, a full-time triathlete, described an even more dedicated training and racing schedule:

> I train like five or six hours a day. In the winter I have, like, I have two months in South Africa ... April I was in Japan and Australia racing, and then I have a three-week camp in France, and then I am away a lot of weekends in between that racing. I train six times a week, sometimes seven. Every other week I usually have a whole day off, or maybe just go swimming, but Monday through Friday I swim in the mornings; Monday, Wednesday and Friday I swim half five until half seven with a club and the other mornings I swim half seven until 9 a.m. just in a public session, and then sometimes I swim on a Sunday night, and then when I come home that's the swimming done which is really good. And then on Monday, Wednesday and Friday, straight away I

will do another session: either an hour's hard running session which may have some repetitions in, or on my turbo trainer on my bike, which is like stationary upstairs. I do a hard session working on my heart rate, and maybe two of those a week. And straight after that I go into town and I go to a gym near where I used to work which has a really good circuit class, and then I do an hour's circuit and then half an hour's weights. And then half an hour's stretching. And I usually get home about half four, feeling pretty knackered! And on Tuesday and Thursday I don't go into the gym and I do longer, easier stuff, like I may do a three-hour bike ride in the morning, and then do an hour's run in the afternoon. And then on a Saturday, I don't swim in the morning, I just get up and do like an hour and a half's running session, an hour's bike, or a two-hour bike, and the same on Sunday. So it's usually about 30 hours a week of training, plus all the driving back and to and things.

Sharon's strict training routine takes up most of her day and impacts on her evenings and her whole social world. She acknowledges that many relationships have broken up over such issues, however, she and her husband had set the 2004 Olympics as a short-term goal.

Sandy is only a novice triathlete but her typical training week is also gruelling. She already runs and cycles each day as well as swims three times a week. All of the women except Claire described how they felt intense agitation (Bordo 1993) on the days when they could not train. The thought of having a few days off filled Deirdre with horror. Martha said 'I go mad if I haven't run or done something for three or four days. I just get (pause) irritable ... I just start getting really restless'. Mood change due to a short withdrawal of exercise may be the first sign that some of the women's exercise programmes are ritualistic. Bordo (1993) suggests that compulsive exercisers are often perfectionists who put an emphasis on control and have little regard for their health. However, existing research on compulsive exercise tends not to consider the complexity of the power relations that surround such behaviour (Bordo 1993). Moreover, Bordo's (1993) concept of 'synchronicity' has relevance for triathlon where other components of cultural forms and practices such as power relations, body image, attractiveness and femininity occur. For example, in triathlon clothing, discourses of femininity, attractiveness and an idealised body image, combine or 'synchronise' with the discourse of performance (having a wet suit improves performance in cold water).

Harriet, Sharon, Betty, Tina, and Deirdre's stories reveal that pushing themselves to the extreme is about being in total control of their bodies. Betty says:

I am much more in control of my life, when I am training. You have got something that you are specifically aiming to do, you feel good, your body feels good, you feel fit, you can eat what you want! I don't know, you feel that you are just working yourself, you are not being lazy, gluttonous, and just drifting along. You have got control of what you are doing, you have got that direction in your life.

Deirdre, Betty, Sharon, Harriet, Trish, Tina and Jackie's stories tell how they often drive themselves to believe that they can overcome all physical obstacles, and how they thrive on pushing their bodies to new limits. Consciously, many of the women are moving their goals to make their bodies go faster for longer. In order to achieve their goals, masculinised behaviours and practices have become normalised into their daily routines. Trish who, at 26, did no sport and is now 37 years old tells how:

> ... the summer of '97 I did the 'End to End' – Lands End to John O'Groats on my bike ... over 2 weeks ... averaging 72 miles a day for a fortnight. Actually my aim – what I am aiming to do for this year is to do the Paris, Brest, Paris (PBP). It is what long-distance cyclists aspire to, because it is 12,000 km without stopping. So it is about, it is a 90-hour limit.

Deirdre prefers to train with men and openly celebrates that she is 'one of the boys' in the triathlon club and at work. She strives for a personal best (PB) in a race, but one PB is not enough. Deirdre then drives herself to achieve that time in at least two more races and then she makes the goal a few seconds faster. Deirdre said:

> I'm someone who, if I race it's with a personal best in mind and I don't feel able to enter a race for the sake of just going through the motions. If I'm entering the race I am going flat out, I am putting myself totally on the line. I'm going to push myself to the limits and I'm not interested in entering a race if I'm not in a state of fitness to be able to do that ... I'd then be looking to follow it with an equal performance in a race in say two, three weeks' time to try and register that I have reached that new level and what I haven't acknowledged is that I think that I'm someone who, having pushed so hard in both training, leading up to the race, and the race itself, certainly needs that period of recovery before I start off again ... I think, as I say, that that has been my major mistake in the past, and I've had sort of significant injury problems as a consequence. I think that my experiences are more of sort of over-training syndrome type problems that have related to a period following sort of sustained, hard training but also a period where I was certainly not getting rest or relaxation from work either.

Thus, Deirdre uses masculinised practices and the physicality of her body to provoke 'a critical, querying reaction' (Lloyd 1996: 258). She is constantly troubling the discourse of femininity by challenging gendered assumptions of women's subject position in sport and the workplace. But her behaviour and ritualistic training practices also convey ways in which she is subject to technologies of power that may, ultimately, have a damaging impact on her body and sense of self.

Elite women triathletes are especially under constant pressure to keep at the top and, in this battle to succeed, they run the risk of outcomes that may be damaging to their health, such as over-training or reducing their weight to harmful levels. In our discussion on the materialisation of the women's body in triathlon, Sharon makes some important points:

> I think that triathlon is healthier because if you look especially at say World Cup races, at the good people, there are all shapes and sizes because you've got to be, you can't be really skinny, the really skinny girls aren't good swimmers often, you know they have got no power and even on the bike you know you need muscle, you can't just be really skinny.

Despite this version of knowledge – that triathlon needs power and strength – all the women's stories (except Paula's and Sandy's) revealed controlled eating. Training to become faster was rationalised through a low-fat diet to reduce body fat and excess weight. They described intense personal battles that centred on the relationships between training and food. Deirdre explains:

> For me, eating is very firmly linked to training, and to 'earning the right to eat' ... I feel guilty about eating if I haven't trained you know and eating is firmly geared – eating follows training, and that is just a cycle that I'm locked in ... the key thing for me is ... I feel guilty about eating what would be considered 'normal', a 'normal eating pattern' and I'd feel guilty following that.

Betty's story shows a similar trend:

> A: So look back to that period when you were not training so much. What was your relationship to your diet and food? How do you feel?
>
> B: I feel fat, unhappy, lazy, completely obsessed with what I eat, guilty if I eat. I suppose it is an unhealthy mental attitude actually. I feel unhealthy, I feel ... I suppose if you analyse it there is a connection between eating too much food and if you don't exercise you can get fat. Your muscle tone goes and you don't feel as good, you haven't got as much energy to do things ... I think it controls my life an awful lot. If I don't exercise I don't feel as if I am in control of anything. I feel dreadful.

Their disciplined behaviour signifies self-control yet Deirdre and Betty also recognise an obsession that may indicate a gradual loss of that control. As Deirdre says: 'I can see a "power" of influences over attitudes and rationality that does "get a grip" on you, so that you are arguably no longer in control ... awareness is certainly a critical first step ...'.

Bordo (1993: 9) suggests that 'young girls begin early in learning to control their weight ... as part of the obscure, eternal arsenal of feminine arts to be passed from generation to generation. Harriet's story told how girls as young as 14 at her old running club viewed dieting as 'normal' even when running long distances. Harriet described how she too got pressurised into controlled patterns of eating:

> When I was at my running club there were a lot of anorexic girls down there, and you just fell into the same trap. Not the same as them but it is always at the back of your mind because they were constantly saying, it was constantly around you 'oh you shouldn't eat that, you will get fat' and when you were 14 I was just hearing this all the time. I went on the odd Slim-Fast for ages ... and it got to a stage that I just kept passing out ...

The young women in the study were at an impressionable age and vulnerable to fashion-related media images of the body beautiful which construct a 'tyranny of slenderness' (Chernin 1986). Here, it can be argued that running acted as a technology of power for these young women (Garner *et al.* 1998). The young women self-regulated by limiting food intake and by increasing running output. Dominant discourses of attractiveness and femininity within contemporary society materialised their bodies into slender bodies. As Bordo (1993: 26) argues, however, the discourse of women's slenderness suggests 'powerlessness in one context ... autonomy and freedom in the next'. Harriet and her friends, for example, celebrated and felt good after losing weight and were oblivious to any negative outcomes or serious health risks from their actions. Trish tells how she also devised very controlled patterns of eating: 'When I was a teenager I think that I was more or less anorexic ... we had a cooked school dinner, I used to hardly eat any of that, and then at tea time again I just ate the minimum that I could get by without mum really noticing.'

In interview Sharon was asked whether she had ever dieted and she replied:

> Yeah ... (laughs, uncertainly) definitely! When I was a runner when I was about 16 ... I did eat really badly for about two years, just had nothing with fat in. I was at boarding school and they only had full fat milk, so then I just didn't have any milk for two years! And I got loads of stress fractures and they don't know if it was kind of to do with not having calcium, or vitamin D and I had like three or four stress fractures in my legs in three years! I did go quite skinny, I don't think that I was ever really bad, but considering how hard I was training, you know I probably was not doing myself a lot of good ... I must have had to be strong mentally because it must have been killing me! To do the running I was doing on the kind of diet I was doing, I mean it must just have been really willpower, willpower.

To eat in such a controlled manner at a time when her body was still growing may have caused Sharon irreparable damage as her life has been plagued with injuries, especially shin splints, which may be linked to her training regimes and lack of calcium over a six-year period at school. As Bordo (1993: 185) states 'fat, not appetite or desire, became the declared enemy'. In Sharon's case the fear of the full fat milk adding a few pounds outweighed her rational knowledge that calcium was a requirement for healthy bones. She rationalised what she was doing by needing to keep her weight down to be like the other girls. Moreover, Sharon and Deirdre were both concerned over the effect of 'throw-away comments' from what they termed 'insensitive men coaches'. As Sharon said:

> Coaches are pretty crap ... as soon as you are looking a bit heavy they will say 'you are carrying a few extra pounds'. And it is so true but there is such a fine dividing line you know that can really tip people over, unless it is carefully monitored then the girls are just convinced that they are too fat ... I think that male coaches are a lot less aware of how women think, you know about their weight, and it is different for guys and girls and so I think that male coaches don't quite understand that if they say one comment it could lead to a lot of mental stress you know ... like 'Oh my God I am fat!' which will lead onto something worse.

Coach tells a story of how she overheard such a comment and of the consequences that followed:

> I know a situation where a male coach said to somebody 'you need to lose 10 pounds'... purely just a throw-away comment it was, 'if you lost 10 lb just think how much faster you would go!' I was actually on an international training camp when that comment was made and I was absolutely disgusted ... I mean that person, she was a young women, she wasn't even mature really ... we were on a two-week training camp and she was trying to survive on nothing, absolutely nothing, like a cream cracker, or a Weetabix, and you are doing three, sometimes four sessions a day! She felt that was sufficient and wondering why, you know, she was passing out, and being violently ill. But yes, you need to be extremely careful with females, we never encourage them to weigh themselves consistently, what we would always say is try a measurement test rather than a weight test.

A: What happened to that athlete?

C: She actually gave up six months later.

Drinkwater et al. (1990, 1995) agree that the adverse health consequences of 'low bodyweight in athletes predisposes women to amenorrhoea and irreversible bone loss as well as susceptibility to stress fractures' (Garner et al. 1998: 845). Discourses surrounding women's reproductive embodiment have historically oppressed women and one topic that has often been used to marginalise women in sport is the discourse surrounding menstruation.

The menstruating woman is considered the norm and is valued in our society yet this research found that *all* of the women had experienced irregular periods at some point in their lives and some (Deirdre, Betty, Tina, Sharon, Martha) had no period for between four months and ten years. Severe deviations that are categorised medically as *amenorrhoea* are defined as *disorders* or *syndromes* and are social signals that warn of a 'dysfunctional' woman. However, the women welcomed amenorrhoea and saw it as a positive relief in their lifestyle (Bordo 1993). Betty, Martha and Deirdre saw the lack of periods as an empowering experience. Harriet admitted that she experienced amenorrhoea for most of her adolescent years and well into her twenties:

> When I was running, when I was younger, yes. It used to be brilliant, I used to say, 'I haven't been on for over 100 days!' I used to tick off the months and say 'Yeah!' This was up until I was about 18 or 19 and then I went to university and started to do triathlon and so I suppose, yes it was still the same really... but when I was younger it was great, great! We used to have competitions in our running group as to who hadn't had it for the longest! We were like 'Yeah!' It was excellent; you could go for months and months ...

Although Harriet did not consciously stop her periods, she consciously chose not to seek medical advice or intervention to reinstate them. She enjoyed resisting the discourse of womanhood and experienced empowerment through her body. Coach's story also told how prevalent these issues are with young women triathletes: 'When we were coaching the National squad ... one of the girls in particular had not had a period for something like 5 years! She had absolutely no idea of the consequences of what was happening to her body!'

Clinically, an 'eating disorder' is considered a mental illness that refers to a spectrum of abnormal eating patterns ranging from atypical behaviour to gross disturbances. A few of the women were losing weight, running faster and feeling more powerful but, simultaneously, may have been becoming less healthy. There is some evidence (Drinkwater *et al.* 1991, Otis *et al.* 1997) that the prolonged cessation of periods may, in fact, be unhealthy and may lead to osteoporosis. Supporting findings from research conducted by Sherlock (1997) and Sherlock and Swaine (1995), this study also challenges the status quo and medical approaches that simply treat the established osteoporosis as a physiological condition. Deirdre has already had three bone scans and between the first two there was a dramatic reduction in bone density; a 9 per cent drop over a two-year period. Deirdre described this as a time when she was training very hard. She was then prescribed hormone replacement therapy for six months and her bone density stabilised. But, Deirdre said, 'I didn't like how I felt during the treatment and it was me that chose to come off the treatment'. This research therefore demonstrates that there is a fine line between sport practices that are healthy and sport practices that are unhealthy. Paradoxically, at the time when Deirdre's body was very unhealthy, and her bone density was at its lowest, she felt at her most powerful and empowered when she was triathlon training:

We were out there cycling about seven hours! (laughs) When you are capable of doing something like that there is such a contradiction with the notion of illness, and that is still hard to get your head round. So, you know you are that fit, but the difference between fitness and health is the ... you know someone can be very, very fit but quite unhealthy.

Conclusions

Deirdre, like many of the other research participants featured in this chapter, is not simply a projection of her inside but rather an interiorisation of the outside. This suggests that she has folded the outside forces (dimensions of truth and power) and related them back to herself (Foucault 1988). Deirdre has transformed herself as 'lean, mean and powerful' even when the language of medicine might construct her as frail, ill and at risk. As Frankenberg (1995) argues, the importance of a way of life is fundamental to a person's being. For Deirdre to change her subjectivities in triathlon and to avoid the risks of osteoporosis and other health issues would be as life-threatening to her as having osteoporosis itself. Without triathlon, Deirdre would lose her sense of self, her subjectivity, her identity and large sections of her social world. To Deirdre, her lifestyle is based upon risk management that is non-negotiable. Thus triathlon can be seen as a strategy of resistance and as a technology of the self (Foucault 1988), but one which can ultimately become its own prison.

Many of the women maintain rigid, ritualistic training routines and all except Martha are entrenched in the discourses of performance and attainment. Deirdre, Betty, Sharon and Trish all follow rituals of controlled eating and they, together with Martha, Tina and Jackie, have all experienced amenorrhoea. Betty and Deirdre are both locked into an eating–training cycle that is based on total control over their bodies, using guilt to control and food as a reward.

The data discussed in this chapter therefore suggest that triathlon practices both function as technologies of power and also operate transgressively as technologies of the self. Technologies of power are maintained through the emphasis that triathlon places upon the ideal female body, both clothed and unclothed, and through its emphasis on training regimes that can be harmful to women's health and well-being. However, it should also be recognised that some of the women's voices convey a 'consciously planned, critical resistance' to such dominant discourses (Markula 2003: 103).

Using the technical apparatus of triathlon, many of the women began to recognise themselves as agents of power and thus countered the technologies of power by developing technologies of the self. It can be suggested that Deirdre, Betty, Paula, Sandy, Martha and Jackie have all developed critical self-awareness that has led to transgressive practices and self-stylisation and that, within the context of triathlon, these transgressive practices constitute technologies of the self.

References

Ashton-Shaeffer, C., Gibson, H. J., Autry, C. E. and Hanson, C. S. (2001) 'Meanings of sport to adults with physical disabilities: a disability sports camp experience', *Sociology of Sport Journal*, 18, 1: 95–114.

Bordo, S. (1993) *Unbearable Weight: Feminism, Western Culture and the Body*, London: University of California Press.

Bourdieu, P. (1984) *Distinction: A Social Critique of the Judgement of Taste*, London: Routledge.

Chapman, G. (1997) 'Making weight: lightweight rowing, technologies of power and technologies of the self', *Sociology of Sport Journal*, 14, 3: 205–23.

Chernin, K. (1986) *Women, Eating and Identity*, London: Women's Press.

Deleuze, G. (1988) *Foucault*, London: Athlone Press.

Donnelly, P. (1993) 'Subcultures in sport: resilience and transformation', in A. Ingham and J. Loy (eds) *Sport in Social Development: Traditions, Transitions and Transformations*, Champaign, IL: Human Kinetics.

Drinkwater, B. L., Bruemner, B. and Chesunt, C. L. (1990) 'Menstrual history as a determinant of bone density in young athletes', *Journal of the American Medical Association*, 263, 4: 545–8.

Drinkwater, B. C., Grimstone, S. K., Cullen, D. M. and Snow-Harter, C. M. (1995) 'ACSM position stand on osteoporosis and exercise', *Medicine and Science in Sport and Exercise*, 24, 4: i–vii.

Foucault, M. (1978) *The History of Sexuality, Vol. 1. An Introduction* (trans. R. Hurley), New York: Vintage Books (originally published 1976).

Foucault, M. (1979) *Discipline and Punish: The Birth of the Prison* (trans. A. Sherridan), New York: Random House (originally published (1975) as *Survellier et Punir: Naissance de la Prison*, Paris: Editions Gallimard).

Foucault, M. (1988) 'Technologies of the self', in L. H. Martin, H. Gutman and P. H. Hutton (eds) *Technologies of the Self: A Seminar with Michel Foucault*, Amherst, MA: University of Massachusetts Press.

Foucault, M. (1997) 'The ethics of concern of the self as practice of freedom' (interview conducted in 1984 by R. Fornet-Betancourt, H. Becker and A. Gomez-Muller; trans. P. Aranov and D. McGrawth) in P. Rabinow (ed.) *Ethics: Subjectivity and Truth*, New York: New Press.

Frankenberg, R. (1995) 'Learning from Aids: the future of anthropology', in A. Ahmed and C. Shore (eds) *The Future of Anthropology: Its Relevance to the Contemporary World*, London: Athlone Press.

Garner, D. M., Rosen, L. W. and Barry, D. (1998) 'Eating disorders among athletes', *Sport Psychiatry*, 7, 4: 839–57.

Guthrie, S. R. and Castelnuovo, S. (2001) 'Disability management among women with physical impairments: the contribution of physical activity', *Sociology of Sport Journal*, 18, 1: 5–20.

Hargreaves, J. (1994) *Sporting Females: Critical Issues in the History and Sociology of Women's Sport*, London: Routledge.

Hebdige, D. (1979) *Subculture: The Meaning of Style*, London: Methuen.

Levi-Strauss, C. (1966) *The Savage Mind*, Chicago, IL: University of Chicago Press.

Lloyd, M. (1996) 'A feminist mapping of Foucauldian politics', in S. Heckman (ed.) *Feminist Interpretations of Michel Foucault*, University Park, PA: Pennsylvania State University Press.

MacSween, M. (1993) *Anorexic Bodies*, London: Routledge.

Markula, P. (1995) 'Firm but shapely, fit but sexy, strong but thin: the postmodern aerobicising female bodies', *Sociology of Sport Journal*, 12, 4: 424–53.

Markula, P. (2003) 'The technologies of the self: sport, feminism, and Foucault', *Sociology of Sport Journal*, 20, 2: 87–107.

Nasser, M. (1997) *Culture and Weight Consciousness*, London: Routledge.

Otis, C, L., Drinkwater, B., Johnson, M., Loucks, A. and Wilmore, J. (1997) 'American College of Sports Medicine position statement: the female athlete triad', *Medicine, Science, Sports Exercise*, 29, 5: i–ix.

Rail, G. and Harvey, J. (1995) 'Body at work: Michel Foucault and the sociology of sport', *Sociology of Sport Journal*, 12, 2: 164–79.

Sherlock, J. (1997) 'Lean, mean and feeling powerful: osteoporosis and the female athlete', paper presented to the British Sociological Conference, 'Body Matters', Edinburgh University.

Sherlock, J. and Swaine, I. (1995) 'The curse of overtraining: cultural processes and physiological manifestations', paper presented to the International Congress for Sports Medicine and Social Sciences, Gothenberg, Sweden.

Wesely, J. K. (2001) 'Negotiating gender: bodybuilding and the natural/unnatural continuum', *Sociology of Sport Journal*, 18, 2: 164–80.

Chapter 6

Gender in sport management

A contemporary picture and alternative futures

Sally Shaw

Introduction

Much of the sport and leisure management literature on gender has assumed that increasing numbers of women in sport organisations will magically cure organisations of gender-related discrimination (Hoeber 2004). This is a limited approach, for three main reasons. First, as a consequence of this dominant focus on women, gender-related issues are perceived in sport organisations to be a minority, or women's, concern, thus relegating gender relations to a women-only issue (Shaw and Hoeber 2003; Staurowsky 1996). Second, a focus on women limits our understanding of gender, as men can also face discrimination based on gendered assumptions (Ely and Meyerson 2000a). Finally, the increasing numbers of women in organisations represents a focus on outcome-based research, which encourages increased numbers of women but has little impact on changing the aspects of sport organisations that have made them inhospitable to women. For example, the second International Conference on Women and Sport in 2000 passed a resolution that urged 'sports organisations … meet the goal of 10 minimum representation of women in decision-making positions by 31 December 2000 … and ensure that the 20 goal [of representation] for 2005 is maintained and attained' (International Olympic Committee 2000). Despite the powerful and positive tone of this statement, and its sanction by the International Olympic Committee, little has changed within sport organisations over this period. Indeed, within the IOC itself, only 6 per cent of the overall membership and one out of ten Board members are female in 2005 (International Olympic Committee 2005).

Women-only, outcome-based, quantitatively oriented policies and statements therefore have significant limitations as a way to combat gender inequity in sport organisations. Their limited impact has encouraged researchers to work towards alternative approaches to understanding gender inequities in sport organisations. Increasingly, researchers are focusing on how gender relations, or the socially constructed relations between women and men (Aitchison 2005; Scraton and Flintoff 2002), are constructed in sport organisations. In order to do this, researchers have moved towards analysing the gendered nature of sport organisations by examining their history, culture, and policies, all of which may work to undermine women and men on the basis of gender, regardless of how many women or men work within an organisation (Hoeber and Frisby 2001; Shaw and Slack 2002; Shaw and Hoeber 2003; Shaw and Penney 2003). By critiquing the historical and contemporary aspects of this environment, researchers may be able to offer alternatives for change, which take into account the subtle and pervasive nature of gender relations.

In this chapter, I will provide an overview of some of this research into gender relations, and indicate how researchers in sport management have attempted to examine some of the complexities of gender relations. First, research that argues for an appreciation and analysis of the enduring, historical nature of discriminatory gender relations is outlined. A description of research into the tensions between masculinities and femininities in sport organisations is then offered, which gives more detail regarding the nature of gender relations as an organisational concern rather than a women-only issue. This is followed by an overview of research into the creation of gender equity policies in sport organisations. Overall, this first section will provide a contemporary view of research into gender relations in sport management. The final section of the chapter will outline an alternative view of how gender relations might be analysed in future, and how this might lead to change over time. Implications of these proposed changes are outlined for practitioners, educators, and researchers.

A historical approach to understanding gender relations

Sport organisations are often steeped in tradition. For example, the 2005 centenary year at Chelsea Football Club has been celebrated with nostalgia for ex-players and historical competition triumphs (Chelsea Football Club 2005). Geographic space is also afforded historical value within many sport organisations, for example the high historical and cultural value that was attributed to the Olympic games 'returning home' to Athens in 2004 (International Olympic Committee 2004). People, too, are afforded historical recognition. For example, Juan Antonio Samaranch was appointed as Honorary President for Life of the IOC as a recognition of his service to the IOC after his term of office finished in 2001 (International Olympic Committee 2005).

Acknowledging and valuing historical events or contributions in sport organisations may seem quite innocuous. It is, however, important to view these events critically and question the versions of history that we are exposed to (Alvesson and Deetz 2000). The people and events in history that find favour in organisations most often reflect the views and values of particular groups of men, usually white, middle class, and ostensibly heterosexual (Ely and Thomas 2001). Furthermore, the implications of favouring such selective historical moments can have long-lasting effects on sport organisations (Hargreaves 1994). For example, Shaw and Slack (2002) found historical evidence of the use of demeaning language in late nineteenth-century discussions about women's sports clubs. This in itself is not surprising, as the mood of the time was to ridicule and even fear women's participation in exercise. Athletics, for example, was 'considered to be a form of exercise unsuited to women's physiques that would produce an unnatural race of Amazons' (Hargreaves 2002: 62). What was surprising to Shaw and Slack (2002), however, was the acceptance of similarly dismissive language regarding contemporary women's involvement as managers within the same organisation. This was evidenced in a description of organisational Presidents that was analysed by Shaw and Slack (2002). Rather than being considered visionary and energetic, both characteristics that were attributed to their male counterparts, 'the only mention of a woman President of the modern organisation was limited to praising "her elegance, calm, and dignity"' (Shaw and Slack 2002: 93). Shaw and Slack (2002) suggested that the descriptors used for modern leaders were historically gendered. That is, men were described by the modern organisation as visionary and energetic and the only woman as more demure, which was in keeping with the dismissive tone taken in the organisation's historical documents. The precedent for this description was historically set, illustrating the strength of discourses in guiding the development of acceptable language and assumptions in the organisation (Shaw and Slack 2002).

As noted in the introduction to this chapter, gender relations have not only developed to discriminate against women. Men who do not fit traditionally 'masculine' roles have also faced historical discrimination in sport organisations. Shaw and Slack (2002) discovered, in their analysis of sport organisations' histories, that it was only high-level administrators who received historical acknowledgement. Leaders and Presidents were explicitly valued in their organisation's literature, rather than men and women who contributed elsewhere. As Shaw and Slack (2002) suggested, men who fulfilled roles further down the organisational hierarchy were rendered invisible by those who wrote organisational histories. It is possible to argue, therefore, that men who did not express conventional 'leadership' skills or values were not considered worthy of mention. Later in the chapter, I discuss how this continues to be the case, and how men who do not conform to conventional masculinity continue to be marginalised on this gendered basis in contemporary organisations.

Contemporary gender relations in sport organisations are therefore strongly influenced by the acceptance of historical discourses, or taken-for-granted assumptions about how men and women are supposed to behave (Hall et al. 1989; Hargreaves 1994, 2002). These assumptions are gendered, that is they are based upon socially constructed expectations of women's and men's behaviour. As Shaw and Slack's (2002) examination of the history of sport organisations indicated, alternative expressions of these social mores are more often than not ignored within organisational history, and thus removed from organisational discourse.

Historical decisions regarding the management of an organisation can also have long-lasting and gendered effects on modern organisations. An organisation in Shaw and Slack's (2002) study, which they called National Governing Body C, was originally composed of two organisations, one representing men and the other women. The women's organisation had made a move to merge with the men in 1895. The men refused, on the grounds that theirs was a men-only organisation. Over the subsequent 100 years, the organisations developed quite distinctly, with the men establishing a structure that enabled the employment of paid staff. In contrast, the women's administrative organisation was much smaller, despite working for similar numbers of participants, and all the organisation's administrative positions (which were occupied by women) were voluntary. The two organisations did not communicate well, other than to develop negative myths about each other which were 'reified by a profound reluctance, within both organisations, to explore and recognize the potential benefits of each others' strengths' (Shaw and Slack 2002: 96).

Eventually, the organisations were forced to merge, encouraged by Sport England, an organisation that saw the futility of two organisations with two different infrastructures bidding for funding for one sport (Sport England 2000). The merger was met with some reluctance, as members of the men's organisation felt that they would have to re-apply for jobs, which they perceived to be theirs, in the newly merged organisation. Equally, women were concerned that their contributions would be under-valued because they had previously been volunteers, rather than paid staff. Part of the reason for organisational members' concerns was based on a reaction to assumptions about each organisation that had been made over their 100-year history. Assumptions about the two separate organisations were therefore reified and were believed to be true, due to 'a profound forgetting of the fact that the world is socially constructed' (Jermier 1991: 231). Over time, gender relations that were based on mistrust became ingrained within the two organisations. This ensured that the process of creating the new, joint organisation was deeply problematic, reflecting a lack of trust between the members.

This section has indicated that the value of historical discourses in modern organisations should not be underestimated and some ways by which the acceptance of historical discourses might be challenged are outlined in the conclusion. In the next section, I turn to some of the other ways in which gender relations are expressed in sport organisations, namely through the expressions of masculinities and femininities.

Masculinities and femininities in sport organisations

As already indicated, gender relations in sport organisations are far from equitable. Inequity is not just the dominance of one group (e.g. men) over another (e.g. women). Rather, gender inequity can be conceptualised as a combination of social processes that lead to the expression of masculinities frequently dominating the expression of femininities, regardless of the gender of the people who express them (Acker 1992). Equity, therefore, is exemplified by the challenges made by individuals and organisations to these social processes.

Masculinity, or masculinities, can be associated with the aggression, strength, competition, and determination required for a successful athletic career in sport (Hall 1996; Hargreaves 1990; Lenskyj 1994; McKay 1997). In turn, masculinities may be adopted into a career in sport management after retirement (Theberge 1994), as many organisations perceive masculinities to be favourable for management (Kerfoot and Whitehead 1998). Masculinities are not just associated with men, and Martin (1996: 191) describes the expression of masculinities by women, stating, 'when a woman adopts a "male interactional style", I have heard men describe her by saying "she kicks ass with the best of them"'. Other researchers, such as McNay (2000), have suggested that women who express masculinities may be perceived as successful people, adapting to the social mores of an organisation.

In contrast, femininities, which also may be referred to in short as femininity (Knights and McCabe 2001), are perceived to include co-operative work practices, consultation, or negotiation skills (Hargreaves 1990; Putnam and Mumby 1993). These practices are often undervalued in sport organisations (McKay 1997) and are understood by many managers to be 'chaotic' and 'irrational' (Putnam and Mumby 1993: 40). Further, femininities may be made invisible in organisations by ensuring that people who express them are employed in private roles such as secretarial or support positions (Fletcher 1999). Femininities are thus associated with what Ely and Meyerson (2000b: 109) claim are dismissed by many managers as 'essentially the "housekeeping" roles of management', thus playing what is perceived to be a minor role in organisations.

Unsurprisingly, women are most often associated with femininities in sport organisations. Not only do they represent the bulk of 'caring' or 'nurturing' roles within sport organisations, they are also most often expected to express femininities outside of paid work, usually taking most responsibility for child and family care (Frisby and Brown 1991; Rehman and Frisby 2000). Men, on the other hand, are often expected to have fewer family responsibilities and can therefore devote more time to their work responsibilities (Hovden 2000). Consequently, men are more often found at the higher levels of sport organisations, in part due to the value that organisations place on masculinities over femininities.

The interaction between masculinities and femininities is not, however, straightforward. When men express femininities, for example by applying to work in more caring roles within organisations, they often face ridicule for being 'soft' (Kerfoot and Whitehead 1998). Shaw and Hoeber (2003) found in their study of three sport organisations that this concern was particularly evident around the position of Regional Development Officer (RDO). This role is one that requires a diplomatic approach, providing a link between national policy decision-making and regional or local level implementation (Shaw and Hoeber 2003). RDOs must therefore be able to communicate with high-level policy development managers as well as people working at the grass roots of sport development. Shaw and Hoeber (2003) found that managers associated these requirements with femininities and women in their study. More specifically, they found that the RDO role was not considered by organisational members to be an appropriate role for men, as respondents suggested it was 'too wimpy' (Shaw and Hoeber 2003: 359). The position was also not considered to be career oriented enough for men, who were 'not expected to stay in that role for long, but to move upward within the organisation to higher ranked positions' (Shaw and Hoeber 2003: 360). Even if men wanted to take on the role of RDO, in which femininities were expressed, they were encouraged not to. Consequently, the association of men with femininities was perceived by these organisations to be problematic, thus limiting the job opportunities available for a specific group of men.

Similarly, Shaw and Hoeber (2003) outlined tensions within organisations when women expressed masculinities. This finding mirrored other researchers' work, for example Martin (1996), who suggested that the expression of masculinities by women is often questioned in organisations. She argued:

> [t]he community of work to which men orient their behaviour ... is ... a world by and for men; women may fit uneasily in this community except in subordinate, supportive positions ... [and] men may view women's enactments of masculinities as illegitimate and/or unattractive.
>
> (Martin 1996: 191)

Shaw and Hoeber (2003) found evidence of this perception of women's expression of masculine discourses within their study. Women were employed in senior management roles with seemingly extreme reluctance on the part of the employing organisations. Indeed a male CEO confirmed that women faced 'extreme pressure' (Shaw and Hoeber 2003: 365) during their interview process, indicating that a woman's interview had been more challenging than the process faced by other, male candidates. This staunch approach was taken in interviewing women because the CEO and other managers did not want to be accused by other organisations of employing a woman as a token gesture (Shaw and Hoeber 2003). This finding clearly indicates that organisational managers were uncomfortable with the perceptions that might be held outside the organisation regarding a woman in a traditionally masculine role.

Coaching, an area that is often overlooked in the sport management literature, was identified as another contested area for masculinity and femininity (Shaw and Hoeber 2003). The coaching role was defined as being 'to develop young or novice athletes after they had learned basic skills by fostering technique and enhancing their competitive edge' (Shaw and Hoeber 2003: 367). Teachers, in contrast, 'were responsible for the early development of athletes' (Shaw and Hoeber 2003: 367). These roles were gendered, as coaching was associated with masculinities, focusing on competition, whereas teachers, expressing femininities, were considered to be more nurturing. Men tended to be more prevalent in coaching and women gravitated towards teaching. As with the RDO role, men who wanted to become teachers were considered to be 'wimpy' and women who had a passion for elite-level coaching were few in number and often faced obstacles to their progression.

Of further interest is Shaw and Hoeber's (2003) finding that if a particular sport evolved from being associated with participatory or health discourses to a competitive purpose, its association with masculinities or femininities changed. For example, when the Paralympics gained more attention from the media after the 1996 Atlanta Games, popular coaching discourses concerning sport for people with disabilities changed from being perceived as therapeutic, and associated with femininities (Ashton-Shaeffer *et al.* 2001) to an area of international competition associated with masculinities. Consequently, coaching athletes with disabilities was perceived to have been legitimised in the coaching world. This might be considered positive, as athletes with disabilities began to receive more of the acknowledgement that they deserve. However, it also serves to outline the gendered nature of coaching, which was clearly outlined by one of Shaw and Hoeber's (2003) male respondents who said that:

> ... disabled sport has been dominated by women teachers. A disabled's suddenly found that they've won a gold medal ... and is gaining elite credibility, so you're seeing male coaches seeing that as a perfectly legitimate, exciting career route.
>
> (Shaw and Hoeber 2003: 368)

This quotation displays a problematic approach on many levels to sport for people with disabilities. However, of importance here is the way in which the respondent outlines the acceptance of eroding teaching, associated with femininities, in favour of coaching, associated with masculinities. Male coaches, most regularly associated with masculinities, stood to gain from this situation, as they could expect more exposure through the successes of their now 'credible' athletes. In contrast, women who were associated with the femininities of teaching, were now even less likely to be associated with successful athletes, and thus receive even less recognition.

This example parallels Acosta and Carpenter's (2004) findings regarding the management of women's sport in American universities. The impact of Title IX, with increased numbers of and profile for women's teams in university sport, has ensured that managing and coaching women's university sport has developed. This previously virtually voluntary role, associated with femininities, is now a higher profile activity that is considered to be legitimate and is characterised by masculinity and profit (Acosta and Carpenter 2004). In the long run, as with coaching athletes with disabilities, this has meant people associated with masculinities have profited from these changes, at the expense of those who express femininities.

The above discussion of masculinities and femininities exemplifies further the gendered nature of sport management. One potential challenge to this is to develop policies that address this dominance. The next section outlines some of the policies that have been developed in sport management and evaluates their impact on gender relations.

Gender equity policies

Gender equity policies have been in existence in the UK in various forms since the 1970s, codified firstly in the Sex Discrimination Act (1975) (Cockburn 1990). Initial policies were largely ineffectual, perceived by many organisations as an extra administrative chore. Cockburn (1990) also argued that they were doomed to failure, as the dominant message in these policies was 'equal pay for equal work' and women's work was rarely perceived in organisations to be as valuable as men's. During the 1980s, attempts were made to recognise and challenge the gendered cultures of organisations, which enabled the progression of some women within organisations. The Sex Discrimination Act (1975) and its successors only applied, however, to the paid workforce. Little attention was paid to the largely voluntary sport sector until 1997 when the English Sports Council (now Sport England) took some steps towards equity, stating that 'everyone deserves the right to enjoy sport and recreation at whatever level of involvement or ability' (English Sports Council 1997: 3). In addition to this, National Governing Bodies (NGBs) had to indicate an acknowledgement and acceptance of equity in order to receive funding (English Sports Council 1997), a move that was designed to ensure compliance with the campaign. To a degree, this strategy worked with NGBs producing equity statements and policies as they complied with Sport England.

There were, however, some shortcomings with the implementation of this Sport England requirement for equal opportunities. First, the programme's focus encouraged a move towards equal numbers of women and men to participate in sport (English Sports Council 1997). As we have seen, such approaches do little if anything to challenge gendered taken-for-granted assumptions in sport organisations. Second, there was little, if any, follow-up by Sport England regarding the sport organisations' policies once they had been written. As has occurred in other fields (Ely and Meyerson 2000b), sport organisations could legitimately write a policy and leave it untouched and unused for some time without any adverse effect on funding (Shaw and Penney 2003). There were also concerns about the general nature of Sport England's guidelines, as Shaw and Penney (2003) discovered in their analysis of gender equity policies in sport organisations. Managers in the NGBs were concerned that there was not enough flexibility within the requirements to address the concerns of their organisations, for example regarding the different ages and cultures of the NGBs. For example, an organisation that was less than 20 years old and had a history of including women on its governing boards was subject to the same requirements as an organisation that was over 100 years old, which had no women on its national executive (Shaw and Penney 2003).

Sport England's (2002: 4) more recent publication targeted 'measurable outcomes' relating to equity. This statement hints that Sport England considered equity to be a tangible entity that can be measured. In turn, the 'achievement' of equity could then be linked to funding. This perspective enabled the creation of a loop-hole in which developing quota-based gender equity policies was perceived by organisational members as a way to achieve funding (Shaw and Penney 2003). Sport England's approach also led some sport organisations to engage in creative accounting, ensuring that numbers of participants reached their quota, rather than taking a more critical approach, such as a focus on undermining the dominance of masculinities in sport organisations (Shaw and Penney 2003).

Furthermore, by imposing a 'national template' (Sport England 2002: 4) for equity in sport organisations, Sport England clearly questioned whether sport organisations were capable of developing their own policies, through alternative means. As Shaw and Penney (2003) suggested, this approach by Sport England represented a lack of trust towards the NGBs, which led to organisational resistance to equity policies. Finally, Shaw and Penney (2003) suggested that the implementation of gender equity policies was considered by organisational members to be a time-consuming and futile chore, which served little purpose to the organisation. Equity policies were therefore limited in their appeal and usefulness to employees (Aitchison 2000, 2005). Ely and Meyerson (2000b) have strongly argued that equity policies do not need to be created and perceived in this way, and can have positive spin-offs for organisations, including a more effective work environment, along with a generally more contented workforce. In the final section of this chapter, I will outline how they suggest this might occur, and offer alternative courses of actions for sport managers to take to encourage equity within their organisations.

Alternative avenues for gender relations in sport organisations

The previous sections have gone some way to explaining the longevity of historical and contemporary discourses that influence gender relations in sport organisations. While sport management research has been generally slow to address the concerns that are highlighted above in a practical manner, there have been some attempts to address similar issues in the critical management literature. This section outlines some of these efforts, and indicates how they might be utilised within sport management. Specifically, Rao et al. (1999) offered an analysis of ways in which alternatives to current gender relations might be developed. They proposed that one way of achieving greater gender equity is by analysing the 'deep structure' (Rao et al. 1999: 2) of organisations, which they conceptualised as the 'collection of values, history, culture and practices that form the unquestioned, "normal" way of working in organisations' (Rao et al. 1999: 2). Rao et al. (1999) suggested that deep structure comprises four gendered elements: valuing heroic individualism; the split between work and family; exclusionary power; and the monoculture of instrumentality. By analysing a combination of these elements, individuals may become more aware of their organisation's gendered nature, and work towards alternative discourses. In the next section, I explain each of the elements of deep structure. Following this, I outline ways by which Rao et al. (1999) suggested changes to deep structure might be conceptualised and practised in organisations, linking their suggestions to sport management.

Heroic individualism

Along with other researchers such as Acker (1992), Rao et al. (1999) suggested that as most organisations were founded on masculine philosophies, it follows that masculinities are prevalent and more highly valued than femininities. As indicated above, masculinities, expressed by specific groups of people, dominate most traditional sport organisations (Aitchison 2005; Hall et al. 1989; Shaw and Hoeber 2003). More specifically Rao et al. (1999: 4) argued that a particular type of masculinity dominates organisations; that of the 'heroic individual'. They suggested that 'organisations tend to value the "hero" who works day and night against tremendous odds to solve a crisis. The person who manages her work smoothly, thereby avoiding such crises, is invisible and undervalued' (Rao et al., 1999: 4).

Heroic individuals are evident in sport organisations, as McKay (1997) has suggested. These individuals may be relatively recent recruits who are favoured by senior managers, and perceived to be in some way heroic in their organisations. In sport, a common example of heroic individualism is evident in the prevalence of ex-elite athletes who are employed at senior managerial levels without a track record in management. Heroes are frequently promoted over other, often female, individuals who have worked for an organisation for many years (McKay 1997). Shaw and Hoeber (2003: 363) discovered some evidence of heroic individualism in their study, in which a Chief Executive Officer suggested that his professional, individualistic approach was more businesslike than the previous, collective, voluntary organisational leadership, characterised dismissively in his own words as a 'bunch of secretaries'. These examples indicate how masculine-dominated heroic individualism in sport organisations can work to undermine employees' efforts that may have a more collective approach, characterised by femininities.

The split between work and family

For women who are in paid employment the tensions between work and family life can be difficult as they try to juggle children, domestic work, and paid work (Rehman and Frisby 2000). Family ties for men may also be considered by many within organisations to be detrimental to their work performance, ensuring that men who express femininities also face difficult career/family decisions. Some managers see the balance between work and family as a problem that can only be overcome if the individuals have no or few family ties (Shaw and Hoeber 2003). Powerful discourses such as these go a long way to ensuring that people who express femininities are in 'no-win' situations in terms of balancing family and career (Cameron 1996).

Exclusionary power

Gender relations are inherently power relations and Rao et al. (1999) outlined their understanding of power as follows. They suggested 'power, like technology, is neither inherently good or bad; it just is' (Rao et al. 1999: 6). It is the use of power that can have positive or detrimental outcomes for certain groups and individuals. As noted, power is expressed frequently and effectively by specific groups of people that express masculinities. Exclusionary power is so entrenched that it dominates the agenda of most sport organisations, whether in a drive to win more gold medals at the expense of grass roots development, or through expressing a desire to have individual, commercial concerns at the expense of a more collective identity, both of which may be understood in terms of the dominance of masculinity (Shaw and Hoeber 2003). Women and men generally accept the taken-for-granted domination by exclusionary power, resulting in a situation in which, 'not only is your issue not on the agenda, you are not even aware that it is an issue' (Rao et al. 1999: 7). In terms of gender relations, this means that individuals are entrenched in their taken-for-granted understandings of gender and may have little conception of it as problematic: advancing change, when people are not even aware of gender relations as 'an issue' becomes extremely difficult.

Monocultures of instrumentality

Finally Rao et al. (1999) suggest that it is necessary to analyse monocultures of instrumentality in order to examine deep structure. This complex title can be simply defined as 'a narrow focus on the accomplishment of quantitative goals' (Rao et al. 1999: 10). Gender equity policies that are deemed to be successful because they increase numbers of women or men in a particular sport are a prime example of this. Yet, as noted above, such policies may do little to address social, cultural, and structural issues within sport organisations (Hoeber and Frisby 2001). Further, a focus on quantitative goals may lead to a superficial veneer of equity, when organisations are far from equitable. Sport England's (2002) measurable equity goals are a good example of this. While sport organisations will be encouraged to increase numbers of women within organisations, there are few mechanisms in place to encourage analysis of inequitable organisational culture.

Promoting change

Rao et al. (1999) offered an opportunity to reflect on gendered deep structure and thereby promote change. In sport organisations, this provides an avenue whereby sport management researchers, educators, and practitioners can be encouraged to take an active role in challenging gender relations. In order to do so, it is necessary to examine different points of view or 'surface multiple perspectives' (Rao et al. 1999: 17). This can be accomplished through five assessment tools: (i) conducting a 'needs assessment' about how gendered discourses affect sport organisations; (ii) analysing 'mental models' or deeply held assumptions about gendered discourses in the organisations; (iii) encouraging sport organisations to 'hold up the mirror'; (iv) examining the 'fourth frame' in organisations, or how gender is an organising category within organisations; and finally (v) appreciating 'invisible work' or those who do valuable work that goes unappreciated and unrewarded. In this section, I address each of these areas in turn, indicating where such moves have been initiated within sport management, and how researchers, educators, and practitioners might contribute to this change project.

For Rao et al. (1999) the first step for an organisation that is moving to develop discourses which positively influence gender relations is to conduct a needs assessment. It is important to 'build broad based knowledge about the organisation and how it is gendered, by raising and engaging with a multitude of perspectives' (Rao et al. 1999: 17). Researchers in sport management can contribute significantly in this area by using their expertise to work within organisations. It is also important that researchers have strong links with their sport management community, enabling and assisting the promotion of meaningful research in organisations. Furthermore, educators who are responsible for teaching future sport managers can also ensure that similar reflexive processes are a part of their curriculum, thus creating a new breed of sport managers who are able to reflect on, and challenge, their organisations' histories and culture.

A good example of educators and researchers working with practitioners on a needs assessment exercise is evidenced by the International Working Group on Women and Sport (IWGWS) efforts at the 2002 International Conference on Women and to assist sport organisations. A programme was developed by the various parties involved, called the 'Montréal Tool Kit', which encourages sport organisations to conduct an audit, or needs assessment, of current gendered discourses (IWGWS 2002a). It offers three steps to creating a needs assessment. These are to 'gather factual information or statistics that demonstrate inequity or lack of fairness ... translate these facts into something interesting, readable ... and communicate your case to those who can influence change' (IWGWS 2002a). This advice is followed by practical steps that members of organisations can take to achieve these aims.

The term 'mental models' is used to describe individuals' assumptions about how an organisation works best. As Rao et al. (1999: 18) suggested, such models 'are not discussed openly yet they are important organising principles'. In some sport organisations, it is assumed that the dominant 'old boys' or 'old girls' networks may be an effective way in which to operate, given their established contacts (Shaw 2001). Moreover, as noted above, masculinities may be accepted as dominant discourses to inform leadership decisions. Again, if practitioners wish to challenge some of these assumptions, they may encourage employees or volunteers to articulate their thoughts on them. Otherwise, if practitioners feel they do not have the skills required to facilitate such a project, or would like outside help, then researchers may be in a position to step in and assist with the process.

As another reflective part of this process of challenge, educators within sport management may question their own assumptions. For example, how do we teach leadership within our curricula? Do we teach the history of leadership in sport organisations as a taken-for-granted list of facts, or do we ask why those leaders were considered to be important? Do we accept masculinity as the premise by which we judge our leaders, and if so, what does that mean for 'other' forms of leadership? Do we encourage networking and, if so, does that mean the exclusion of people who do not 'fit' within our networks? If educators, researchers, and practitioners can begin to ask some of these questions, then the sport management community may be in a place to start making some resistance to gendered discourses.

Feedback, or 'holding up the mirror', is central to Rao et al.'s (1999) proposals. Once a needs assessment and reflection of mental models has been conducted, the information from these sessions is provided in a feedback session to the organisation. Feedback sessions lend themselves to promoting change by enabling previously unheard perspectives to be articulated in a public setting. People who wish to conduct such sessions need to have specific skills in negotiating and facilitating. Consequently, educators in sport management need to work towards encouraging students to acquire such skills. As those students progress into the workforce, they will have the background and ability to provide useful feedback sessions. The Montreal Tool Kit offers some assistance in planning a 'holding up the mirror' session, with guidelines and suggestions for discussing gendered discourses with organisational members (IWGWS 2002a, 2002b).

Rao et al. (1999) emphasise the complexity of gender relations and related discourses when they discuss the importance of the fourth frame. Elsewhere, the fourth frame has been described as a way of analysing the ways in which gender acts as 'an organizing category that shapes social structure, identities and knowledge' (Kolb and Meyerson 1999: 139). Individuals need to ask questions of their own assumptions, such as 'what discourses do I expect my leaders to express?', 'what do we expect from Regional Development Officers?' or 'how do we perceive women who are in positions of power?' Such questions need to be asked in order to promote discussions about gender, and therefore to highlight alternatives to taken-for-granted assumptions. It is this area of offering workable alternatives that represents current, significant limitation in the research literature. Researchers need to engage in an attempt to theorise alternatives, along with practitioners, and work with them towards promoting change.

Invisible work is that which is often hidden in organisations, such as secretarial, facilitation or planning work. It is often associated with femininities, and also often ignored (Fletcher 1999). As noted above, this is largely because historical and contemporary accounts of organisations usually focus on those who express masculinities, most often in leadership roles. In contrast, invisible work is rendered so within organisations that prefer to express active leadership and outcome-based performance as their defining features. According to Rao et al. (1999) it is important to ensure that invisible work is made visible, so that organisational members receive the acknowledgement they deserve. Some attempts have been made by practitioners to achieve this, such as Sport England's campaign to increase the profile of volunteers (Sport England 2005). In order for invisible work to become visible, it is also important for educators to reflect the value of jobs within their teaching. For example, highlighting the opportunities for male students in roles traditionally associated with femininities may have some long-term potential for change in industry perceptions of those roles.

Conclusion

In this chapter, I have outlined one view of the contemporary situation of gender relations in sport management. Using recent research, I have suggested that sport organisations are gendered, with discourses that are expressed in history, the interactions of masculinities and femininities, and gender equity policies all contributing to this state. There are, however, alternatives to this, and Rao *et al.*'s (1999) framework outlines how change in organisations might be developed. Further, I have outlined how researchers, educators, and practitioners might work towards challenging the gendered discourses within organisations by critiquing gender relations and working towards some alternative view. Change can only be enacted through creative thinking and application regarding gender, and a move away from the outcomes-based approaches that have dominated much of the sport management literature for the past thirty years.

References

Acker, J. (1992) 'Gendering organisational theory', in J. Mills and P. Tancred (eds) *Gendering Organisational Analysis*, Berkeley, CA: Sage.

Acosta, R. V. and Carpenter, L. J. (2004) *Women in Intercollegiate Sport: A Longitudinal Study – Twenty-seven-year Update*, West Brookfield, MA: The Project on Women and Social Change of Smith College and Brooklyn College of the City University of New York.

Aitchison, C. C. (2000) 'Women in leisure services: managing the social–cultural nexus of gender equity', *Managing Leisure*, 5, 4: 181–91.

Aitchison, C. C. (2005) 'Feminist and gender research in sport and leisure management: understanding the social–cultural nexus of gender–power relations', *Journal of Sport Management*, 19, 4: 222–41.

Alvesson, M. and Deetz, S. (2000) *Doing Critical Management Research*, London: Sage.

Ashton-Shaeffer, C., Gibson, H. J., Autry, C. E. and Hanson, C. S. (2001) 'Meaning of sport to adults with disabilities', *Sociology of Sport Journal*, 18, 1: 95–114.

Cameron, J. (1996) *Trailblazers: Women who Manage New Zealand Sport*, Christchurch: Sports Inclined.

Chelsea Football Club (2005) *History*. Available at: http://www.chelseafc.com/article.asp?article= 270987.

Cockburn, C. (1990) 'Men's power in organisations: "equal opportunities" intervenes', in J. Hearn, and D. Morgan (eds) *Men Masculinity and Social Theory*, London/Winchester, MA: Unwin Hyman.

Ely, R. J. and Meyerson, D. E. (2000a) 'Advancing gender equity in organisations: the challenge and importance of maintaining a gender narrative', *Organisation*, 7, 4: 589–608.

Ely, R. J. and Meyerson, D. E. (2000b) 'Theories of gender in organisations: a new approach to organisational analysis and change', *Research in Organisational Behaviour*, 22, 103–51.

Ely, R. J. and Thomas, D. A. (2001) 'Cultural diversity at work: the effects of diversity perspectives on work group processes and outcomes', *Administrative Science Quarterly*, 46, 2: 229–73.

English Sports Council (1997) *England, The Sporting Nation: A Strategy*, London: English Sports Council.

Fletcher, J. K. (1999) *Disappearing Acts. Gender, Power, and Relational Practice at Work*, Cambridge, MA: MIT Press.

Frisby, W. and Brown, B. A. (1991) 'The balancing act: women leisure service managers', *Journal of Applied Recreation Research*, 16, 4: 297–321.

Hall, M. A. (1996) *Feminism and Sporting Bodies: Essays on Theory and Practice*, Champaign, IL: Human Kinetics.

Hall, M. A., Cullen, D. and Slack, T. (1989) 'Organisational elites recreating themselves: the gender structure of national sport organisations', *Quest*, 41: 28–45.

Hargreaves, J. (1990) 'Gender on the sports agenda', *International Review for Sociology of Sport*, 25, 4: 287–309.

Hargreaves, J. (1994) *Sporting Females: Critical Issues in the History and Sociology of Women's Sports*, London: Routledge.

Hargreaves, J. (2002) 'The Victorian cult of the family and the early years of female sport', in S. Scraton and A. Flintoff (eds) *Gender and Sport: A Reader*, London: Routledge.

Hoeber, L. (2004) 'Putting organisational values into practice: gender equity for athletes in a Canadian university', unpublished thesis, Vancouver: University of British Columbia.

Hoeber, L. and Frisby, W. (2001) 'Gender equity for athletes: rewriting the narrative for this organisational value', *European Sport Management Quarterly*, 1, 3: 179–209.

Hovden, J. (2000) 'Heavyweight men and younger women? The gendering of selection processes in Norwegian sport organisations', *NORA: Nordic Journal of Women's Studies*, 1, 1: 1–32.

International Olympic Committee (2000) *2nd Conference on Women in Sport*. Available at: http://www.olympic.org/ioc/e/org/women5Fconf2000/women5Fconf5F80320005Fe.html.

International Olympic Committee (2004) *Athens 2004*, Available at: http://www.olympic.org/uk/games/past/index_uk.asp?OLGT=1&OLGY=2004.

International Olympic Committee (2005) *Members*. Available at: http://www.olympic.org/uk/organisation/ioc/members/index_uk.asp.

International Working Group on Women and Sport (2002a) *The Montreal Tool Kit*. Available at: http://www.canada2002.org/e/toolkit/index.htm.

International Working Group on Women and Sport (2002b) *Tools for Advocating Change*. Available at: http://www.canada2002.org/e/toolkit/advocating/index.htm.

Jermier, J. M. (1991) 'Critical epistemology and the study of organisational culture: reflections on street corner society', in P. J. Frost, L. F. Moore, M. R. Louis, C. C. Lundberg and J. Martin (eds) *Reframing Organisational Culture*, Newbury Park, CA: Sage.

Kerfoot, D. and Whitehead, S. (1998) '"Boys own" stuff: masculinity and the management of further education', *Sociological Review*, 46, 3: 436–58.

Knights, D. and McCabe, D. (2001) '"A different world": shifting masculinities in the transitions to call centres', *Organisation*, 8, 4: 619–45.

Kolb, D. M. and Meyerson, D. E. (1999) 'Keeping gender in the plot: a case study of the Body Shop', in A. Rao, R. Stuart and D. Kelleher (eds) *Gender at Work: Organisational Change for Equality*, West Hartford, CT: Kumarian.

Lenskyj, H. (1994) 'Sexuality and femininity in sport contexts: issues and alternatives', *Journal of Sport and Social Issues*, 18, 4: 356–76.

Martin, P. Y. (1996) 'Gendering and evaluating dynamics: men, masculinities and management', in D. L. Collinson and J. Hearn (eds) *Men as Managers, Managers as Men: Critical Perspectives on Men, Masculinities and Management*, London: Sage.

McKay, J. (1997) *Managing Gender: Affirmative Action and Organisational Power in Australian, Canadian, and New Zealand Sport*, New York: State University of New York.

McNay, L. (2000) *Gender and Agency: Reconfiguring the Subject in Feminist and Social Theory*, Cambridge: Polity Press.

Putnam, L. L. and Mumby, D. K. (1993) 'Organisations, emotion, and the myth of rationality', in S. Fineman (ed.) *Emotion in Organisations*, London: Sage.

Rao, A., Stuart, R. and Kelleher, D. (eds) (1999) *Gender at Work: Organisational Change for Equality*, West Hartford, CT: Kumarian Press.

Rehman, L. and Frisby, W. (2000) 'Is employment liberating or marginalizing? The case of women consultants in the fitness and sport industry', *Journal of Sport Management*, 14, 1: 41–63.

Scraton, S. and Flintoff, A. (2002) 'Sport feminism: the contribution of feminist thought to our understandings of gender and sport', in S. Scraton and A. Flintoff (eds) *Gender and Sport: A Reader*, London: Routledge.

Shaw, S. (2001) 'The construction of gender relations in sport organisations', unpublished thesis, Leicester: De Montfort University.

Shaw, S. and Hoeber, L. (2003) '"A strong man is direct and a direct woman is a bitch": analyzing discourses of masculinity and femininity and their impact on employment roles in sport organisations', *Journal of Sport Management*, 17, 4: 347–76.

Shaw, S. and Penney, D. (2003) 'Gender equity policies in national governing bodies: an oxymoron or a vehicle for change?', *European Sport Management Quarterly*, 3, 1: 78–102.

Shaw, S. and Slack, T. (2002) '"It's been like that for donkey's years": the construction of gender relations and the cultures of sport organisations', *Culture, Sport Society*, 5, 1: 86–106.

Sport England (2000) *A Sporting Future for All*, London: Sport England.

Sport England (2002) *No Limits: Sport England's Equity Policy*, London: Sport England.

Sport England (2005) *Extra Funds to Boost Volunteering*. Available at: http://www. sportengland.org/news/press_releases/extra_funds_to_boost_volunteering.htm.

Staurowsky, E. J. (1996) 'Blaming the victim: resistance in the battle over gender equity in college athletics', *Journal of Sport and Social Issues*, 22, 2: 194–210.

Theberge, N. (1994) 'Toward a feminist alternative to sport as a male preserve', in S. Birrell and C. Cole (eds) *Women, Sport and Culture*, Champaign, IL: Human Kinetics.

Part III

Performing sexualities in sport

Chapter 7

Gender, sexuality and queer theory in sport

Corey W. Johnson and Beth Kivel

Introduction

Why struggle for liberation in the context of leisure and sport research? Usually the argument for ending the marginalization, discrimination and violence enacted toward sexual minorities in leisure and sport is enough to justify a need for such work. However, the complex tensions raised in our critique of the leisure and sport studies literature on lesbian and gay people has changed how we think about emancipation for sexual minorities (and sexual majorities for that matter). This is not to say that we do not believe we can strive for equality and first-class citizenship rights for sexual minorities through institutional policies and/or the effective training of 'leisure service professionals'. Rather, tensions located in our examination of the research literature on this issue point to Vaid's (1995) assertion that the mainstreaming of lesbian/gay culture may have yielded a better cultural and political life for lesbians/gay men, but that those improvements are merely shifts in discourse and nothing more than a virtual equality. Consequently, we suggest the use of Queer, as both theory and practice, for transforming the oppressive/marginalizing structures of leisure and sport, as a means of both subverting the privilege and entitlement earned through heterosexuality and masculinity and for questioning the heteronormative behaviours which function to maintain heterosexuality's dominance.

The purpose of this chapter is to introduce a theoretical perspective that can broaden our thinking about leisure, sport and sexual identity that shifts us away from a narrow social psychological commitment in the study of leisure and sport behaviour in relation to sexual identity toward a more critical sociological analysis that problematizes the rigid and mutually exclusive categories of identity that organize contemporary social science research, including leisure and sport studies. We believe this shift in analysis can result from the critical employment of *queer theory*.

Leisure research and people with marginal sexual identities

Although prior to the mid-1990s there was a notable absence of scholarly work from a gay/lesbian theoretical perspective in North America, some attention has been given to sexual minorities by recent scholars (Kivel 1994, 1996, 1997; Bialeschki and Pearce 1997; Caldwell *et al.* 1998; Hekma 1998; Jacobson and Samdahl 1998; Kivel and Kleiber 2000; Johnson 2001, 2005). These studies have, to varying degrees, launched a critique against the heterosexual/homosexual binary that perpetuates mainstream inequality and institutional injustice. However, looking at the current leisure studies literature that focuses on sexual identity, we would not be able to discern much heterogeneity in the participants' identity categories according to their intersections with gender (or other salient categories for that matter). Most of the research on sexual orientation in the leisure studies literature combines men and women together and does not consider the masculine/feminine binary and its perpetuation of heteronormativity in leisure.

Moreover, within this previous literature, researchers have focused on people who identify as lesbian/gay/bisexual without using a framework that is based in lesbian and gay theory. In contrast, gay and lesbian theory places sexuality at the centre of a critique of the cultural and historical reproduction of heterosexuality's dominance. The literature has focused on the leisure experiences of people who identify as lesbian/gay/bisexual without examining the meaning of lesbian and gay theory as it is applied to their experiences.

This distinction is important as we turn our focus toward the literature on gay men and lesbians by leisure and sport studies scholars. Caldwell, Kivel, Smith, and Hayes (1998) provide one example of an exploratory study of the leisure and sport behaviour and experiences of youth who identified as lesbian, gay male, bisexual, or questioned their sexual identities. This quantitative study focused on a broad spectrum of sexual identity issues and concluded that leisure and sport may not always be positive for sexual minorities. Indicating that lesbian, gay, bisexual, and questioning youth are aware of their differences from the dominant culture, the authors argue that these youth are often excluded or exclude themselves from sport and leisure. This study, similar to some of the earlier qualitative work by Kivel (1994, 1996), highlights some interesting connections to the problems that non-heterosexual youth encounter in their free time; problems the authors identify as linked to a pervasive heterosexual society and institutionalized homophobia and heterosexism. However, these studies fail to lodge any substantial critique against the homosexual/heterosexual binary. Consequently, such research does little to challenge the stability of heteronormative leisure.

Several other studies identified in the leisure and sport literature are more effective in their ability to document and critique the heterosexual/homosexual binary. Johnson (2001) and Kivel (1996, 1997) have both argued that gay and lesbian young adults and adolescents are similar to heterosexuals in their leisure and sport, but have the added challenge of battling homophobia and heterosexism.

These studies convey how society's heterosexist values are created, enacted, and reinforced in leisure and sport, as well as the ways in which leisure, in particular, is used by gay men and lesbians to resist heterosexist values. Yet, all of these studies use a social-psychological approach that focuses almost entirely on the individual. Consequently, the discussions are limited to challenging the heterosexual/ homosexual binary as it applies to individual identity development, and offer little insight into the cultural forces and structural inequalities that create and reproduce that binary. However, despite her lack of attention to those macro levels of structural inequality, Kivel (1996) recognized the need for advancing this theoretical work when she wrote:

> Leisure as a context for identity formation should not only focus on the individual, but should also focus on the cultural ideologies which shape and influence the individual ... the next step is to begin to understand how leisure contexts contribute to a hegemonic process which creates 'insiders' and 'outsiders'.
>
> (Kivel 1996: 204)

The aforementioned studies illustrate how heterosexism serves as an obstacle for gay and lesbian adolescents and young adults in pursuit of personal growth, creativity, self-expression, and camaraderie provided by leisure and sport. However, some studies have also identified examples of a larger ideological resistance to the heterosexual/homosexual binary, both implicitly and explicitly. Qualitative studies conducted by Bialeschki and Pearce (1997), Hekma (1998) and Jacobson and Samdahl (1998) elucidate an interaction between individual agency and social structure. All three of these studies move toward a more critical perspective of the homosexual/heterosexual binary, looking at how it is both resisted and reinforced by gay men and lesbians as they negotiate heteronormative ideologies.

In their study on leisure in the lives of lesbian mothers, Bialeschki and Pearce (1997) examined how leisure was understood and assigned meaning when both parents were lesbians. This process grew more interesting as the authors began to make sense of how lesbians' leisure and family responsibilities were negotiated in a society where heterosexual gender roles guided typical family responsibilities. Based on their findings, Bialeschki and Pearce (1997) argued that social messages about heterosexuality are both explicitly and implicitly conveyed throughout cultural discourse and that messages and meanings about alternative family structures are excluded from that discourse. By interviewing lesbian mothers and making interpretations based on their lives, Bialeschki and Pearce illuminate how leisure might serve as an exit point from heterosexuality, where lesbian mothers design and negotiate strategies and make conscious decisions around household and child-care responsibilities. This process helped these lesbians develop their own sense of family and challenge heteronormativity by being socially visible. Such a study might therefore be deemed to provide a good example of how the heterosexual/homosexual binary is confronted in and through leisure.

Focusing on leisure's potential to have negative as well as positive consequences, Hekma (1998) conducted an extensive critique of the heterosexual/homosexual binary in the context of organized sports. Hekma combined qualitative and quantitative methods to investigate reports of discrimination, forms of discrimination and the effects of discrimination in athletic organizations. Using a gay and lesbian theoretical framework, Hekma anticipated that the masculine/feminine binary would influence the heterosexual/homosexual binary in relation to the amount of discrimination experienced in sports. What Hekma found most revealing was that a gay or lesbian (sexual) identity was hazardous because of a fear of eroticism sparked by the homophobia present in heterosexuals. Hekma concluded that sport possesses gender enactment and privileges that reinforce the dominant ideologies of opposite-sex sexual behaviour and heterosexuality. Deviations from those dominant heterosexual ideologies led to forms of discrimination that mirrored in broader society. As a result, Hekma (1998: 20) argued that there really is 'no safe and readily accessible space for homosexual involvement in sports'.

Like Bialeschki and Pearce (1997) and Hekma (1998), Jacobson and Samdahl (1998) focused their investigation on how the homosexual/heterosexual binary operates in sexual minorities' efforts to resist or negotiate dominant heterosexual ideologies. In their investigation of lesbians over the age 60, the authors found that the women's experiences with discrimination produced negative feelings but also motivated their involvement with activist organizations. Unable to find a public space where they could be free from harassment, these women created their own spaces where they could control, negotiate, and/or possibly resist heterosexual traditions. Jacobson and Samdahl, encouraged and surprised by their findings, suggested that leisure scholars might examine how leisure is used to resist and reinforce heterosexual ideologies by looking at leisure in the context of people's everyday lives, the lives of both those who are dominant and those who are marginalized.

However, while Bialeschki and Pearce (1997), Hekma (1998) and Jacobson and Samdahl (1998) all do an excellent job of examining, and to some extent critiquing, the heterosexual/homosexual binary, they do little in the way of deconstructing or challenging our current heterosexual ideologies and/or the socially constructed heterosexual/homosexual binary. Incorporating a gay and lesbian theoretical perspective requires a shift in thinking beyond studies of those individuals who identify as gay or lesbian, toward the deconstruction of the heterosexual/homosexual, masculine/feminine dichotomies and how they take shape in the cultural contexts of leisure and sport. This type of thinking can reveal the important dialectical relationship between structure and agency and show how meaning systems within gay and lesbian communities are located along axes of difference (Kivel 2000). We want to offer a framework to discuss topics that expand the opportunities and resources for non-oppressive interaction by critiquing the underlying ideology that surrounds dominant heterosexual attitudes, values, and beliefs. Sexual identity and sexual orientation are already present in our daily lives through individual actions, institutional practices, media representations and interaction with people in the community. Leisure and sport scholars and service providers must move beyond the resting-place of tolerance and inclusion and prepare for a world where there can be a celebration around difference.

Tracing the origins of queer theory

Gender and sexuality are inextricably linked in our Western culture. The dominant ideological messages around gender and sexuality are created, perpetuated, maintained, and enforced in the social institutions and social structures of society, making dominant hegemonic categories seem natural and/or unproblematic. Though there are many different ways to conduct oneself as a man or a woman, one's gender is always grounded in the interpretation of two exclusive sexes: male or female. However, gender is not inevitable but may be challenged, transformed, and reconstructed distinct from one's biological sex (Butler 1990, 1991). For example, dominant social messages tell men that based on their biological sex (male) they are supposed to enact the 'masculine' to fulfil the socially constructed ideals of being a man and that one of the most powerful ideologies of their manhood is the attraction/desire to be sexual with a woman. However, the existence of 'gay' men within this same Western culture creates a site of philosophical as well as actual conflict in relation to this essentialized perspective. The consequences for these gay men are unknowable because of an unlimited number of variables, which may include visibility, geographic location, race, class, and so the list goes on.

These theoretical arguments are based primarily on the work of Foucault (1978) and Butler (1991) who argue that sex is not an *effect* but rather a *cause* of gender relations. Foucault's (1978) *History of Sexuality* encouraged sexuality researchers to reason that sexuality is always historically based on and produced by the dominant culture's use of power. Using their power, the dominant culture creates and organizes social systems, social discourses, social process, and social products. The dominant culture then uses these structures to influence or guide individuals' production and consumption of ideologies about social identities and, in this case, gender and sexuality (Butler 1990, 1991; Harding 1998). Consequently, at least in Western society, people are both explicitly and implicitly compelled *to be* a gender, and *to express* that gender through the appropriate dominant cultural expressions of sexuality at that historic moment.

Homosexuality

Foucault (1978) theorized that homosexuality was constructed as a modern invention created by the medical profession to define a person by the very sexual acts in which he or she participates (Jagose 1996; Rubin 1975/1997). Notwithstanding arguments over language use, homosexuality has commonly and widely been used to describe same-sex sexual behaviour. However, the theoretical goal of deciding what constitutes homosexuality or who is a homosexual is much more ambiguous. In fact, historical arguments indicate that the designation of homosexuality, and consequently the identity categories of gay, lesbian, bisexual, and straight have only been constructed during the past century (Jagose 1996; Laumann *et al.* 1994/1997).

Even though homosexual activity was subject to sodomy laws in England before 1885, those laws were only directed against specific 'acts' between women and women and men and men. 'Homosexual' was not ascribed as an identity category until the era surrounding the Oscar Wilde trials at the end of the nineteenth century. During that historical period, the medical profession began to claim cultural authority for the explanation of sexual behaviour by creating a designation and/or classification for homosexuality (Foucault 1978; Jagose 1996).

While there is ongoing debate over the exact historical (trans)formation of the 'modern homosexual', homosexuality continues to remain theoretically elusive. In trying to determine an essentialized homosexuality, scholars must examine both the singular and complex elements used by the individuals who self-identify and/or by society's attempt to appropriate the label or associated labels of homosexuality. Researchers have used a variety of determinants in an attempt to identify 'homosexuals'. These determinants include behaviour, desire, and self-identification just to name a few. Traditionally, homosexual behaviour has been used to categorize specific actions conducted with a partner of the same gender. These actions include, but are not limited to, active and receptive oral sex, active and receptive anal sex, and other forms of genital stimulation.

Although homosexuality as behaviour seems to require physical activity, the determinants of homosexuality as desire and/or identity are considered more complex. Homosexual 'desire', for instance, encompasses a spectrum from finding the same sex appealing, to actually becoming involved with individuals of the same sex, to an uncontrollable attraction for same-sex sexual activity.

Homosexual 'identity', on the other hand, seems to indicate the ability of the individual to self-report that he or she ascribes to some label of same-sex sexual orientation (e.g. gay, lesbian, and bisexual). It is critical to recognize that when sexuality is used as a signifier for identity, the agent acquires social and/or political capital offered by the sexual identity category. Self-identification often demonstrates an affinity for grounding personal politics in relation to an individual's sense of personal identity. The politics of sexual identity allow individuals to determine or negotiate a common ground where they might construct visible and active communities. That common ground provides an organizational and political framework for individuals to become part of communities and create distinct cultures.

Despite the perceived power generated through identity politics, some theorists argue that the way in which those politics are applied and substantiated toward defining a 'true' or essentialized identity is problematic. Identity politics are constantly shifting because of their subjective nature and therefore do not account for how identity is constructed naturally, historically, physically or linguistically.

This makes the use of identity (or self-identification) as the only means for defining homosexuality troublesome. For instance, several years ago in a very personal, but groundbreaking interview, James Baldwin discussed the perplexities surrounding the categorization of homosexuals. He stated,

> Men have been sleeping with men for thousands of years – and raising tribes. [Homosexuality] is a Western sickness, it really is. It's an artificial division … It's only this infantile culture which has made such a big deal of it … Homosexual is not a noun.
>
> (Goldstein 1989: 77)

Baldwin's quote illustrates how the determinants of behaviour, desire and identity used to describe and characterize homosexuality are problematic; homogenizing individuals without consideration for the variability in the application of these definitional tools to the larger population. This variability should be a key consideration for anyone investigating sexuality in today's 'postmodern' society (Kelly 1998; Laumann *et al.* 1994/1997).

Compulsory heterosexuality and heteronormativity

Understanding that homosexuality itself is a modern categorical construction also suggests that heterosexuality is a modern categorical construction. However, heterosexuality, also dependent on changing cultural models, has been naturalized, viewed as unproblematic and seems to require no explanation or justification for its existence (Jagose 1996). Instead, the dominant culture's ideologies, which are based on heterosexuality, serve as powerful, pervasive mechanisms of social control, using the already powerful cultural constructions of gender (masculine and feminine) to subjugate persons who are not heterosexual.

Maintaining the idea of a naturalized heterosexuality takes considerable investment on the part of the dominant culture, but is necessary to create and enforce the perceptions of a radical and demonstrable difference between heterosexuals and homosexuals. The idea of a naturalized or unquestioned heterosexuality is maintained in the production of discrete and polar categorizations of gender and sexuality. These categorizations conceal power relationships by bringing issues of anatomy, biology and sensations of pleasure together in an 'artificial unity' through the act of sex (Foucault 1978). This artificial unity not only permits but also encourages heterosexual desire to be naturalized and perpetuated as normal and compulsory. 'Compulsory heterosexuality' then is the portrayal or enactment of a heterosexual identity. It is perceived as the only correct or normal way to be, coercively encouraging individuals to live their existence according to the duty that heterosexuality and a heterosexual gender order prescribe.

In her influential essay *Compulsory Heterosexuality and Lesbian Existence*, Adrienne Rich (1993) examined how cultural processes are used to forcibly and subliminally control women. Consequently, when women resist or revolt from those cultural processes they are punished. Rich (1993) also indicated that, more recently, heterosexuality has been romanticized to represent an idealistic life for women (and we would add men). She argued that this lie could be felt in all aspects of women's lives when she wrote,

> The lie of compulsory female heterosexuality today afflicts not just feminist scholarship, but every profession, every reference work, every curriculum, every organizing attempt, every relationship or conversation over which it hovers. It creates, specifically, a profound falseness, hypocrisy, and hysteria in the heterosexual dialogue, for every heterosexual relationship is lived in the queasy strobe light of that lie. However we choose to identify ourselves, however we find ourselves labelled, it flickers across and distorts our lives.
>
> (Rich 1993: 61)

Rich speaks from an activist and political space within her essay but her writing also serves to inform our theoretical understandings of the powerful forces of compulsory heterosexuality. Rubin (1975/1997) has similarly examined the social construction of compulsory heterosexuality and its relationship to gender:

> Gender is not only an identification with one sex; it also entails that sexual desire be directed toward the other sex. The sexual division of labour is implicated in both aspects of gender – male and female it creates them, and it creates heterosexual.
>
> (Rubin 1975/1997: 40)

These authors argue that our social organization and institutional processes enable a hierarchical power structure whereby heterosexuality is favoured as the norm and non-heterosexuality is situated as deviant and/or un-permissible.

Radicalesbians (1997) described how, as a result of compulsory heterosexuality, a lesbian cannot perform her naturalized sex role and be considered a real woman. The Radicalesbians (1997) wrote,

> In popular thinking there is only one essential difference between a lesbian and other women: that of sexual orientation – which is to say, when you strip off all the packaging, you must finally realize that the essence of being a 'woman' is to get fucked by men.
>
> (Radicalesbians 1997: 154)

The arguments by Radicalesbians, Rubin, and Rich illustrate how the socially constructed role of a woman cannot be examined without deconstructing its relationship to heterosexuality. Other feminists such as Wittig have also tackled the issue of women and their link to compulsory heterosexuality. Wittig (1993) indicated that, as a result of their homosexuality, lesbians also refuse heterosexuality and thus reject the ideological and economic power associated with the connection to a man. Wittig (1993) argued that any woman who refused servitude to men, rejected the connection to men's power, or asserted her own personal/political independence, would be labelled by dominant society as a homosexual, lesbian, or dyke. Thus, even the labels surrounding homosexuality are used to categorize and marginalize people, keeping both women and non-heterosexuals in subordinate or less-valued roles. Radicalesbians (1997) indicated that this heterosexual male classification system is

> The condition which keeps women within the confines of the feminine role, and it is the debunking/scare term that keeps women from forming any primary attachments, groups, or associations among ourselves ... As long as the label 'dyke' can be used to frighten woman into a less militant stand, keep her separate from her sisters, keep her from giving primacy to anything other than men and family – then to that extent she is controlled by male culture.
> (Radicalesbians 1997: 155)

As indicated by these arguments, heterosexuality gives power and privilege to men first. Lesbian relationships are simply perceived as alternative sex acts, not valued for the independent psychological and emotional relations that are separate from or absent of men. Therefore, lesbianism itself would seem to serve as a challenge to the compulsory heterosexual processes of women's insubordination. Turning this argument onto the gay male subject, we can see how, for men, the building block that links gender with heterosexuality is their masculinity. It is through masculinity that men construct their sexuality and, through that sexuality, confirm their gender identity (Fracher and Kimmel 1998). However, when a man is 'homosexual' or 'gay' these issues become complicated. Some theorists posit that the hegemonic ideals of the male sex role make it more difficult for men who deviate from the traditional roles to challenge them. Instead, those men will often feel personally inadequate and insecure, and frequently face acts of discrimination and hate. However, Connell (1995) suggested that gay men do find a common ground in their collective knowledge of gender ambiguity, tension between their bodies and identities, and a realization of traditional masculine contradictions. Consequently, he argued that the problems associated with gay life could be traced to the elements of heteronormativity that prove difficult for gay men as they attempt to transgress the gender and sexual norms of compulsory heterosexuality.

So far we have explained several foundational concepts for understanding the way in which the current constructed categorical binary of sexuality can be viewed as mythical and inextricably tied to gender. From the time we are born our sexuality involves the acceptance and absorption of these ideological myths about what it means to be heterosexual, homosexual, men and women. Those myths are embedded in both our conscious and unconscious, directing us in how we should behave, think, feel, desire, want, love and so on. Although, we will continue to argue that sexuality is socially constructed, we do not believe that it is untrue or unreal. For most of us, our sexuality is *very real* and often feels innate. However, critically examining how and why gender and sexual ideologies are shaped to form complex structures of heteronormativity that ensure their continued dominance is a necessary step toward emancipation of lesbians and gay men. In order to escape the confining and oppressive structures of gender and sexuality we suggest that leisure and sport research needs to be driven by an intellectual and political mobility that encourages more equitable social change.

Queer

We see this intellectual and political mobility entering into leisure and sport studies, and leisure and sport in general, through conceptualizations inspired by Queer (cf. Dilley 1999; Gamson 2000; Jagose 1996; Talburt 2000). Queer, previously used as a marker for that which was considered abnormal, was reclaimed by activists and academics in the late 1980s for the express purpose of political mobility and social change. In its most simplistic form, queer offers a new way to think about the production of culture and what difference *difference* makes. Queer presents an opportunity to complicate the unquestioned understandings and intersections of the sex-gender-sexuality-desire matrix. As a form of identity (Queer), a system of thinking (queer theory), and a means of action (queering), queer subverts the privilege, entitlement, and status obtained through compulsive heterosexuality and questions how heteronormative behaviours enacted by both heterosexuals and homosexuals function to maintain heterosexuality's dominance. Queer moves us beyond the limits of difference offered by sexual orientation (straight, gay, lesbian, etc.) and instead interrogates sexual orientation's existence. Queer does this in an attempt to become more transgressive and socially transformative, forcing us to consider the social responsibility we have to ourselves, to those who came before us, and to those who will come after us (Grace *et al.* 2004).

Queer theory arose in a context of debates between feminists, critiques of feminism, the rise of constructivist sociology, postmodern theory and the anti-gay and anti-AIDS right-wing backlash of the 1980s. The most influential feminist debates and critiques seemed to centre on heterosexuality as the cornerstone of male supremacy, women's oppression and, more specifically, lesbian oppression. Adrienne Rich (1980) constructed a 'lesbian continuum' where a political movement for lesbians should be centred on gender, not sexuality, since men, straight and gay, were committed to patriarchy and misogyny. In her groundbreaking essay, Rich wrote that heterosexuality, like other forms of oppression, is a set of power relations:

> The failure to examine heterosexuality as an institution is like failing to admit that the economic system called capitalism or the caste system of racism is maintained by a variety of forces, including both physical violence and false consciousness.

> (Rich 1980: 648)

The analysis Rich encouraged was radical in its critique of the normative status, or 'compulsory' nature of heterosexuality and its framing of sexuality as institutional rather than personal. The lesbian feminist movement developed an identity politics based on a fixed lesbian identity that was stable and coherent so that it could classify lesbians as a 'minority' deserving of protection against discrimination. This lesbian identity was fairly narrow and women often found themselves unable to measure up to the 'ideal' although they may have expressed what was, to them, a lesbian identity. In these ways, lesbian feminism anticipated queer theory in that it foreshadowed queer theory's critique of heteronormativity but simultaneously initiated queer theory's attention to anti-essentialism and troubling of the hetero/homobinary.

Queering leisure and sport: implications for research, professional practice and activism

In conjunction with Foucault's (1983) conceptualizations of power relations in social contexts, leisure and sport studies, scholars might use queer theory to extend our examination of leisure and sport constraints to explore how power relations reflect issues of negotiation (control and evading control) in leisure and sport. Leisure and sport scholars could ask how lesbian, gay, bisexual and transgendered people are policed in their leisure and sport, especially when the space is constructed in and among heterogendered discourses. Leisure and sport scholars need to ask, when and how are people Othered in leisure and sport? How do leisure and sport serve a 'disciplinary space' (Foucault 1983)? How do participants navigate the terrain of meanings associated with appropriate behaviours around gender and sexuality? How can we recreate leisure and sport spaces so that they are not disciplining but, instead, foster a celebration around difference? Using queer theory in leisure and sport research might also allow researchers more mobility for moving into, out of and among multiple identities in order to understand the increasing complexities of leisure and sport relations and practices (Grace et al. 2004). Queer theory encourages researchers to combine diverse subjectivities with multiple theoretical utilities, studying phenomenon such as leisure and sport in ways that challenge normative discursive ideologies and arouse political activism in an effort to eliminate injustice and create social change; a social change that can be galvanized through the research efforts of leisure and sport studies scholars.

Another important implication is the need for us to extend beyond the scope of looking at leisure and sport from a queer *theoretical* perspective, but also how we might 'be queer' in our leisure and sport. Being queer in our leisure and sport – by either heterosexuals or non-heterosexuals – provides an opportunity to consciously and actively disrupt the legitimacy of heterogendered power. Pushing boundaries often illuminates who has the power, why they have the power and how they keep the power. Being queer in our leisure would mean we intervene and disrupt dominant systems of power, creating social change that (re)shapes leisure and sport in a more equitable fashion; a fashion that considers the dissident voices and multiple subjectivities that exist in leisure and sport. Queering our leisure and sport will cut paths across leisure and sport spaces, practices and products to make a difference in the leisure and sport communities for both the Queer and not-Queer, opening up possibilities for creative ways of being. Queering our leisure and sport identifies and scrutinizes those practices and policies that need to change in order to make leisure and sport equitable and safe for individuals and groups of individuals across race, class, ability, gender, and sexual orientation, 'generat[ing] new knowledge, … reform[ing] "common sense" and inform[ing] critically public policies, existent social movements, and daily community life' (Fine et al. 2000: 124). Queer would encourage us to act in ways that do more than create a 'virtual equality' by creating an equality that resonates in us through a celebration of our difference.

References

Bialeschki, M. D. and Pearce, K. D. (1997) '"I don't want a lifestyle – I want a life": the effect of role negotiations on the leisure of lesbian mothers', Journal of Leisure Research, 29, 1: 113–31.

Butler, J. (1990) Gender Trouble: Feminism and the Subversion of Identity, New York: Routledge.

Butler, J. (1991) 'Imitation and gender insubordination', in D. Fuss (ed.) Inside/out, New York: Routledge.

Caldwell, L. L., Kivel, B. D., Smith, E. A., and Hayes, D.M. (1998) 'The leisure context of adolescents who are lesbian, gay male, bisexual and questioning their sexual identities: an exploratory study', Journal of Leisure Research, 30, 3: 341–55.

Connell, R. W. (1995) Masculinities, Cambridge: Polity Press.

Dilley, P. (1999) 'Queer theory: under construction', International Journal of Qualitative Studies in Education, 12, 5: 457–72.

Fine, M., Weis, L., Weseen, S. and Wong, L. (2000) 'For whom? Qualitative research, representations, and social responsibilities', in N. K. Denzin and Y. S. Lincoln (eds) Handbook of Qualitative Research (2nd edn), Thousand Oaks, CA: Sage Publications.

Foucault, M. (1978) The History of Sexuality (1st US edn), New York: Pantheon Books.

Foucault, M. (1983) 'The subject and power', Afterword in H. L. Dreyfus and P. Rainbow (eds) Michel Foucault: Beyond Structuralism and Hermeneutics, Chicago, IL: University of Chicago Press.

Fracher, J. and Kimmel, M. (1998) 'Hard issues and soft spots: counselling men about sexuality', in M. S. Kimmel and M. A. Messner (eds) Men's Lives (4th edn), Boston, MA: Allyn and Bacon.

Gamson, J. (2000) 'Sexualities, queer theory, and qualitative research', in N. K. Denzin and Y. S. Lincoln (eds) Handbook of Qualitative Research (2nd edn), Thousand Oaks, CA: Sage.

Goldstein, R. (1989) '"Go the way your blood beats": an interview with James Baldwin', in W. Rubenstein (ed.) Cases and Materials on Sexual Orientation and the Law, St Paul, MN: West Publishing.

Grace, A., Hill, B., Johnson, C. and Lewis, J. (2004) 'In other words: queer voices/dissident subjectivities impelling social change', *International Journal of Qualitative Studies in Education*, 17, 3: 301–24.

Harding, J. (1998) *Sex Acts: Practices of Femininity and Masculinity*, London/Thousand Oaks, CA: Sage.

Hekma, G. (1998) '"As long as they don't make an issue of it …": gay men and lesbians in organized sports in the Netherlands', *Journal of Homosexuality*, 35, 1: 1–23.

Jacobson, S. A. and Samdahl, D. M. (1998) 'Leisure in the lives of old lesbians: experiences with and responses to discrimination', *Journal of Leisure Research*, 30, 2: 233–55.

Jagose, A. (1996) *Queer Theory: An Introduction*, Washington Square, NY: New York University Press.

Johnson, C. W. (2001) 'Living the game of hide and seek: leisure in the lives of gay and lesbian young adults', *Leisure*, 24, 2: 255–78.

Johnson, C. W. (2005) '"The first step is the two-step": hegemonic masculinity and dancing in a country western gay bar', *International Journal of Qualitative Studies in Education*, 18, 4: 445–64.

Kelly, G. F. (1998) *Sexuality Today: The Human Perspective*, Boston, MA: McGraw Hill.

Kivel, B. D. (1994) 'Lesbian and gay youth and leisure: implications for practitioners and researchers', *Journal of Park and Recreation Administration*, 12, 4: 15–28.

Kivel, B. D. (1996) '*In on the Outside, Out on the Inside: Lesbian/Gay/Bisexual Youth, Identity, and Leisure*, unpublished manuscript: University of Georgia.

Kivel, B. D. (1997) 'Leisure, narratives and the construction of identity among lesbian, gay and bisexual youth', *Journal of Leisurability*, 24, 4: 31–8.

Kivel, B. D. (2000) 'Leisure experience and identity: what difference does difference make?', *Journal of Leisure Research*, 32, 1: 79–81.

Kivel, B. D. and Kleiber, D. A. (2000) 'Leisure in the identity formation of lesbian/gay youth: personal, but not social', *Leisure Sciences*, 22, 4: 215–32.

Laumann, E., Gagono, J., Michael, R. and Michaels, S. (1994/1997) 'The social organisation of sexuality', in W. Rubenstein (ed.) *Cases and Materials on Sexual Orientation and the Law*, St Paul, MN: West Publishing.

Radicalesbians (1997) 'The woman identified woman', in L. J. Nicholson (ed.) *The Second Wave: A Reader in Feminist Theory*, New York: Routledge.

Rich, A. (1980) 'Compulsory heterosexuality and lesbian existence', *Journal of Women's History*, 15, 3: 11–48.

Rich, A. (1993) 'Compulsory heterosexuality and lesbian existence', in H. Abelove, M. A. Barale and D. M. Halperine (eds) *The Lesbian and Gay Studies Reader*, New York: Routledge.

Rubin, G. S. (1975/1997) 'The traffic in women', in L. J. Nicholson (ed.) *The Second Wave: A Reader in Feminist Theory*, New York: Routledge.

Talburt, S. (2000) 'Introduction: some contradictions and possibilities of *Thinking Queer*', in S. Talburt and S. R. Steinberg (eds) *Thinking Queer: Sexuality, Culture and Education*, New York: Peter Lang.

Vaid, U. (1995) *Virtual Equality: The Mainstreaming of Gay and Lesbian Liberation*, New York: Anchor Books.

Wittig, M. (1993) 'One is not born a woman', in H. Abelove, M. A. Barale and D. M. Halperin (eds) *The Lesbian and Gay Studies Reader*, New York: Routledge.

Chapter 8

'Queers, even in netball?'

Interpretations of the lesbian label among sportswomen

Kate Russell

This chapter addresses the positive and negative experiences of being labelled as lesbian among sportswomen in general and female rugby players, cricketers and netballers in particular. What follows is an exploration of how the lesbian stereotype develops within sport and how women who play rugby, cricket and netball experience those stereotypes. The discussion is illustrated with empirical data from 30 interviews conducted with women who played rugby, cricket and netball and this discussion is informed by literature spanning the last 20 years in the sociology and psychology of sport.

Development of the lesbian stereotype

Much has been written concerning the development of the lesbian stereotype of women in sport (Griffin 1992; Lenskyj 1994; Krane 1996; Halbert 1997; Young 1997; Veri 1999; Wright and Clarke 1999; Choi 2000). The focus of such direct labelling stems from the acceptance or rejection of women's participation in traditionally-defined male activities such as body building, football, rugby, boxing and wrestling: all of which contain large amounts of physical contact or the presentation of a strong and muscular body. It is clear that the level of physical power these women need to play such sports, or even the outward display of a muscular body, does not reflect the hegemonic masculinity of Western societies in which women are essentially regarded as passive and weak and men as strong and powerful (Sabo and Messner 1993). Sport is often regarded as a male preserve (Dunning 1994), an area in which images of ideal masculinity are constructed and promoted (Connell 1987). In a similar fashion, sport also forms many of the ideals and beliefs we have concerning female athletes' 'femininity' and how these perceptions are constructed and supported.

Muscles equals lesbian

Investigating the sporting experiences of women in three sports that differ in levels of physicality (contact – rugby, or non-contact – cricket and netball) and social acceptance (whether considered 'masculine' – cricket and rugby, or 'feminine'

– netball) highlights how the lesbian stereotype exists irrespective of sport choice. What does differ, however, is how and why these stereotypes develop within each sporting community. For rugby players, the most striking aspect of the labelling process begins and ends in the physicality of the sport and the assumption that muscles equates to lesbianism. Perceptions of muscular women are often fixed by the strong link between masculinity and 'butch' women. Women with muscle definition are considered a novelty and treated with surprise, in particular when compared with male rugby players:

> I suppose it's completely the opposite, it's like a macho thing so they [men] can't be gay but for women it's a macho thing so they must be. ... the number of people that have said 'who's that girl with the muscles?'... nobody's sort of really said it negatively but ... they were surprised because she has got a lot of definition ... I think the main thing that it is like associated with lesbianism, you know people automatically assume women rugby players 'oh you must be butch and a lesbian' (laugh) more than the muscle thing really ... I think people who don't know anything about rugby think ... you must be butch and you must be lesbian and people who know about women's rugby think you must be fairly fit and you must be gay (laugh). (Suzie: Rugby)

For rugby women in general there does tend to be a strong connection made between lesbianism and the display of power and, in this particular instance, the open display of a muscular body. The explanation provided by others is that this is a result of or a development from her lesbianism. Whether or not this is true does not really matter, her sexuality exhibited through the display of physical prowess and control poses a threat to both women and men. Suzie's sexuality is assumed either because she is physical or because she is a rugby player. In her research on female bodybuilders, Choi (2000) points to the threat of over-developed muscularity and the fear of appearing unfeminine. In this context unfeminine equates with lesbianism. Research on other sports, including football (Kolnes 1995) and boxing (Halbert 1997), also indicates a similar perceptual relationship between women's physical expressions, the assumptions of unfeminine behaviour and the short leap to lesbian definitions. Veri (1999) points to the definition of the female athlete as deviant because of her open defiance of the discipline of femininity. Any transgression from the traditional ideals of what the feminine body should be doing labels itself as deviant, masculine and thus homosexual.

Cath, a cricketer, also recognises the link between power and lesbianism, not as an indicator of women cricketers' lesbianism but as a more general statement about women in sport. Here Cath is referring to the French tennis player Amélie Mauresmo:

> ... take, for example, the fuss there was over the French girl ... you know people openly know that there are a lot of gay tennis players and don't talk about it at all, but the minute someone appears on the ... court looking

powerful ... and that was what people got, you know about the size of her arms ... her sexuality suddenly became a huge issue whereas nobody really asks ... about the others who look more petite, so here again you have a woman who is strong ... who is competitive, who is aggressive ... and people immediately want to talk about who she prefers to sleep with. (Cath: Cricket)

The influence of the media in the development and maintenance of the lesbian stereotype in sport is demonstrated through the trivialisation and marginalisation of women's sporting experiences (Griffin 1992; Pirinen 1997; Lenskyj 1998; Koivula 1999; Wright and Clarke 1999). In general sportsmen have been portrayed as active, strong and competent, with female athletes defined by their heterosexual attractiveness. There appears to be a strong resistance by the media to present athletic women as athletes without first identifying them as either acceptably feminine or dangerously deviant. What occurs through this 'symbolic annihilation' (Lenskyj 1998) is the exclusion of female talent as worthy, with attention, instead, directed towards her sexuality.

Lesbian label as inevitable

This research highlighted how sportswomen are all too aware of the existence of the lesbian label within their own and other sports and also provided evidence of the association of greater physical contact with the likelihood of the assumption of lesbianism. This was particularly evident in the case of the netballers who accepted that if they chose to play rugby or football, the perception of lesbianism would increase. Mary discusses this point when considering whether to start playing rugby or football at her local club and the reasons behind her reluctance to do so:

I suppose if anything, people look upon netball as being more of a feminine sport rather than rugby and football, which are typically male sports ... I found it quite difficult to talk to people to say that ... I was interested because I suppose I have always had this concept that rugby is a male thing and ... I'd be looked at differently. I would, you know feel as if I had to justify why I played it ... whereas I don't feel I have to justify why I play netball ... when I started playing five a side on a Friday it was a case of 'oh you're not going to join a women's football team are you?' basically and 'oh no you can't join a women's football team, they're all gay', oh God! Whereas I think it's definitely not seen in netball ... it's definitely seen as more of an acceptable ladies sport. (Mary: Netball)

Many of the cricketers, however, also attested to the notion that it was participation in sport in general (not just contact sports) that amplified the perception of lesbianism among the group from observers:

I mean they always think that you're a lesbian; obviously if you play cricket you've got to be gay ... and I'm sure it's the same in many sports that are so sort of engendered as male sports ... I would say cricket, hockey, rugby they're always the sports that people go 'oh yeah you know', they always challenge your sexuality if you play those sports, you play in all three and you've had it (laugh). (Cheryl: Cricket)

For some of the women this was a difficult issue to reconcile because they wanted to play any sport they chose but were aware that by doing so they would attract certain sexual associations. Participants in all three sports attested to the inevitability of the questioning of their sexuality because of their participation, confirming similar findings with other sportswomen (Young 1997). Although there is an acknowledgement that there are gay women who play rugby, cricket, football, tennis, netball, swimming and just about any other sport you could mention, there was also a strong feeling of having to explain and rationalise why this was so. In particular, it was women who identified themselves as heterosexual who commented most on this topic. This suggests that even when rejecting traditional ideals of acceptable behaviour, by choosing to play rugby or cricket, these women were still struggling to accept that there were gay women in their teams. Rather than just playing the game they were attempting to rationalise why this was happening and, in doing so, identifying their own prejudices. Griffin (1992) highlights the nonsensical nature of trying to ascertain the number of lesbians within sport. For her 'women in sport must come to understand that it wouldn't matter if there were no lesbians in sport. The lesbian label would still be used to intimidate and control women's athletics' (Griffin 1992: 260). For Griffin, the real question that needs addressing is why women are subject to such analysis in the first place. Only by examining those motives will the prejudices faced by women in sport be tackled.

Intrusion into the male domain

For some respondents, an explanation of the assumption of homosexuality through playing sport rests on male resentment of women's participation in 'their' activity. Clare recalls how her participation in cricket at school resulted in a wealth of verbal and physical abuse from her male peers because she had intruded on their sporting space. This continued into adulthood with male competitors in mixed cricket teams attempting to mock her performance through any means:

I did experience those sorts of comments playing cricket, even at that age ... but not [for] any other sport that I played for school ... because it's threatening isn't it? It's got to be, I couldn't explain it no other way ... they've got to find it threatening ... that I was good at a sport that is allegedly just for them ... I have found people, other blokes, abusive and offensive, whether it be about sexuality or ... just the standard of cricket ... it makes no difference really. (Clare: Cricket)

Such accounts indicate how fear of women's success in sport is utilised by men to justify their ridicule of female performance and to suggest that women do not have the physical or psychological capacity to play in a sport dominated by men (Young 1997). Young (1997) also points to the transparency of such male attitudes towards women in sport and which women actively resist by developing alternative competitive philosophies. Taken to an extreme, Halbert (1997) notes the tension exhibited between men and women boxers when it comes to sparring practice. In order to demonstrate their physical superiority and to express their unhappiness at the female intrusion into their 'world', female boxers recall beatings received at the hands of more experienced men. This was regarded as an attempt by the men to persuade women that they did not belong in that environment. Young (1997) demonstrated similar findings in his research with female participants in rugby, ice hockey, wrestling, mountain climbing and martial arts. Wright and Clarke (1999) further illustrate this point by highlighting the media's rationalisation of women's participation in rugby by confirming to (male) readers that these women are not making any (feminist) statement. Rather they are playing because of a love and appreciation of the sport. This justification is rarely, if ever, given or deemed necessary when discussing male participation in rugby or any other physically demanding sport.

Sportswomen and sexuality

When discussing sexuality it is clear that the lesbian stereotype is prominent in sport, but it would be inappropriate to continue this discussion without recognising that for the netballers their identity was rendered ambiguous as they were often perceived as being both gay and straight. These assumptions were based on two different assumptions: first, that women together are already or will ultimately become lesbians, and second, that netballers were 'up for a good time' with men. In the UK, where only women play netball competitively, it is one of the most stereotypically feminine sporting activities and it is therefore surprising to note that the lesbian label was as prominent in this sport as in many others that women play. Nanette noted that the perception of netballers as lesbians was actually founded on the 'women only' nature of the sport:

> Blokes think there's ... a lot of queers as well in the game.
> Kate: In netball?
> Yeah because it's all women. (Nanette: Netball)

Taking this and other accounts into consideration, it would appear that women are regarded as lesbian purely on the basis of physical activity rather than as a consequence of participation in 'male' sports such as rugby and cricket. This could reflect wider assumptions that women who are together for any length of time regardless of activity are seen as lesbian, for example, in the case of female prisoners. Here the explanation does not depend on the level of physicality needed to play a sport but merely the fact that women are playing it.

However, contradicting this notion, many netballers also discussed the perception of their sexuality by men as reflecting a heterosexual ideal of women. Nicki recalls that the expected behaviour of netballers, especially at university, was one of overt heterosexual activity in the pursuit of men:

> I think, you know, if you talk to people and you say oh you're in a netball team, especially blokes are like 'oh the netball team hey you're up for a good time aren't you' ... sort of thing, you know, also the social side ... having competitions on how many blokes you can pull or stuff like that. (Nicki: Netball)

It is clear that the male perceptions noted here reflect deep-seated fears of being ignored when women develop friendships, as demonstrated by the netballers. There is support for this perception of the female athlete as a sexualised object in research relating to the marginalisation of women's sport and the trivialisation of their performances by media reporters (Duncan and Hasbrook 1988; Griffin 1992; Kane and Greendorfer 1994; Lenskyj 1998; Wright and Clarke 1999). This does, however, relate mainly to those women in sports deemed as appropriate to female participation whereas women in traditional male activities suffer from a similar sexualisation but one which focuses on their potential lesbianism.

Justifying participation

Having to justify participation in an activity considered to be inappropriate by others can also bring an insight into how and why definitions of femininity are constructed. Men and women can be regarded as having different perceptions as to why someone would choose to play rugby, for example:

> ... men tend to be a bit more ... suspicious because you've entered into that male territory ... and want you to prove that you know what you're talking about, you know ... they say stupid things that piss me right off like 'do you do tackling?' ... 'do you play for 40 minutes each way?' ... women are thinking what's your real reason, what's your real motivation, do you play rugby because you want to be one ... of the rugby girl entourage? (Sue: Rugby)

Other players felt that there were constant questions as to why they would want to choose such an activity, when really it was very simple. Sue was vehement in her annoyance:

> I think this is a really important thing, people assume that you're making a massive statement about your life because you play rugby, that you're trying to prove something ... and the only reason I play rugby is because ... I enjoy it, I like the game, I like getting dirty, I like the aggression. I'm an aggressive

person on the pitch but not off ... I like the girls, I like the people and that's why I play rugby. I don't play rugby to make a statement about my life, don't play rugby to make a statement about the fact that I can play a man's sport so there! ... don't play rugby because I can say I'm not homophobic and I can get in the shower with a bunch of lesbians ... I don't do it for any other reasons than that I enjoy the game and I like the people who play. (Sue: Rugby)

Having to face such prejudice, together with the constant examination of motives, makes it unsurprising that some women prefer not to discuss their sporting activities within certain gatherings. One cricketer, Denise, commented on how her international status could be used as a way to diffuse the assumptions placed on her participation:

... sometimes I don't always bring it into the conversation ... because it sort of still gets frowned upon ... just like football and rugby, like a masculine sport and it seems bizarre that women actually play it ... but I think because I've done quite well in the sport people accept me more ... but I think if ... I just played like recreationally or something I'd get, you know ... well masculine ... and 'oh you play women's cricket – you must be a lesbian'. (Denise: Cricket)

Similar findings have come from work investigating the experiences of female wrestlers (Sisjord 1997). When meeting new people, participation in wrestling was hidden by both the wrestler and her family, focusing conversation instead on other activities such as horse riding that were considered more appropriate. It has been suggested by attributions research (e.g. Jones and Davis 1965; Lau and Russell 1980; Weiner 1985) that individuals tend to look for reasons or causes for unexpected events more than for expected events. It would seem that people question why women play rugby much more so than they question why men play rugby and, subsequently, female rugby players/cricketers more so than female netballers. No one is surprised that men play rugby or cricket or that women play netball. The fact that these women are constantly expected to justify their participation shows that people believe it to be an unexpected activity which, in turn, reflects stereotype formation and maintenance. For Denise, being an international player justified her participation when talking to men. However, when talking to other sportswomen her self-presentation may well focus on her team-mates and enjoyment of cricket rather than on 'proving' her ability. Demonstrating an undeniable level of expertise or fitness within a sporting activity deemed appropriate for men has been one avenue through which women have gained acceptance, albeit a reluctant acceptance (Halbert 1997). In contrast, none of the respondents in this study could recall a male athlete ever having to prove himself to the same extent as women do within a training session.

Justifying the presence of lesbians

These sportswomen also sought to clarify why the lesbian stereotype was so rife. Cath, a cricketer, spent a great deal of time trying to intellectualise why there was a large number of gay women in her sport in an attempt to reconcile it for herself:

> ... women who play the major men's sports [rugby, cricket, football] ... are seen as being women who want to prove something, who are out to be tougher than everybody else ... there are a lot of gay women who take a lot of pride or enjoyment in being physically fit, are ... almost more in control of their body ... not as a, I don't know a signal for sex in that sense ... but more a kind of just of feeling it being fit, or powerful, or being able to do something that I would argue a lot of straight women aren't able to do ... a pride in ... yourself and also ... you know, being gay, therefore, you're on the fringes of society, therefore, you form a team. (Cath: Cricket)

There is some evidence to suggest that lesbian women differ from heterosexual women in relation to body image (Striegel-Moore et al. 1990). Striegel-Moore et al. provide an explanation of this in that lesbians do not have to appeal to the heterosexual ideal of attractiveness. Gay women may be rejecting traditional notions of acceptable physical appearance in addition to the rejection of traditional sexual relationships. In studies comparing lesbian and heterosexual women, lesbians were found to be significantly heavier than heterosexual women and preferred larger physiques. This was combined with a greater satisfaction of their bodies and less concern about their physical appearance (Brand et al. 1992; Herzog et al. 1992; Siever 1994). For women in heterosexual and men in homosexual encounters the display and maintenance of a certain image is valued in terms of a sexual signal (Silberstein et al. 1988; Brand et al. 1992). There is no reason to suggest that the pursuit of a mate for lesbian women would not be associated with physical attraction any less so because of their sexual orientation; it may simply be in a different way than that which appeals to heterosexual men.

Changing the lesbian image

In considering the prevalence of the lesbian stereotype within women's sport there appears to be a clear directive concerning a change of image. One factor involved may well be as a result of government funding for these sports and the subsequent movement towards a more professional and marketable image. There is certainly an undercurrent, however, of moving towards what Griffin (1992) describes as the heterosexualisation of women's sport. Femininity serves as a code word for heterosexuality especially within the domain of sport. She states that:

... the underlying fear is not that a female athlete or coach will appear too plain or out of style, the real fear is that she will look like a dyke or, even worse, is one. This intense blend of homophobic and sexist standards of feminine attractiveness remind women in sport that to be acceptable, we must monitor our behaviour and appearance at all times.

(Griffin 1992: 254)

In rugby there was an appreciation of how the physical qualities required of a female rugby player were changing due to the increase in standards throughout the world. Women had to be far fitter, stronger and more athletic than in previous years. A number of the women remarked that the image of the 'lardy' prop that trundled from one point on the pitch to the next was long gone. For the cricketers there was also a real sense that the image was being changed, directed by a need to rid the game of the lesbian ticket:

... well I think there's like sort of lesbianism around and ... you know sort of butch and sort of bigger women. Short hair, that sort of image but I think now as well ... we're [younger women] coming through, that's sort of filtering out because of the fitness side and you don't get so much the bigger, larger women now. I think maybe to play sport you have to be, you know, hard, bigger and, you know, physically fit. I don't know why you have to be gay ... I have an image of just really any female sport [being gay]. I mean netball I wouldn't think because it's sort of feminine ... like you wear a skirt. (Danny: Cricket)

What is evident from such comments is the process of 'victim blaming' that occurs within some sports, suggesting that it is the women themselves that are hurting their sports because of the image they present (Halbert 1997). Danny's comment is also interesting because, in her definition of what it is to be feminine, she uses the symbol of the skirt as a way to identify netballers as more feminine than cricketers. The irony here is that, until very recently, female cricketers have always worn skirts (teams were able to choose to wear skirts or trousers from the 2000–1 season). Clearly this symbol of femininity is not transferred to women who play cricket but it clearly demonstrates how some female cricketers perceive the lesbian label.

The need to change the image of female cricketers is reflected in the wider discussion of how sport is promoted and who is considered to be a marketable product. Kolnes (1995) points to the development of sexualised sportswear and how a woman's sexuality can be openly displayed. She highlights the case of Florence Griffith-Joyner as the ultimate exponent of sexual presentation. Duncan's (1990) analysis of Griffith-Joyner's media coverage in the 1988 Seoul Olympics describes how her clothes, make-up and sexual attractiveness were discussed at every opportunity rather than highlighting her athletic abilities. A similar presentation was used with Australian pole-vaulter, Tatiana Grigorieva, and her sexualised image used to promote the 2000 Olympic Games in Sydney (see Robinson 2002). Sponsorship in elite sport promotes the use of sexualised images and in doing so directs the athlete to appear in such a way that emphasises this aspect of their performance (Kolnes 1995). Women both confirm and accept that they have to display their heterosexual attractiveness or fail to secure sponsorship to compete. Halbert (1997) explicitly noted this dilemma for the female boxers in her work and identified how those women who appear more 'feminine' (i.e. heterosexually attractive) are more likely to receive backing from promoters. Both Halbert and Kolnes also note how women can become complicit in this form of sexism. For example, one boxer in Halbert's research referred to the need to rid the sport of those women who appear like men or feel they can compete with the men in favour of more traditionally accepted displays of femininity. Halbert refers to this as 'internalised belief' of so-called 'appropriate' behaviour.

Taking this into consideration it is clear that women in many sports deemed inappropriate, either on the basis of physicality or social acceptability, are fully aware of the stereotypes in place. This fully supports Goffman's (1963) notion of the hierarchy of body idioms that individuals embrace and use to judge themselves and others. The women within these sports recognise those physical characteristics that are valued above others and use these to determine 'appropriate' sporting appearance. Griffin (1992) suggests that by becoming active in the process of trying to change the image of some women's sports, women are taking an active role in the continuation of such stereotypes. She argues 'the energy expended in making lesbians invisible and projecting a happy heterosexual image keeps women in sport fighting among ourselves rather than confronting the heterosexism and sexism that our responses unintentionally serve' (Griffin 1992: 260–1).

Lesbianism as a positive identity?

Not all women found the presence of lesbians to be such a negative experience. For some the assumption that there might be gay women within a sport team provided a way into a social scene that suited them; a social environment where it was safe to be 'out' and which provided a friendship network based on similar life styles was highly sought by some women:

> I think there's a lot of people as well who come into it because it is predominantly gay, the social life is really important and I also think the extension of that is that if they are gay they find an identity there because it's a scene. (Sue: Rugby)

For many women, having a recognised or known assumption about the presence of gay women in sport can result in a positive experience through membership. Having a safe environment in which to express their sexuality was very empowering for these women. Many discussed the ways in which the team provided opportunities for acceptance and recognition as a gay woman within sport. Lenskyj (1994) highlights the potential for positive experience through her investigation of the Notso Amazon Softball League in Toronto. Here the women-only recreational league provided an avenue for lesbian and lesbian-friendly women to gather together and share their love of sport. This ultimately provided an avenue for social support, friendship development and partner finding.

However, for some rugby women the open display of their sexuality was seen as damaging to the game, as in cricket, and used as a source of resentment and suspicion within the higher ranks of female sport. There was a real sense of having to explain and justify in some way why there was such a large number of gay women within certain sports. Griffin (1992) discusses the so-called predatory lesbians who seek out the naive and vulnerable as an argument put forward by the heterosexual majority to prevent young women from participating in sporting activities. This assumption was clearly identified in 1994 when Denise Annetts had been dropped from the Australian women's cricket team. She alleged that her sacking was due to her heterosexual preference and marital status (Burroughs *et al.* 1995). Although never proven, the speculation provided an avenue for rumours to abound concerning the sexual preference of all the women within the cricket team. Incidents such as these not only serve to question the sexuality of any athlete in a traditionally male-dominated sport, but also suggest that the presence of lesbian athletes is wrong and damaging.

It is clear from the rugby and cricket women in this study that the majority who watch and participate in those sports perceive the assumption of homosexuality negatively. For cricketers, in particular, there is an acceptance of the need to change the image in order to promote the sport to younger women and rid the game of the older more 'butch' woman. The demarcation of the lesbian stereotype is demonstrated clearly when discussing the perceptions of netballers as lesbian. For the women interviewed there was a recognition of the presence of the stereotype of them as gay because they were 'all women together', as distinct from that focused on the rugby players and cricketers. Here the perception of lesbianism within netball had a more positive association for male observers because it appealed to men's own heterosexual ideals of sexual fantasy. Nicola notes how the men she talked to were fascinated by the prospect of there being gay women within netball because it fitted a heterosexual fantasy of the 'lipstick lesbian' who would perform for their pleasure:

> ... from men one of the things they probably think, they're hoping that you're either going to be gay, whether there's a lot of gays or whatever lesbians would be in that sport because it's an all female sport
> KATE: Even in netball?
> ... because it's a female sport, they think straight away they think 'oh right' ... but they ... I think they like to imagine, you know 'cos it's one of their fantasies. (Nicola: Netball)

It would appear that the presence of gay women in netball is more acceptable than in rugby and cricket if netball women are regarded as attractive in a heterosexual framework. This would mean that they were subsequently open, therefore, for sexual appreciation and objectification. We find further explanation of this phenomenon in the work of Veri (1999) who notes how the male heterosexual gaze is uninterrupted when athletes participate in sports traditionally reserved for women (e.g. figure skating, gymnastics and netball). Here the female athlete is still able to be objectified as a sexual object because she has not removed herself from what Veri calls 'compulsory heterovisuality'. This supports the notion that when women do participate in activities which are more masculine (e.g. rugby, cricket or football) the gaze, which holds her as sex object and not athlete, is disrupted.

Limiting perceptions of femininity

In considering the limiting perceptions of femininity, Halbert describes the marketing situation in women's boxing whereby appearing more feminine results in more fights. Here there is only one definition of femininity as meaning 'not manlike' which prevents any other possible expression of femininity. Being regarded as feminine by male observers and promoters produces a clash with what Halbert calls 'heterosexist logic'. This asserts that women who participate in the masculine sport of boxing must themselves not be feminine (Halbert 1997). This correlates strongly with the dynamics of women's rugby when women who appeal to male heterosexual ideals of attractiveness elicit surprise by those watching and all the more so if they are talented. What is clear, however, is that these remarks do not reflect the experiences of women who play these sports. As found with female bodybuilders (Marsh and Jackson 1986), perceptions of their own femininity are no less so because of their sports participation. Clearly the women who are actively involved in these sports are able to develop multidimensional constructs of femininity and ones which do not rely on restrictive codes of acceptable heterosexual identities.

Women's ideals of sportswomen

It should be recognised that women within sport also contribute to the exclusion of women who do not fit *their* ideal of what it is to be a sportswoman. One cricketer recalls how shameful it would be to be bowled out by someone she called a 'dolly bowler'. The bowler in question was tall, slim, had long blond hair and was not considered to be a serious competitor solely because of her physical appearance:

> … you may have the worse bowler in the world bowling at you but they might just come up with one corker of a ball and it'll get you out and … a lot of that as well is pride because you think 'oh God I've just been out by a dolly bowler', you know and the shame of it. (Delia: Cricket)

It is clear that, for this particular cricketer, there is as much fear exhibited by her need to avoid defeat by a 'dolly bowler' as there is for a man to avoid defeat by a 'girl'. For Delia, an exit at the hand of this bowler can only be evaluated through a mocking of her appearance rather than as an acceptance of her superior playing skills.

Expectations of physical appearance permeate all levels of the sports presented here and by all competitors. However, there is an evident tension between maintaining an image which is appropriate for the sport and seeking an image that appeals to potential participants. Whilst there is recognition of the heterosexist definitions of female sport participants as lesbian there also appears to be an exclusion by the participants themselves of women who do not fit that image. For women within the sport there is a rejection of those they consider to be too feminine: the 'dolly bowlers', the 'mud wrestlers' and the 'Foxee' boxers. This is based not only on the presence of these women as supposed ridiculers of their sport but also on what the female participants consider to be appropriate physical appearance. What is evident is that for these sportswomen there is a conflict between rejecting traditional ideals of acceptable behaviour, demonstrated by their choice of sport, but also in accepting women into their sport who choose to conform to ideals of heterosexual attractiveness.

There is an expectation for the 'real' sportswomen to reject traditional ideals of what a woman should look like by simply imposing one set of rules for another. The irony would appear to be that it is at times the women within the sport itself who prevent inclusiveness. Thus women who participate in sport have complex views of what femininity means to them and what it should mean to others. This situation suggests that there may well be two sets of body idioms or shared vocabularies, which are used to judge the presentation of the self (Goffman 1963). On the one hand there is an agreed set of society idioms that are adopted and used to judge others and ourselves. On the other hand there may well be specific sport-based idioms that direct the judgements of sportswomen to either accept or reject a presented physical appearance.

Conclusion

This chapter has focused on how sexuality comes to bear such an influence on the enjoyment and participation of women in sport. The underlying link of women's physical activity to lesbianism has been identified revealing that women in sport are regarded as potential lesbians regardless of their activity being seen as gender-appropriate or not. Moreover, the chapter has demonstrated how the development of positive and negative lesbian stereotypes is formulated through the perception of male observers with netballers being described as lesbian and promoting a male fantasy which appealed to heterosexual ideals of female attractiveness. For rugby players and cricketers, however, the assumption of lesbianism was strongly related to the image of women in those sports as 'butch' and muscular and, therefore, not attractive to heterosexual men. This led to many women feeling that they had to justify their participation in these two sports and search for an approval through sporting excellence.

It is clear that the ways in which socially constructed ideals of femininity are formed permeate all levels of society. Even when resisting social standards of acceptable physical behaviour, by playing cricket and rugby, the women within these sports still find themselves judging others by constructed notions of physical attractiveness with the irony that it is often sportswomen themselves who create alternative body idioms to judge members of their own teams. It is also clear that certain social processes prescribe what those bodies should look like. In particular, it is often the marketing and promotion of sports that have determined which bodies are viewed as successful and financially viable. Although, as Goffman (1963) argues, individuals usually have the ability to control and monitor their bodily performances in order to interact with other people, the meanings attributed to that performance are not determined by the individual. Meanings are the result of negotiated constructions and reconstructions by individuals as they interact with other people. If one sport performance is valued over another, such as 'feminine' over 'masculine', women may come to be categorised as failed members of society or sport society by others. This may result in an internalisation of that label and incorporation of it into a 'spoiled' self-identity (Goffman 1968). In these ways, in and through sport, dominant and subordinate body stories and identities are created and maintained (Sparkes 1997).

References

Brand, P., Rothblum, E. and Solomon, L. (1992) 'A comparison of lesbians, gay men and heterosexuals on weight and restrained eating', *International Journal of Eating Disorders*, 11, 3: 253–9.

Burroughs, A., Seebohm. L. and Ashburn, L. (1995) '"A leso story": a case study of Australian women's cricket and its media experience', *Sporting Traditions*, 12, 1: 27–46.

Choi, P. Y. L. (2000) *Femininity and the Physically Active Woman*, London: Routledge.

Connell, R. W. (1987) *Gender and Power: Society, the Person, and Sexual Politics*, Stanford, CA: Stanford University Press.

Duncan, M. C. (1990) 'Sports photographs and sexual difference: images of women and men in the 1984 and 1988 Olympic Games', *Sociology of Sport Journal*, 7, 1: 22–43.

Duncan, M. C. and Hasbrook, C. A. (1988) 'Denial of power in televised women's sports', *Sociology of Sport Journal*, 5, 1: 1–21.

Dunning, E. (1994) 'Sport as a male preserve: notes on the sources of masculine identity and its transformations', in S. Birrell and C. L. Cole (eds) *Women, Sport, and Culture*, Champaign, IL: Human Kinetics.

Goffman, E. (1963) *Behaviour in Public Places: Notes on the Social Organisation of Gatherings*, New York: Free Press.

Goffman, E. (1968) *Stigma: Notes on the Management of Spoiled Identity*, Harmondsworth: Penguin.

Griffin, P. (1992) 'Changing the game: homophobia, sexism, and lesbians in sport', *Quest*, 44, 2: 251–65.

Halbert, C. (1997) 'Tough enough and woman enough: stereotypes, discrimination, and impression management among women professional boxers', *Journal of Sport and Social Issues*, 21, 1: 7–36.

Herzog, D. B., Newman, K. L., Yeh, C. J. and Warshaw, M. (1992) 'Body image satisfaction in homosexual and heterosexual women', *International Journal of Eating Disorders*, 11, 4: 391–6.

Jones, E. E. and Davis, K. E. (1965) 'From acts to dispositions: the attribution process in person perception', in L. Berkowitz (ed.) *Advances in Experimental Social Psychology* (vol. 2), New York: Academic Press.

Kane, M. J. and Greendorfer, S. L. (1994) 'The media's role in accommodating and resisting stereotyped images of women in sport', in P. Creedon (ed.) *Women, Media and Sport: Challenging Gender Values*, Thousand Oaks, CA: Sage.

Koivula, N. (1999) 'Gender stereotyping in televised media sport coverage', *Sex Roles*, 41, 7/8: 589–604.

Kolnes, L. J. (1995) 'Heterosexuality as an ongoing principle in women's sport', *International Review for the Sociology of Sport*, 30, 1: 61–75.

Krane, V. (1996) 'Lesbians in sport: toward acknowledgement, understanding, and theory', *Journal of Sport and Exercise Psychology*, 18, 3: 237–46.

Lau, R. R. and Russell, D. (1980) 'Attributions in the sports pages', *Journal of Personality and Social Psychology*, 39, 1: 29–38.

Lenskyj, H. (1994) 'Sexuality and femininity in sport contexts: issues and alternatives', *Journal of Sport and Social Issues*, 18, 4: 356–76.

Lenskyj, H. (1998) '"Inside sport" or "on the margins"? Australian women and the sport media', *International Review for the Sociology of Sport*, 33, 1: 19–32.

Marsh, H. W. and Jackson, S. A. (1986) 'Multidimensional self-concepts, masculinity, and femininity as a function of women's involvement in athletics', *Sex Roles*, 15, 3: 391–415.

Pirinen, R. (1997) 'Catching up with men?: Finnish newspaper coverage of women's entry into traditionally male sports', *International Review for the Sociology of Sport*, 32, 3: 239–49.

Robinson, L. (2002) *Black Tights: Women, Sport and Sexuality*, Toronto: Harper Collins.

Sabo, D. and Messner, M. A. (1993) 'Whose body is this? Women's sports and sexual politics', in G. L. Cohen (ed.) *Women in Sport: Issues and Controversies*, Thousand Oaks, CA: Sage.

Siever, M. D. (1994) 'Sexual orientation and gender as factors in socioculturally acquired vulnerability to body dissatisfaction and eating disorders', *Journal of Consulting and Clinical Psychology*, 62: 252–60.

Silberstein, L. R., Striegel-Moore, R. H., Timko, C. and Rodin, J. (1988) 'Behavioural and psychological implications of body dissatisfaction: do men and women differ?', *Sex Roles*, 19, 3/4: 219–32.

Sisjord, M. K. (1997) 'Wrestling with gender: a study of young female and male wrestlers' experiences of physicality', *International Review for the Sociology of Sport*, 32, 4: 432–8.

Sparkes, A. C. (1997) 'Reflections on the socially constructed physical self', in K. R. Fox (ed.), *The Physical Self: From Motivation to Well Being*, Champaign, IL: Human Kinetics.

Striegel-Moore, R. H., Tucker, N. and Hsu, J. (1990) 'Body image dissatisfaction and disordered eating in lesbian college students', *International Journal of Eating Disorders*, 9, 5: 493–500.

Veri, M. J. (1999) 'Homophobic discourse surrounding the female athlete', *Quest*, 51, 4: 355–68.

Weiner, B. (1985) '"Spontaneous" causal thinking', *Psychological Bulletin*, 97: 74–84.

Wright, L. and Clarke, G. (1999) 'Sport, the media and the construction of compulsory heterosexuality: a case study of women's Rugby Union', *International Review for the Sociology of Sport*, 34, 3: 227–43.

Young, K. (1997) 'Women, sport and physicality: preliminary findings from a Canadian study', *International Review for the Sociology of Sport*, 32, 3: 297–305.

Chapter 9

Driving down participation

Homophobic bullying as a deterrent to doing sport

Celia Brackenridge, Ian Rivers,
Brendan Gough and Karen Llewellyn

Introduction

The authors of this chapter came together from very different starting points but with a common interest in how gender, sexuality and sexual orientation are used as weapons of exploitation in various arenas and, particularly, in sport where such behaviour deters sports participation and enjoyment. Ian Rivers and Brendan Gough, although adopting two very different methodological approaches to their research, share a common interest in the ways in which homophobia manifests itself within contemporary society (Rivers 2001a, 2001b, 2004; Gough 2002, n.d.). Celia Brackenridge and Karen Llewellyn have approached their previous work from feminist sociological perspectives. Karen Llewellyn has always been interested in gender relations and their influence within physical education and sport and Celia Brackenridge's work on sexual exploitation (1997, 2001, 2003), which has focused largely on sexual harassment and abuse, was the springboard for her interest in sport as a site of homophobic bullying.

Discussing the extent and types of homophobic bullying outside sport, it became clear to us that the issue begged further investigation within the sporting context. Indeed, a major stimulus for this collaboration was the proposition that sport is a prime site for homophobic bullying and that the social and personal consequences of homophobic bullying associated with sport are severe.

Drawing on previous work in education and the wider community, this chapter opens with an examination of different meanings of bullying, homophobia and homophobic bullying. This discussion is set within a paradigm wherein we argue that sexual identities are socially constructed, multiple and malleable, built upon the needs and understandings of the individual set with a cultural framework (Rivers 1997). Consequently, we acknowledge that, to adequately gauge the prevalence of homophobic bullying within sport, it is important to review and build upon those studies that provide the social, educational and professional contexts within which sport is played. In providing this background, our intention is to demonstrate how awareness of the issue far exceeds observers' readiness to act upon or against it by intervening, challenging or reporting perpetrators.

We move on to review some of the now extensive literature on sexuality and sport and to outline why it is so important for sport scholars and policy makers to acknowledge and address homophobic bullying. Whilst homophobia in sport *per se* has been a focus of academic attention for some three decades (see Griffin 1998; Pronger 1990), homophobic bullying has not previously been linked overtly to work on sexual violence and abuse in sport. Using data from an earlier survey on homophobic bullying (Rivers 2004), figures specifically relating to sport are extrapolated and presented here for the first time.

Anti-bullying initiatives and prevention policies and action are slowly emerging among sport organisations. The way that homophobic bullying has been addressed through policy within and outside sport is briefly explored here. There is a great deal to learn from the education service in the way it defines, manages and responds to homophobic bullying: sport is found to be seriously lagging in this regard. The chapter closes by posing some research questions about homophobic bullying in sport that we hope to explore in the future, that may provoke further work in this field by others and that may eventually inform a more effective policy infrastructure for protecting Lesbian, Gay, Bisexual and Transgender (LGBT) athletes and encouraging higher participation rates.

What is homophobic bullying?

Homophobia is a dislike or fear of someone who is lesbian, gay or bisexual (LGB). At its most benign it involves passive resentment of LGB men and women. In its most destructive form it involves active victimisation.

(DfES/DoH 2004: 6)

Homophobic bullying is often found in environments where there is a failure to respond to attitudes, beliefs or behaviours that denigrate or otherwise pathologise non-heterosexuals. The children's charity *Kidscape* has defined homophobic bullying thus:

Any hostile or offensive action against lesbians, gay males or bisexuals or those perceived to be lesbian, gay or bisexual. These actions might be: verbal, physical, or emotional (social exclusion) harassment, insulting or degrading comments, name calling, gestures, taunts, insults or 'jokes', offensive graffiti,humiliating, excluding, tormenting, ridiculing or threatening, refusing to work or co-operate with others because of their sexual orientation or identity.

(Kidscape 2004)

Although a great deal of the research on homophobic bullying has focused on the school environment, it is not solely confined to the classroom or playground. It is endemic and owes its continued presence to debates surrounding the acceptability of homosexuality as a typical expression of human sexual orientation. Indeed, the fear of those who identify as anything other than heterosexual is based on unjustified assumptions of indiscriminate and sexually voracious or predatory behaviour (see Gough 2002). In addition, the commonly cited but, as yet, scientifically unsubstantiated association between homosexuality and paedophilia has resulted in both public and self-imposed restrictions placed upon lesbians and gay men who are teachers, mentors and coaches, and who are often automatically and irrationally presumed to be a threat to all children and young people whether opposite- or same-sex. It is not surprising, therefore, that among those who suffer homophobic bullying, feelings of self-loathing and worthlessness are commonplace (Rivers 2004: 2). Indeed, one of the best predictors of mental health among lesbian, gay and bisexual young people is self-acceptance (Hershberger and D'Augelli 1995), which, for victims of homophobic bullying, is often a struggle.

To understand the way in which homophobic bullying pervades not only our school systems but any environment in which young people are brought together, it is necessary to understand the presuppositions that inform the nature and structure of the institution, place or activity in which they participate. Comparable with Goffman's (1961) classic description of the total institution, where the inmate is de-individualised, those environments in which young people often find themselves (schools, colleges, recreational and sports clubs) are predicated on the presumption that heterosexuality is not simply the norm but the irredoubtable absolute. Any variation from the norm among the client group brings with it flux and an inability of the supervising organisation or individual to function effectively. If one looks at the language of the school yard, the pitch or the sports arena, those who do not act or perform to a given standard are labelled deviant, abnormal and not 'one of us'.

Among males, descriptors such as 'girly', 'poofy' or 'gay' appear not only in the banter of peers but also in the encouragement, feedback and, most commonly, the castigation of young men by teachers and coaches in the hope that future behaviour and performance will be more in keeping with that of the majority. Mac an Ghaill's (1994) sociological study of masculinity in the school environment demonstrates how gender stereotypes are reinforced, not only through the curriculum but also in the way teachers and pupils interact. However, this study, and subsequently that of Duncan (1999), shows us that there are boys who are labelled 'gay' and then there are real 'gay' boys: the former need to be brought into line, the latter need to be excluded. Among girls, terms such as 'lezzie' or 'dyke' can be heard in the school yard or playground and among peers where one girl challenges the status quo, or where she prefers the company of one as compared with a group of others. Interestingly, however, Duncan (1999) suggests names such as 'slag' are used more commonly as the descriptors for one who contravenes the unofficial rules of the school yard or playground. 'Lezzies' and 'dykes' become social outcasts, often because of the intimate nature of their relationship with one other person, or because they do not conform to stereotypical ideals about the way a young woman must act, dress and portray herself.

It is recognised that physical education and school sport, in particular, are established sites for the privileging of particular forms of heterosexism and homophobia. These forms apply to the experiences of both teachers (Sparkes 1994, 1997; Squires and Sparkes 1996; Brown 1999; Clarke 1998, 2001) and young people (Parker 1996; Clarke 2003; Paechter 2003). Recent writings on the 'schooling of bodies' and the 'sexualisation of space' reveal a homophobic terrain and subsequent hostility to those who challenge these narrowly defined '(hetero) sexual boundaries' (Clarke 2004: 191).

Whilst educators have a responsibility to create safe spaces, homophobic and heterosexist behaviours in schools do not lend themselves to an inclusive climate, particularly for lesbian and gay school students (Morrow 2003). In challenging this situation, Sykes' (1998) work demonstrates that anti-homophobic pedagogies by physical educators in relation to name-calling, whilst preventing 'injury' to their students, result in greater personal risk of harm to the teachers themselves.

So when does a name or label, or an action or behaviour cease to be banter and become harassment? Any assessment of harassment is, invariably, based upon subjective interpretation. Behaviours that might be deemed appropriate in one venue may be wholly inappropriate in another. However, researchers agree upon three fundamental criteria in determining what constitutes harassment, victimisation or bullying: it has to be repeated, deliberate and with the intention of harming its target ('the victim'). Homophobic bullying is, in essence, the exploitation of an individual's actual or perceived sexual orientation with the intention of belittling or otherwise denigrating her/his status as an equal, often with the intention of inflicting mental as well as physical harm. It can be seen as a subset of harassment which sits part way along the 'sexual exploitation continuum' (Brackenridge 1997). Behavioural illustrations or acts of perpetration might therefore include any or all of the following based on perceived or alleged homosexual and, perhaps, transsexual orientation:

- staring/looking
- psychological harassment
- ridiculing or caricaturing someone's physical, sexual or social features
- stealing possessions
- name calling (dyke, queer, lezzie, poof, weirdo)
- joking about someone's sexual orientation
- using physical threats or actual physical violence.

Admittedly, this conceptual structure is limited by its linearity and by its perpetrator perspective. It also defines what a homophobic bully might *do* but not necessarily how a victim of homophobic bullying might *feel* or, indeed, the relational processes through which homophobic bullying is constructed. Different victims of homophobic bullying might therefore experience these kinds of practices in very different ways, depending on their own social and sexual histories. For some, they result in a sense of 'unremitting oppression' (Duncan 1999) or feeling forced to lie to cover up shame or feelings. In other words, it is difficult to offer a singular, objective definition of homophobic bullying. However, this conceptual structure does provide an index of the types of behaviour that are acknowledged to relate to both overt and covert acts of aggression that represent the daily discrimination faced by lesbians and gay men in the developed world (Hershberger and D'Augelli 1995; Pilkington and D'Augelli 1995; Rivers 2001a).

Another limitation of defining homophobic bullying according to single instances or acts is reductionism: descriptions of individual homophobic behaviours capture neither the pervasive cultural negativity that homophobic bullying engenders (the 'repeated' episodes), nor the ways in which rapid cultural shifts from tolerance to intolerance can occur through collusive silences. In other words, homophobic bullying becomes a continuous process and not a series of solitary and seemingly unrelated events. The processes of stigmatising someone because of their perceived or actual sexual orientation can be subtle and long term: something as innocuous as a look or stare if delivered by a key protagonist can be just as effective a weapon as a fist or a foot. The often subtle nature of homophobic bullying means that it can go undetected for years – there are no visible injuries on the victim and there are no names to overhear. Indeed, the system failures that lead to and reinforce homophobic bullying are often not revealed by the particularisation of behaviour. Understanding a cultural climate that is intolerant of sexual diversity is thus just as important as understanding the individual motivation of the homophobic bully. It could be argued that changes in the laws promoting equality in terms of the age of consent, human rights and civil partnerships indicate a change in cultural attitudes towards women and men who define as non-heterosexual and should thus result in a reduction in homophobic bullying. Yet twenty years after the original study which showed that 39 per cent of 416 young people who identified as lesbian and gay had experienced problems and bullying at school (Warren 1984), Ellis and his colleagues demonstrated that homophobic bullying is now more prevalent among young people than perhaps at any other time (Ellis and High 2004).

Other studies reiterate the prevalence of homophobic bullying. According to Rivers and Duncan (2002), it affects approximately one-third of all young people who later identify as lesbian and gay. It also affects a small minority of young people whose only crime is that they do not conform to the stereotypes their parents, peers and teachers understand. A survey by Stonewall published in 1994 reported that homosexuals under the age of 18 were experiencing more violence than any other part of the gay community (Coates 1998). Half of the attacks on gay children were perpetrated by other pupils. In 1997, the University of London produced a report on secondary school teachers' experience of homosexual pupils and bullying. It found that 82 per cent of teachers were aware of gay name-calling at their schools and 26 per cent were aware of violent incidents accompanied by homophobic comments (University of London 1997). Strikingly, whilst 99 per cent of schools had a policy on bullying, only 6 per cent had a policy that dealt specifically with gay and lesbian school students. In a UK study, Rivers (2004) found that post-traumatic stress was an issue for 17 per cent of self-identified adult gay men, lesbians and bisexuals who had experienced frequent and prolonged bullying during their schooldays.

These statistics are vividly illustrated and elaborated in critical qualitative research on heterosexism and homophobic bullying, particularly in educational contexts. In his groundbreaking qualitative study of sexual bullying in a secondary school, Duncan (1999: 126) reported that sexuality was 'a motor for disruptive behaviour' among the pupils. He found that there were many different meanings and interpretations of 'gay', including:

- low-status male
- male homosexual
- failing to meet 'even the lowest standards of "laddishness"'
- an apology for the male sex
- someone who could legitimately be beaten up – this was not personal but seen as an imperative and done in order to defend oneself against the possibility of personal attack
- 'niceness' to girls
- antithetical to sporting prowess.

What Duncan's work illustrates very sharply is that, when aimed at boys at least, the label of 'homosexual' is a powerful weapon: 'The most prevalent and hurtful accusation that could be levelled at boys by both sexes was to be called "gay"' (Duncan 1999: 106).

This concept of homophobic bullying as negative labelling is reinforced by Richardson (2004: 20) who says:

> ... homophobic bullying is not confined to the playground; and it isn't only inflicted on gay children. One of the most popular playground insults now is 'gay', which – like 'poof' in the 70s – doesn't mean homosexual so much as different and weak ... With that mindset it doesn't take much mental effort to see all gay men as vulnerable, as people deserving to be picked on.

Such was the impact of the term 'gay' among Duncan's respondents that they said they would rather be called 'nutter'. The tactical use of homophobic bullying to 'other' people in this way has been mastered adeptly by children and young people, many of whom have little or no idea of the meanings of the sexual language they adopt, and many of whom have not yet developed or confirmed their own sexual identity, let alone realised it in practice. However, this usage of homophobic bullying raises the interesting possibility that it is based on hatred of difference/love of sameness rather than sexual orientation *per se*, and that it might therefore be a kind of pseudo-homophobia. The transposition of 'gay' into 'weak and vulnerable' generalises the hatred but is no less offensive to the victim. Even attempting to seek clarity of definition may be a fruitless exercise in an area which is characterised by category errors and confusion: 'Definitions imposed on "gay" pupils were often incoherent, and they were infected by the language of oppression that they reserved for the alien' (Duncan 1999: 108).

The 'gender policing' that Duncan describes was itself differentiated by both gender and age. Boys and girls gave different sexual insults and responded differently to receiving them:

> The possibility of gays' presence in the school was loathed far more strongly by the boys than by the girls, and perhaps it was only their incredulity [that there might be real gays in their school] that prevented a witch-hunt.
>
> (Duncan 1999: 109)

The girls were far more tolerant of the idea of homosexuality than the boys (Duncan 1999: 123) and both genders were more accepting of lesbianism (the boys for voyeuristic reasons), although the younger girls were more threatened than their older peers by being called a lesbian. While younger pupils traded homophobic insults in a more matter-of-fact way, 'sexual bullying which [the boys] endured from some older boys was ... normal, pervasive, systemic and covert' (Duncan 1999: 113); as they advanced up the school, these same older boys adopted very narrow forms of heterosexual hegemonic masculinity:

> The notion that boys bully mainly by physical force appeared to be nonsense ... boys and girls exchanged vague gendered unpleasantries in the lower years ... As they underwent pubertal change the boys' ... insults [to girls] became more sexualised and funnelled through two major modes of expression: misogyny and homophobia.
>
> (Duncan 1999: 130)

The use of insults like 'poof' and 'nancy-boy' by males has been documented in both primary (Epstein 1997) and secondary school (Mac an Ghaill 1994; Frosh *et al.* 2002) contexts through ethnographic observation of male interactions and recording the stories of 'victims' of such abuse. Consider the comments of Miles, a secondary school pupil who did not inhabit a traditionally masculine position within the school:

> It's a sort of stigma, ain't it? A quiet person in a class would be called 'gay' or summat. I was for a time 'cos I was fairly quiet in the classroom and for a while everyone was callin' me gay ... I think my grades have suffered because of disruptive members of the class ...
>
> (Kehily and Nayak 1997: 83)

Research by Gough (2002) also highlights the use of homophobic discourse within higher education. Other research investigating homophobia as a social practice has further elaborated on the relationship to hegemonic forms of masculinity, with evidence suggesting widespread prejudice amongst groups of (mainly young, working-class) heterosexual men located at various institutional sites. Research with adolescent males in a work context also points to frequent instances of homophobia to maintain hierarchies between different groupings (see Haywood and Mac an Ghaill 1997). With regard to recent changes in USA government legislation concerning gays in the military, Britton and Williams (1995) have noted implicit (irrational) constructions of gay wo/men as threats to discipline and cohesion, even in spite of simultaneous commendation for services to the state. Clearly, talk and 'humour' based on homophobia and directed at 'other' males is used by boys and men to define and regulate hegemonic, heterosexual masculinities – with painful consequences for non-macho men.

Of interest to us here is whether and how far these social patterns might also be apparent in sport. Does the inherent/structural competitiveness of sport exacerbate this type of culture and lead from physical to sexual competitiveness? To what extent does homophobic bullying damage the enjoyment of young athletes or even deter young people from engaging in sport at all? These and other questions are addressed below.

Homophobic bullying in sport

Resistance to homosexuality within sport, especially mainstream sports, is well known. As Mennesson and Clement (2003: 316, 319) point out: 'Homophobia manifests itself in a particularly violent manner in sports in general, and in certain 'major' team sports in particular ... The vast majority of soccer [female] players are stigmatised by the scornful attitudes of men'.

The dominant gender culture and cultural climate of sport is homo-negative. In his work on hegemonic masculinity, Connell (1990) argues that sport is a cultural idealisation of masculinity. Although the mass media can be a site for contesting and renegotiating traditional sexual and sporting stereotypes, Nylund (2004) argues that they more often reinforce the culture of hegemonic heterosexual masculinity, with radio sports talk shows affording the 'covert intimacy' (Messner 1992) of the locker room to heterosexual male listeners where they can escape the 'political correctness' of public spaces. Pressure to 'come out' works in favour of heteronormativity because it requires someone first to claim a sexual orientation as gay/lesbian (Nylund 2004): there is no such pressure on heterosexuals. Visibility as gay/lesbian brings possibilities for liberation but also new oppressions of surveillance and discipline.

For males, to be disinterested or perform poorly in sport is to risk ridicule in the form of homophobic terminology such as 'poof' and 'queer', especially in the context of youth sports, whether taking place at school or in the community (Swain 2000). Since gay men are popularly associated with softness and effeminacy, they too are either excluded or devalued within the hetero-normative world of sport. Wendel, Toma and Morphew (2001: 470) found that heterosexual athletes were 'unwilling to confront and accept homosexuality'. Indeed, a man who is both gay and athletic transgresses pervasive understandings of homosexuality and sport and may well provoke negative press as a result. Various examples over the years reinforce this point. There is the tragic story of Justin Fashanu, for example, a talented British football (soccer) player who ended up committing suicide in 1998 after a troubled career, while the gifted Australian rugby player Ian Roberts experienced much animosity after coming out in 1991.

There is a growing body of work that documents and theorises instances of homophobia and heterosexism in a variety of sporting arenas (Pronger 1990; Griffin 1998; Caudwell 1999; McKay et al. 2000). For lesbian athletes, there are pressures associated with 'hegemonic femininity' whereby resistance, for example in the form of muscularity, is pathologised while conformity, for example in presenting a 'feminine' appearance, risks trivialisation (see Krane 2001). Similarly, qualitative research with pre-adolescent girls who played football at school (Jeanes 2004) found that all aspired to heterosexual marriage and having children and all had concerns about 'being manly'. In an interview study with closeted gay male athletes, Hekma (1998) illustrated the persistence of homophobic language and 'hyper-heterosexuality' within sport. In their study of women's soccer in France, Mennesson and Clement (2003: 317) found that homophobia was operational policy in many soccer clubs and that the clubs' male managers adopted assiduous policies of 'weeding out', 'cleaning up' or 'eradicating' the 'problem', organising 'girls days' where players had to wear skirts, paying expenses for boyfriends to travel to matches with the women players and so on. This is institutionalised homophobia.

A study by Andersen (2002), a highly respected coach and activist who has now become an academic working in California, was one of the first to recruit and interview openly gay athletes. Key themes derived from the qualitative analysis suggest a lack of overt prejudice against these athletes but this was linked to a suppression and silencing of gay sexualities within the sporting environment. So, while straight sportsmen continue with locker room 'chick talk', their gay counterparts have little choice but to stay silent about their own sexual life, or to mask it in other ways. Anderson concludes that this amounts to tolerance rather than acceptance, and that much more work needs to be done before spaces within sport can be opened up where gay as well as straight masculinities can flourish. It is worth noting, for example, that out gay athletes tend to converge on individual sports rather than more prestigious (and more conventionally masculine) team sports, and there is some evidence that many gay sportsmen remain in the closet for fear of their status and, in some cases, careers being irreparably damaged.

Another study by Shire et al. (2000), of female field hockey players, found that although the 'heteros' and 'homos' got along well together, they sometimes split into two sociability groups and frequented different social and recreational spaces such as discos or gay bars. The women appeared to prefer a male-free space and suggested that the presence of men changed the dynamic of the sociability in unwanted ways. Assigning of bus seats and hotel rooms on away trips was done on the basis of perceived sexual preference; thus, sexuality was used as an organising principle, with bisexual women on the team acting as intermediaries between the two groups, who teased each other. This contrasts with the 'brutal rejection of homosexuality' reported in men's team sports, including soccer (Theberge 1995).

The impact of heterosexism and homophobia is so pervasive that anyone opting out of hegemonic gender prescriptions attracts questions about their sexual orientation:

> The post-match drink where the discourse often centres around everyday issues of relationships, break ups, house buying, family and sex for example, is a discourse closeted gay or lesbian athletes are unable to participate in.
>
> (Borrie 1999: 117)

> ... these deep closets are full of not only lesbians, but also heterosexual women who fear that women's sport is only one lesbian scandal away from ruin.
>
> (Griffin 1998: ix–x)

> All lesbians and gay men should have the right to participate openly in sport, not just as sports people but as gay and lesbian athletes – to be visible, to be supported, and to be valued, without the threat of vilification, harassment or violence.
>
> (Borrie 1999: 117)

Elling et al. (2003: 441) question the 'social integrative meanings and functions' of sport through their examination of the growing trend for separate events for LGBT athletes, such as the Gay Games. They argue that social integration might mean different things for ethnic and for sexual preference minorities. They separate clubs into 'mainstream' (i.e. socially heterogeneous) and 'categorical' (i.e. based on an ethnic or sexual signifier) clubs. Overall participation figures (in the Netherlands) show no differences between heterosexual and LGBT participants but there were sport-specific and context-specific differences. Although large numbers of gay clubs now participate in mainstream leagues and competitions, they question whether this is part of an emancipatory project or an exclusionary one. They also suggest that 'legislation that forbids discrimination seems to have limited influence on [sport] club culture' (Elling et al. 2003: 452). The culture of exclusion that they observed affects the comfort level for LGBT athletes and influences their choices to join separate teams or clubs, despite the apparent openness of Dutch sport and despite claims to be socially inclusive. The prospects for resistance by integrating are thus countered by the heterosexist climate of the sports clubs: rather than leading to acceptance, this can lead to even greater homophobia by the general 'public' as a form of backlash. The onus for integration and change is thus put on the LGBT athletes, who risk rejection, rather than on the mainstream athletes and sports organisers, who risk nothing. At best, this leads to accommodation rather than assimilation.

In women's professional golf, sexual orientation is ever-present but barely acknowledged. It was described as the 'image problem' by the respondents in Crosset's study (1995) and engendered fear among most of them. The golfers were avowedly apolitical and deliberately ignored opportunities to build the solidarity that might enable them to exercise collective challenges to the structural inequities they faced. In contrast, lesbian and bisexual women competing in the Gay Games reported greater collective esteem as a result of participating. They also reported willingness to engage in social change, to educate others and to work through political channels, reflecting the politicising influence of their participation (Krane et al. 2002). The commercial importance of the professional golf tour is one possible explanation of why these two groups of women athletes responded so differently to their participation in sport but the presence or absence of institutionalised homophobic bullying is another. The positive homosocial culture of the Gay Games could hardly compare more starkly with the homo-negative culture (Krane 1997) of the women's golf tour.

Mennesson and Clement (2003) studied what they called the 'unique form of sociability' in women's sport and found that it acted as a facilitating environment for homosexual identity formation. 'This unique type of sociability makes room for the homosexual practices of female players acting by enabling its discovery for some and acting out for others' (2003: 411). In contrast, 'learning to suffer, submission to training and male solidarity characterise the sociability of male team sports' (Sabo and Panepinto 1990: 412). Indeed, these authors argue that homophobic homosociability is virtually a norm in male team sports yet in women's team sports homosexuality is almost protected – which they describe as a kind of 'permissive homosociability'.

As described above, there is a good deal of research into homophobia in sport but this is not directed specifically at homophobic bullying and its effects upon participation. The prevalence of homophobic bullying in sport is not known and, to our knowledge, has not been measured but extrapolating from previous studies of homophobic bullying in education, in which some situational data were collected, it is possible to gauge a limited idea of the extent of sport-related homophobic bullying. Extrapolating from data collated from a three-year longitudinal cohort study of the incidence of bullying in schools conducted by Rivers and colleagues in UK schools (Rivers 2004), it is possible to determine the frequency of homophobic bullying within sports environments (see Tables 1–3).

Table 1 shows that 50 per cent of these young people's experiences of homophobic bullying took place in the context of sport. Table 2 shows that 51 per cent of those reporting that they perpetrated homophobic bullying did so in the context of sport, and Table 3 indicates that 70 per cent of those witnessing homophobic bullying did so in the context of sport. There is also an interesting contradiction in the data, in that nearly 15 per cent of respondents reported seeing someone bullied homophobically yet only a tiny percentage reported being involved in homophobic bullying, either as a victim or a bully. These data might therefore indicate that homophobic bullying is a minority behaviour but something

Table 1 Young people's experience of homophobic bullying in the context of sport in UK schools (extrapolated from Rivers 2004)

N = 1,860	n (%)
Were called homophobic names by others	38 (2.1)
Of which: were bullied on the playing fields	10 (0.5) (all boys)
Of which: were bullied in the changing rooms	9 (0.5) (8 boys, 1 girl)

Table 2 Young people as perpetrators of homophobic bullying in the context of sport in UK schools (extrapolated from Rivers 2004)

N = 1,860	n (%)
Bullied others homophobically	55 (3.1)
Of which: bullied others on the playing fields	15 (13 boys, 2 girls)
Of which: bullied in the changing rooms	13 (11 boys, 2 girls)

Table 3 Young people as witnesses of homophobic bullying in the context of sport in UK schools (extrapolated from Rivers 2004)

N = 1,860	n (%)
Saw someone bullied homophobically	266 (14.7)
Of which: saw someone bullied on the playing fields	90 (64 boys, 26 girls)
Of which: saw someone bullied in the changing rooms	97

of a spectator sport for this group of young people. The general trend for bullying in sporting contexts is shown in Table 4.

These data demonstrate clearly that, whilst a minority of pupils (0.8–2.2 per cent) engage in bullying behaviour, between 11.6 and 12 per cent of the school population have witnessed such behaviour, with upwards of 5 per cent of the school population suffering it regularly.

These prevalence data reveal a worrying picture of homophobic bullying, especially for boys. Our conclusion from the qualitative studies reported above, and from the limited quantitative data available, is that homophobic bullying influences the quality of sport participation for both males and females but in different ways. For boys, what is important is success in sport (Duncan 1999: 27) with 'group membership earned via a sporting skill' (Duncan 1999: 77) and 'modes of appreciation ... always mediated through sporting references' (Duncan 1999: 89). Homophobic bullying is used as a weapon to encourage conformity to a hypermasculine sporting ideal and to vilify those who deviate from it. For girls, homophobic bullying is also used as a weapon, but to discourage sporting engagement and achievement. In both cases, the government's aim to 'drive up participation' (Rowe 2004) is thwarted.

Table 4 General trends for bullying in the context of sport (extrapolated from Rivers 2004)

Status	Sport context	Figures
Victims of bullying	Playing fields	range 4.1%–5.4%
	Changing rooms	range 2.5%–3.8%
Bullies	Playing fields	range 2.2%–2.2%
	Changing rooms	range 0.8%–1.8%
Witnessing bullying	Playing fields	12%
	Changing rooms	11.6%

The policy response to homophobic bullying

Anti-bullying networks in education and the workplace abound. After pressure from Stonewall and others, the UK's first Anti-Bullying Week was launched on 22 November 2004. Schools minister Stephen Twigg (himself out gay) 'set out plans to help schools tackle homophobic bullying'. Nine regional anti-bullying conferences were held across the UK during 2003–4, all of which ran workshops on preventing and responding to homophobic bullying (www.teachernet.gov.uk 2004). A Schools Anti-Bullying Charter was distributed to all maintained schools in 2004 and guidance on whole-school behaviour and attendance underlined the importance of keeping records of all instances of homophobic bullying (www.teachernet.gov.uk 2004). In the same year, Education Action Challenging Homophobia (EACH), a national charity, was established to challenge homophobia through education and it offers advice, support and a helpline (www.teachernet.gov.uk 2004).

Name-calling is perhaps the most widely used medium for bullying in general and homophobic bullying in particular. In the USA, a national 'No name-calling week' (24–28 January 2005) was organised across the nation, and supported by dozens of organisations including the US Women's Sports Foundation and the Gay, Lesbian and Straight Education Network (www.nonamecallingweek.org).

The launch of a new UK Commission for Equality and Human Rights to act as a single point of reference for rights, including those of sexual minorities, should give added protection through policy provisions. Although Sport England foreshadowed the Commission by bringing together its equality work into a single Equality Charter in 2004, the rights of LBGT people in sport have not had a high profile in national sports policy.

Despite a surge of interest in and policy development on child abuse and protection, fair play and violence in sport since the mid-1990s (Brackenridge and Fasting 2002; Dunning 1999; McNamee and Parry 1999; Ruskin and Lammer 2001), homophobic bullying has been ignored as a policy matter. This is largely because sexuality *per se* has been frequently omitted from policy documents on gender (and women) in sport. Some sport organisations overseas have established their own policy frameworks for defending the rights of LGBT athletes (for example, www.homophobiainsports.com and the Women's Sports Foundation in the USA, www.womensportsfoundation.org). Innovative work has also been started by the Football Association (2003, 2004a, b, c, d) and the UK Women's Sports Foundation (Donohue 2003) but such initiatives are still relatively rare in the UK.

A research agenda

A research agenda on homophobic bullying could explore a number of assumptions about LGBT athletes, partly through reviews of extant literature and partly through new empirical investigations. We hypothesise, for example, that lesbian and gay athletes:

- form a minority of athletes
- have been part of a sport system for years that has done little to tackle their social exclusion
- face pressure to conform because of their gender atypical behaviour
- experience higher rates of harassment and bullying than heterosexual athletes
- suffer enforced invisibility if male but enforced visibility if female
- have faced homophobic bullying as a part of their sport experiences from a very young age
- experience fear of harassment, assault and/or social isolation as a strong form of social control, regardless of actual experience
- therefore, attempt to hide their sexual orientation
- experience loss of friendships and significant other support as a result of their sexual orientation
- experience victimisation by athlete peers that is matched by both active and passive support for homo-negativity from their coaches and other authority figures in sport
- may be less likely to report harassment and bullying if from an ethnic or cultural minority because of the convergent silences of racism and homophobia.

Conclusions

Only through systematic qualitative and quantitative research will the pattern and dynamics of homophobic bullying in sport be uncovered. And only then will sports policy become properly evidence-based and therefore effective in challenging and reducing homophobic bullying.

Silence on the matter of homophobic bullying in sport merely serves to collude with the bullies. People inside sport need both the confidence and the tools to challenge such practices, and lesbians and gay men deserve the same protection policies and procedures as are now afforded to disabled people and children in sport.

Government imperatives for a healthier, fitter and more sport-active nation are not differentiated by sexual orientation but they are being undermined by homophobic bullying. Rather than driving up participation, homophobic bullying is driving down the chances that LGBT athletes will start, stay or succeed in sport.

References

Andersen, E. (2002) 'Openly gay athletes: contesting hegemonic masculinity in a homophobic environment', *Gender and Society*, 16, 6: 860–77.

Borrie, S. (1999) 'Being visible: towards gay games VI and cultural festival, Sydney 2002', paper presented at *'How You Play the Game: The Contribution of Sport to the Promotion of Human Rights Conference'*, Sydney, Australia 1–3 September.

Brackenridge, C.H. (1997) '"He owned me basically": women's experience of sexual abuse in sport', *International Review for the Sociology of Sport*, 32, 2: 115–30.

Brackenridge, C.H. (2001) *Spoilsports: Understanding and Preventing Sexual Exploitation in Sport*, London: Routledge.

Brackenridge, C.H. (2003) 'Dangerous sports? Risk, responsibility and sex offending in sport', *Journal of Sexual Aggression*, 9, 1: 3–12.

Brackenridge, C.H. and Fasting, K. (eds) (2002) 'Sexual harassment and abuse in sport – the research context', in C. Brackenridge and K. Fasting (eds) *Sexual Harassment and Abuse in Sport – International Research and Policy Perspectives*, Special issue of *Journal of Sexual Aggression*, 8, 2: 3–15.

Britton, D.M. and Williams, C.L. (1995) '"Don't ask, don't tell, don't pursue": military policy and the construction of heterosexual masculinity', *Journal of Homosexuality*, 30, 1: 1–21.

Brown, D. (1999) 'Complicity and reproduction in teaching physical education', *Sport Education and Society*, 4, 2: 143–60.

Caudwell, J. (1999) 'Women's football in the United Kingdom: theorizing gender and unpacking the butch lesbian image', *Journal of Sport and Social Issues*, 23, 4: 390–402.

Clarke, G. (1998) 'Queering the pitch and coming out to play: lesbians in physical education and sport', *Sport, Education and Society*, 3, 2: 145–160.

Clarke, G. (2001) 'Outlaws in sport and education? Exploring the sporting and education experiences of lesbian physical education teachers', in S. Scraton and A. Flintoff (eds) *Gender and Sport: A Reader*, London: Routledge.

Clarke, G. (2003) 'There's nothing queer about difference: challenging heterosexism and homophobia in physical education', in S. Hayes and G. Stidder (eds) *Equity and Inclusion in Physical Education and Sport*, London: Routledge.

Clarke, G (2004) 'Threatening space: (physical) education and homophobic body work', in J. Evans, B. Davies, and J. Wright (eds) *Body Knowledge and Social Control*, London: Routledge.

Coates, T. (1998) weblog www.plastic.bag.org/archives/1998/11/on_homophobic_bullying. shtml, dated 17 November, accessed 21 July 2004.

Connell, R. (1990) 'An iron man: the body and some contradictions of hegemonic masculinity', in M. Messner and D. Sabo (eds) *Sport, Men and the Gender Order*, Champaign, IL: Human Kinetics.

Crosset, T.W. (1995) *Outsiders in the Club House: The World of Women's Professional Golf*, Albany, NY: SUNY Press.

DfES/DoH (2004) *Stand Up For Us: Tackling Homophobia in Schools*, Wetherby: Health Development Agency.

Donohue, K. (2003) *Transsexuality and Sport: Women's Sports Foundation Response to the Department for Culture, Media and Sport, December 2002*, London: WSF: www.wsf.org.uk.

Duncan, N. (1999) *Sexual Bullying: Gender Conflict and Pupil Culture in Secondary Schools*, London: Routledge.

Dunning, E. (1999) *Sport Matters: Sociological Studies of Sport, Violence and Civilisation*, London: Routledge.

Elling, A., de Knop, P. and Knoppers, A. (2003) 'Gay/Lesbian sport clubs and events: places of homo-social bonding and cultural resistance', *International Review for the Sociology of Sport*, 38, 4: 441–56.

Ellis, V. and High, S. (2004) 'Something more to tell you: gay, lesbian or bisexual young people's experiences of secondary schooling', *British Educational Research Journal*, 30, 2: 213–25.

Epstein, D. (1997) 'Boyz' own stories: masculinities and sexualities in schools [1]', *Gender and Education*, 9, 1: 105–15.

Football Association (2003) 'FA supports Mardi Gras festival', http://www.TheFA.com/TheFA/Ethicsand SportsEquity/28 July, accessed 8 December 2004.

Football Association (2004a) 'Sexual identity', http://www.TheFA.com/TheFA/Ethicsand SportsEquity/, accessed 8 December 2004.

Football Association (2004b) 'FA stage homophobia summit', http://www.TheFA.com/TheFA/Ethicsand SportsEquity/May 7, accessed 8 December 2004.

Football Association (2004c) 'FA tackles homophobia', http://www.TheFA.com/TheFA/Ethicsand SportsEquity/28 Sept, accessed 8 December 2004.

Football Association (2004d) *Ethics and Sports Equity Strategy: Football for All*, London: The FA.

Frosh, S., Phoenix, A. and Pattman, R. (2002) *Young Masculinities*, Basingstoke: Palgrave.

Goffman, E. (1961) *Asylums: Essays on the Social Situation of Mental Patients and Other Inmates*, Garden City, NY: Doubleday.

Gough, B. (2002) "'I've always tolerated it but ...": heterosexual masculinity and the discursive reproduction of homophobia', in A. Coyle and C. Kitzinger (eds), *Lesbian and Gay Psychology*, Oxford: BPS Books/Blackwell.

Gough, B. (n.d.) 'Coming out in the heterosexist world of sport: a qualitative analysis of web postings by gay athletes', unpublished.

Griffin, P. (1998) *Strong Women, Deep Closets: Lesbians and Homophobia in Sport*, Champaign, IL: Human Kinetics.

Haywood, C. and Mac an Ghaill, M. (1997) 'A man in the making: sexual masculinities within changing training cultures', *Sociological Review*, 45, 4: 576–91.

Hekma, G. (1998) "'As long as they don't make an issue of it ...": gay men and lesbians in organised sports in the Netherlands', *Journal of Homosexuality*, 35, 1: 1–23.

Hershberger, S.L. and D'Augelli, A.R. (1995) 'The impact of victimization on the mental health and suicidality of lesbian, gay, and bisexual youths', *Developmental Psychology*, 31, 1: 65–74.

Jeanes, R. (2004) 'Girls, football participation and gender identity', paper presented to the Leisure Studies Association annual conference *Active Leisure and Young People*, Leeds Metropolitan University, 13–15 July.

Kehily, M.J. and Nayak, A. (1997) 'Lads and laughter: humour and the production of heterosexual hierarchies', *Gender and Education*, 9, 1: 69–87.

Kidscape, www.kidscape.org.uk/professionals/homophobicbullying.html, accessed 21 July 2004.

Krane, V. (1997) 'Homonegativism experienced by lesbian collegiate athletes', *Women in Sport and Physical Activity Journal*, 6, 2: 141–63.

Krane, V. (2001) 'We can be athletic and feminine, but do we want to? Challenging hegemonic femininity in women's sport,' *Quest*, 53, 1: 115–33.

Krane, V., Barber, H. and McClung, L. (2002) 'Social psychological benefits of Gay Games participation: a social identity theory explanation', *Journal of Applied Sport Psychology*, 14, 1: 27–42.

Mac an Ghaill, M. (1994) *The Making of Men: Masculinities, Sexualities and Schooling*, Buckingham: Open University Press.

McKay, M.A., Messner, M.A. and Sabo, D.F. (eds) (2000) *Masculinities, Gender Relations, and Sport*, Thousand Oaks, CA: Sage.

McNamee, M.J. and Parry, S.J. (eds) (1998) *Ethics and Sport*, London: Routledge.

Mennesson, C. and Clement, J.-P. (2003) 'Homosociability and homosexuality: the case of soccer played by women', *International Review for the Sociology of Sport*, 38, 3: 311–30.

Messner, M. (1992) *Power at Play: Sports and the Problem of Masculinity*, Boston, MA: Beacon Press.

Morrow, R.G. (2003) 'Perceptions of homophobia and heterosexism in physical education', *Research Quarterly for Exercise and Sport*, 74, 2: 205–14.

Nylund, D. (2004) 'When in Rome: heterosexism, homophobia and sports talk radio', *Journal of Sport and Social Issues*, 28, 2: 136–68.

Paechter, C. (2003) 'Power, bodies and identity: how different forms of physical education construct varying masculinities and femininities in secondary schools', *Sex Education: Sexuality, Society and Learning*, 3, 1: 47–59.

Parker, A. (1996) 'The construction of masculinity within boys' physical education', *Gender and Education*, 8, 2: 141–57.

Pilkington, N.W. and D'Augelli, A.R. (1995) 'Victimization of lesbian, gay, and bi-sexual; youth in community settings', *Journal of Community Psychology*, 23, 1: 33–56.

Pronger, B. (1990) *The Arena of Masculinity: Sports, Homosexuality and the Meaning of Sex*, New York: St Martin's Press.

Richardson, C. (2004) 'After school, clubs: queerbashing is a habit that is acquired in the playground but refined on the way home', *Guardian*, 15 November: 20.

Rivers, I. (1997) 'Lesbian, gay and bisexual development: theory, research and social issues', *Journal of Community and Applied Social Psychology*, 7, 5: 239–43.

Rivers, I. (2001a) 'The bullying of sexual minorities at school: its nature and long-term correlates', *Educational and Child Psychology*, 18, 1: 33–46.

Rivers, I. (2001b) 'Retrospective reports of school bullying: recall stability and its implications for research', *British Journal of Developmental Psychology*, 19, 1: 129–42.

Rivers, I. (2004) 'Recollections of bullying at school and their long-term implications for lesbians, gay men and bisexuals', *Crisis*, 25, 4: 169–75.

Rivers, I. and Duncan, N. (2002) 'Understanding homophobic bullying in schools: building a safe educational environment for all pupils', *Youth and Policy*, 75 (Spring): 30–41.

Rowe, N. (ed.) (2004) *Driving up Participation: The Challenge for Sport*, London: Sport England.

Ruskin, H. and Lammer, M. (eds) (2001) *Fair Play: Violence in Sport and Society*, Jerusalem: Cosell Centre for PE, Leisure and Health Promotion.

Sabo, D. and Panepinto, J. (1990) 'Football ritual and the social reproduction of masculinity', in M. Messner and D. Sabo (eds) *Sport, Men and the Gender Order: Critical Feminist Perspectives*, Champaign, IL: Human Kinetics.

Shire, J., Brackenridge, C.H. and Fuller, M. (2000) 'Changing positions: the sexual politics of a women's field hockey team', *Women in Sport and Physical Activity Journal*, 9, 1: 35–64.

Sparkes, A.C. (1994) 'Self, silence and invisibility as a beginning teacher: a life history of lesbian experience', *British Journal of Sociology of Education*, 15, 1: 93–118.

Sparkes, A.C. (1997) 'Ethnographic fiction and representing the absent other', *Sport Education and Society*, 2, 1: 25–40.

Squires, S.L. and Sparkes, A.C. (1996) 'Circles of silence: sexual identity in physical education and sport', *Sport, Education and Society*, 1, 1: 77–101.

Swain, J. (2000) '"The money's good, the fame's good, the girls are good": the role of playground football in the construction of young boys' masculinity in a junior school', *British Journal of Sociology of Education*, 21, 1: 95–110.

Sykes, H. (1998) 'Turning the closet inside/out: towards a queer-feminist theory in women's physical education', *Sociology of Sport Journal*, 15, 2: 154–73.

Theberge, N. (1995) 'Gender, sport and the construction of community: a case study from women's ice hockey', *Sociology of Sport Journal*, 12, 4: 389–402.

University of London (1997) *Playing it Safe*, London: University of London, Institute of Education.

Warren, H. (1984) *Talking about School*, London: London Gay Teenage Group.

Wendel, W., Toma, L. and Morphew, C. (2001) 'How much difference is too much difference? Perceptions of gay men and lesbians in intercollegiate athletics', *Journal of College Student Development*, 42, 5: 465–79.

Chapter 10

Challenging homophobia and heterosexism in sport

The promise of the Gay Games

Caroline Symons

Introduction

Gay Games founder, Dr Tom Waddell, considered the Gay Games to be an excellent vehicle for proving to mainstream society that gay people were just like everybody else: they played sport. He wanted to bring to the gay and lesbian communities of the world what he saw as the health-promoting powers of sport participation and the community building embodied in a charismatic event. He also wanted to dispel myths about gay men being un-masculine. After all, sports, especially those involving the demonstrations of strength, power, speed and combat, were excellent social practices to affirm one's masculinity as a male. But these sports were more usually developed within sites that acted as training grounds and celebratory public arenas for supremist forms of heterosexual masculinity. Sport has also become one of the most mediatised, consumed and naturalising social institutions 'for defining preferred and disparaged forms of masculinity and femininity, instructing boys and men in the "art" of making certain kinds of men' (Rowe and McKay 1998: 118). Homosexual men were definitely suspect in this macho sports world, and women were rendered the naturally inferior 'other'. Homophobia and heterosexism place significant constraints on the ways straight but especially gay, lesbian, bisexual, transgender and queer (GLBTQ) people engage in and seek pleasure, achievement and careers within the mainstream sporting arena. The international Gay Games were founded to provide a uniquely affirming environment for such sporting enjoyment and achievement. So, have these Games challenged the gender order and opened up different ways of experiencing gender, sexuality and sport?[1]

Gender, sexuality and sport

Sport is still considered one of the central shapers of masculinity in present-day Western society (Bryson 1987: 349–60; Connell 1987; Dunning 1986: 79–90; Duppert 1979; Hargreaves 1994; Messner and Sabo 1990; Nelson 1994; Pronger 1990). In a time when there are few opportunities to display and be rewarded for physical prowess, sport can be seen as one of the last bastions of traditional masculinity where men can prove themselves as 'real' or 'inferior' men and differentiate themselves from women. In fact, sport has become the main public and popular arena of bodily display, in which the complexities of sex, gender and sexuality are simplified and naturalised. It has become such a strong and lasting symbol of hegemonic masculinity because it 'literally embodies the seemingly natural superiority of men over women' (Rowe and McKay 1998: 118). This supposed superiority is translated into other sport and cultural arenas such as politics, business management and ownership, and mainstream media coverage. The gendering of sport also underlines the efforts sportswomen have had to make over the past century to secure even a measure of parity in sports facility and funding provisions, sponsorship, media coverage, sports management and institutional representation, in addition to their attempts to secure opportunities to participate (Hargreaves 1994). Sport has thus been marked out as the principal masculine preserve.

Sportswomen contest this gender ordering of sport through political activism and leadership in sports organisations, passionate participation, muscularisation and sheer athleticism. Women and men who question traditional gender expectations in society generally and in sport in particular, are often thought of as dangerous and in need of control. This is where homophobia and heterosexism can enter the picture.

Homophobia, heterosexism and sport

Homophobia refers to 'the fear of gays and lesbians and the hatred, disgust and prejudice that fear brings' (Canadian AIDS Society 1991: 65). The dominant view that heterosexuality is and should be the norm continues to be the organising principle of the gendering process. Accordingly, there can only be two dualistically related and natural sexes and genders, and one natural (heterosexual) and one deviant (homosexual) sexuality. Furthermore, women who are independent from men sexually, economically and socially are considered a threat to the gender order. Men who love, desire and have sex with other men, and/or act in 'effeminate' ways, also undermine hegemonic masculinity (Messner and Sabo 1994: 106–9). Homophobic beliefs are strong amongst young heterosexual males demonstrating their gender identity, when 'to behave like a man means not to behave like women' (Messner and Sabo 1994: 103). Indeed, some young men are so homophobic that they resort to physical violence and even murder to prove and revenge their masculinity (Mason and Tomsen 1997). Heterosexism is also maintained by force and violence. Recent research into the lives of same-sex-attracted Australian youth aged 14–22 indicates that this bullying and victimisation starts at a young age even in a comparatively tolerant society (Hillier et al. 1999: 12–15). Research into the experiences of gay, lesbian and bisexual youth in US schools reveals a similar picture. Rienzo et al. (1997: 20–5) found that such youth are at risk of a variety of health problems including higher rates of substance abuse, victimisation through verbal and physical harassment, isolation, alienation, leading to higher rates of low self-esteem, dropping out of school, depression and attempting and committing suicide.

Homophobic discrimination is a worldwide human rights issue. As Hargreaves so succinctly states: 'In all countries in the world lesbians and gay men face discrimination; in most countries they experience physical violence; and in some countries their lives are threatened by government policy and ideology' (Hargreaves 2001: 129). Discrimination based on the grounds of sexual orientation is not explicitly prohibited or even mentioned in any international treaty or standard adopted by the United Nations. Yet, in most Middle Eastern and African and some Asian countries punitive criminal sentences ranging from prison sentences to execution can be imposed on those caught engaging in homosexual relations.

The politics of homophobia and heterosexism are particularly pronounced in mainstream sport, which highlights and reinforces sexual difference and inequality, and especially hegemonic masculinity, in a number of ways. Most of the literature documenting these politics and the experiences of gay and lesbian sportspeople emanates from the US. However, there are some discernible patterns that are similar in practically all Western countries, including Australia. For example, the popular conception of the most masculine man as the team sport hero – strong, courageous, relatively wealthy and able to attract and have sex with many desirable young women – forms a dominant discourse (Messner and Sabo 1994: 36–42). In contrast to this is the popular stereotype of the effeminate, soft and swishy gay man. The gay male athlete contradicts these cultural myths and, as such, must be rendered invisible in order to maintain the dominant cultural discourses. Women are frequently marginalised in sport to produce the same effect and the fear of the 'lesbian label' is one of the favourite strategies used to achieve this. Transgendered people do not fit the neatly dualistic two-sexed model underpinning mainstream sport and are therefore frequently excluded outright from competition (Opie 2001; Skirstad 1999).

In general, homophobia creates a hostile environment for lesbian and gay sportspersons, especially at the elite and professional levels where the glare of the media and the opportunities for glory and financial rewards are greatest. There is the daily threat of stigma, ostracism and discrimination (Lenskyj 1991: 61–9). This hostile atmosphere can affect these athletes' performances, their general enjoyment of their sport, and their career prospects and financial returns. They may even be forced to drop out of their sport and most remain deeply closeted (Griffin 1998: 48; ESPN 1999). For example, as recently as 2002 there were no professional or international level male athletes playing the valorised team sports who were publicly 'out' as gay. By making their sexuality public, top athletes such as Martina Navratilova, Billie Jean King and David Kopay have lost lucrative endorsement and have suffered stigmatisation (Kopay and Young 1977; Navratilova with Vecsey 1985). There are no Australian Rules Football players or cricketers who have publicly revealed their homosexuality. The only known gay male professional team sportsman to 'come out' during his career was Australian Rugby League front-rower Ian Roberts. He found the closet far too destructive and publicly announced his homosexuality in 1995. This was during the last three years of his illustrious twelve-year sports career. Roberts appears to have managed this emergence carefully and reported few financial losses. His biography documents the widespread homophobia and misogyny of the rugby culture as well as the ongoing homophobic verbal and physical abuse that he received. This abuse mainly came from opposing supporters and young males out to prove themselves on the streets. Roberts recalls the conditional and sometimes respectful tolerance he received from some of the key players of his team. He has also received positive acclaim for his courage in being one of the only world-class male athletes to stand tall as a gay man (Freeman 1997). The first professional soccer player from the Netherlands to 'come out', albeit on retirement, had this to say about the homophobic and misogynistic world of this most celebrated and richest of men's sports:

> The soccer world is a heterosexual world. Macho behaviour and women predominate. Whenever soccer players are together they get vulgar, they talk about women and having sex. As a young boy I felt uncertain in that context. That's why I didn't want my fellow players to know it. Eight hours a day I passed. I couldn't do anything else.
> (Algemeen Dagblad, 25 February 1997: 17, quoted in Ellings 1998: 6)

This is telling, considering that the Netherlands is considered one of the most tolerant countries in the world for gay and lesbian people.

Gay men in mainstream sport

Woog (1998: xiv) suggests that the climate for individual gay male athletes within the US may not be as hostile as that experienced in team sports. Sociological research by Messner and Sabo (1994: 109–12) has demonstrated that male bonding required in teams involves a very close homosociability based significantly on the strong adherence to group values and norms, the exclusion of women, the denigration of the feminine and the homosexual and an underlying erotic bond between men in the team. The playing field is where boys and men can be obviously physically and emotionally affectionate to each other and they are often naked together in the locker room. Overt homophobia and locker room talk and practice that treats women as sex objects safely frames and deflects this homoeroticism. Some coaches are also known to use homophobia and sexism as a motivational and team-building tool (Messner and Sabo 1994: 108). This reinforces the already existent anti-gay feelings of the team and plays on the vulnerabilities of gender identity and sexual development of boys and young men. Messner and Sabo (1994: 47) also observe that it is through these sports practices, of denigration and expulsion of the feminine and the homosexual from within and without, that heterosexual masculinity is collectively constructed. Homophobia itself comes to be equated with 'true' masculinity.

It is understandable that gay men remain invisible in this hostile and potentially dangerous environment. Some closeted gay men engage in the most masculine of sports to prove their masculinity to themselves and conceal their secret from the world. Ian Roberts adopted this strategy for most of his rugby career. Gay Games founder and past US Olympian, Tom Waddell, used American Football and the gruelling decathlon as his closet during his 20s and early 30s. Fear of exposure can accentuate homophobic behaviour. In this masculine proving ground of close bodies, denial, fear and the public gaze it is not surprising that sports, particularly of the team varieties, are seen as one of the last acceptable, and even celebrated, realms of homophobic discrimination and abuse.

Lesbian women in mainstream sport

Compared with the main game of men's sport, homophobia and heterosexism have significantly different histories and effects for women. Following World War Two, the mannish lesbian athlete became a widespread stereotype in the US (Cahn 1993: 348; Griffin 1998). Women's sports advocates took up a defensive position of trying to prove women athletes' heterosexual appeal and success. Sport did provide an important haven for women who did not fit into the heterosexual ideal. This was especially so for many lesbians who found community, friendships, loving and sexual relationships within sports teams, as long as they kept their sexual orientation concealed from the public gaze. During the dangerous times of the 1950s and 1960s, lesbian athletes supported each other in these closeted circles and developed a code of silence that enabled survival. A history of women's sport in Australia that explores the politics of normative sexuality and the experiences of lesbian sportswomen is yet to be written.

The second-wave feminist movement of the 1970s promoted social and political changes that improved women's access to and acceptance in sport. The fitness boom of the 1980s also encouraged more women to take up sport and fitness. Title IX, legislated in the US Senate in 1972, was significant in opening up sports opportunities for girls and women (Griffin 1998: 41). Women's sport promotion programmes have also had positive results in Australia, Europe, Canada and England. It has become much more socially acceptable for women and girls in most Western countries to engage in all kinds of sport, and the athletic and mildly muscular look is certainly in vogue (Hargreaves 1994: 180–4).

Despite these social advances for women in sport and a greater social acceptance of lesbians in many Western societies, the use of the lesbian label to preserve traditional gender boundaries, control sportswomen and stigmatise lesbians is still a dominant practice. By being involved in the masculine territory of certain sports, particularly those emphasising strength, power and muscularity, women sports administrators, coaches and athletes of all sexual orientations have to continually prove their 'femininity' to be acceptable (Kolnes 1995). Lenskyj links these physical traits of hegemonic masculinity developed by sport with supposed masculine personality traits such as 'risk taking, dominance and aggression' (1992).

When sportswomen excel in these areas their minds and bodies can be changed resulting in an empowerment that, according to Lenskyj, could jeopardise 'the entire balance of power of the sexes' (1992). Kolnes (1995) suggests that within sport femininity acts as a code word for heterosexuality. Sportswomen emphasise their femininity to avoid being labelled butch or, even worse, a lesbian. Examples of emphasised femininity and heterosexual normalcy are numerous and include the makeup, feminine dress and deportment classes that have been a regular feature of a number of national women's sporting teams; the heterosexy calendars featuring individual and teams of sportswomen; and the emphasis in media coverage on the heterosexual relationships of sportswomen (Griffin 1998: 68–75; Lenskyj 1995: 47–60).

This fear of the 'lesbian label' is based on deep-seated prejudices and negative stereotypes. Griffin (1998: 57) outlines a number of these including the 'sexual predator' and the 'poor role model', both seen as especially dangerous for young female athletes. The myth of the lesbian as super-athlete, supposedly more masculine, extraordinarily strong, confident, competent and more aggressive than heterosexual sportswomen, was played out in the media coverage of the 1998 Australian Open Tennis Championships. During these championships the tabloid press and television sensationalised French tennis champion Amélie Mauresmo's lesbianism, linking it to masculine strength and predatory power on the court. This occurred in the headlines after Martina Hingis had likened Mauresmo to a half-man for having a girlfriend, and Lindsay Davenport had described her tennis contest with Mauresmo as being like playing against a man. If we contrast such sensational accounts with the positive and affirming attention that the media overly pays to the love interests and 'normal' domestic arrangements of heterosexual sportswomen, it becomes apparent who the good girls and the bogeywomen are (McKay 1991; Griffin 1998: 68–70; Kell 2000: 128–36). Such myth-making has been used to call into question the degree to which these outstanding sportswomen are 'real' women and suggests that heterosexual and, by implication, appropriately feminine sportswomen are naturally inferior in the realm of serious sport.

Conventional gender boundaries are also maintained in women's sport and controlled through the reinforcement of the myth that lesbians wield significant power and influence (Griffin 1998: 60–2). The media, general public and sport administrators' responses to cricketer Denise Annette's accusation that she had failed to gain selection for the Australian women's cricket team scheduled to tour New Zealand in 1995 on the grounds of her heterosexuality, illustrates this fabrication beautifully (Burroughs et al. 1995: 27–46). Prior to this 'scandal' Australian women's cricket received very limited media coverage even though the team had won many world cup victories. A media feeding frenzy and sanctimonious editorials ensued, with some of the country's leading newspapers calling for the sport to 'examine its conscience' and 'face up to prejudice charges'. Burroughs et al. (1995) convincingly argue that this widespread media attention was not only motivated by homophobia and male reporters' prurient fascination with lesbians but also a heterosexual backlash at the increasing visibility and demands for anti-discrimination and harassment-free work and sport environments of lesbians and gay men.

The cricketers that competed on this tour were besieged and harassed continually by the media to single out who was gay, and the whole of women's cricket underwent an inquiry into the charges of prejudice. A Code of Conduct was introduced which, among other things, aimed to 'eliminate the existence of any overtones of a homosexual culture that may exist in the sport' (Burroughs *et al.* 1995: 43).[2] Not one sports organisation came forth to defend the Australian Women's Cricket Council, not even the main advocate for women's sport: the Australian Sports Commission's Women and Sport Unit. Predictably, the Women in Sport Unit itself has been referred to as the 'Lesbian in Sport Unit' by male sports administrators (McKay 1997: 92–3). Lesbians are easy scapegoats for image issues and a variety of other perceived problems in women's sport.

Considering that most lesbian sportswomen, sports administrators and coaches, particularly at the elite level, are not public about their sexual orientation, it is interesting that they are seen to be so powerful in the sports world. When they are open, they are vulnerable to negative media coverage, negative stereotyping, actual discrimination and harassment, lack of understanding, support and respect from fellow athletes, coaches and managers, a potential if not real loss in financial rewards and greater vulnerability in their employment security. This is definitely not the position of the powerful and the specially privileged.

Sporting climates for lesbian and gay people

Griffin (1998: 92–107) identifies three main climates that permeate the cultural, institutional and competitive contexts for lesbians involved with 'mainstream' sport from school through to the professional level. These climates are not formalised, having developed out of everyday social practices, and their boundaries are previously constituted. The first and most difficult climate for lesbian sportswomen is characterised by hostility, discrimination and harassment. It is one in which lesbian participation in sport, whether their sexual identity is concealed or not, is considered a major and unwanted problem. To even be suspected of being a lesbian is dangerous in a hostile climate, and many lesbians have to not only conceal their significant life partners, lovers and general private lives but also put on elaborate performances to continually confirm their heterosexuality. Other researchers have also documented this hostile sports environment for lesbians within Canada, Australia, England and the Netherlands (Hargreaves 1994: 260–4; Squires and Sparkes 1996; Clarke 1999: 45–58; Lenskyj 1992: 19–33; McKay 1997; Hekma 1994). In countries with anti-discrimination laws that cover sexual orientation such as Australia, Scandinavia, the Netherlands, Germany, Canada and South Africa, in addition to some states of the US, blatant discrimination may not be as prevalent. Factors such as regionality and the religiosity of an area can also affect the level of hostility experienced by lesbians and gay men. The sports environment of gay men, especially in mainstream team sports, can also be characterised as hostile and sometimes downright dangerous.

The second climate for lesbian sportswomen identified by Griffin (1998: 93–103) is one characterised by conditional tolerance: 'it's all right if you are on the team, but please keep yourself invisible'. Sports organisations use this strategy particularly in their marketing practices of women's sport. Such collaborative denial means that heterosexual sportswomen do not really have to question the nature of systematic prejudice experienced by their lesbian team mates and this practice also places lesbians once again in the position of having to continually monitor their appearance and social relationships so as not to call attention to their sexual orientation. Choosing to remain in the closet is both an accommodating and a limiting strategy.

The most affirming climate for sporting lesbians and gay men is characterised by openness and inclusion. Coaches, administrators and players are welcoming of diversity in the sexual orientation of their athletes and colleagues. They are prepared to open up the dialogue concerning homophobia, understanding that prejudice can have a limiting effect on all participants and that positive leadership is necessary to ensure this process of openness and inclusion is effective. However, Griffin (1998: 103–6) notes that there are few open and inclusive climates in mainstream US sport. This appears to be the case in Australia as well. Most sport-related environments are hostile at worst or conditionally tolerant at best and, especially with women's sport, the more media-profile and image conscious a sport is, the less open and inclusive of lesbians it becomes. The most open and inclusive sports environments for lesbians and gay men are those created by gay people, and the international Gay Games is one such environment.

The Gay Games

The Gay Games were founded in 1982 on the principle of inclusivity. Inspired by the Olympics, but disillusioned by their apparent racism, sexism, nationalism, homophobia and elitism, Tom Waddell envisaged the Gay Games as people's games. They were open to all sexual orientations, genders, races, nationalities, ages, and abilities. The first Gay Games were held in San Francisco, organised by a small group of volunteers and involved 1,300 athletes, mainly from California and a few Western countries. These Games have grown over ten-fold, becoming the largest international queer event engaging people from practically all aspects of the diverse GLBTQ communities spanning the five continents of the world. Each Gay Games – San Francisco (1982, 1986), Vancouver (1990), New York (1994), Amsterdam (1998) and Sydney (2002) – has been organised, politicised and enlivened by the gay and lesbian community of the host city. An extensive and participatory cultural and social issues programme was added to the Gay Games during the 1990s. GLBTQ people could engage in their preferred sports, watch queer-themed and queer-performed plays, music recitals, dance performances, participate in human rights workshops and/or Queer Studies conferences, attend parties, gay and lesbian affirming ceremonies, film festivals and generally have the strong sense of being visible or even 'taking over' the host city and making it queer for the week of the Games (Symons 2002, 2003).

Research spanning the Vancouver, New York and Amsterdam Games strongly corroborates their positive social impact in reinforcing self and community identity and esteem amongst participants where many lesbians and gays could be publicly visible – a major contrast with the experiences of many gay and lesbian people within mainstream sports (Krane and Romont 1997; Krane and Barber 2001; Pronger 1990). They could more freely express themselves and their sporting passions without concern for heterosexist prejudice and could meet others with similar interests, all in an environment of inclusion, encouragement and celebration. This can be seen as marking a shift in gay liberation: from the 1970s concern about the politics of oppression to greater concern for the personal experience of being gay and of gay pride (Pronger 1990: 251). In a social psychological study of 125 lesbian and bisexual athletes competing in Gay Games V, respondents reported gaining strong personal and social identity and self and collective esteem from their Games involvement. They also revealed 'that following the Gay Games they felt more likely to work towards social change by becoming more out, educating others and working through political channels' (Krane and Barber 2001: 3). Such empowerment may challenge homophobia in sport and wider society at both personal and local political levels.

The first three Gay Games provided a catalyst and model for the development of gay and lesbian sports organisations within the US, Canada, Europe and Australia (Hargreaves 2001: 170; Symons 2003). City teams established to participate in the Games of the 1990s have sprung up throughout these countries. Gay and lesbian sports people can engage in their sport on a regular basis as well as participate with their queer team in mainstream sports competitions and leagues. The European Gay and Lesbian Sport Federation (EGLSF) was founded in 1989 and determines which European city will host the EuroGames, a gay and lesbian sport and cultural festival similar to the Gay Games and held every two years (Tent 1996). The EuroGames have been described as the largest event of the gay and lesbian community in Europe (Hargreaves 2001: 156). Whilst there is no co-ordinating national body within Australia, well-established city teams such as Team Sydney, Team Melbourne and Team Perth have been hosting an annual, multi-sport 'for all' festival named the Australia Gaymes since the late 1980s.

A logical follow-on to this increase in participation in gay and lesbian sport organisations and events at local, regional and national levels is the establishment of specific international gay and lesbian sport peak bodies and championships. Swimmers who had met at the first two Gay Games, and were keen to establish regular gay swimming championships within the US, organised their first meet in San Diego in 1987 and by Gay Games III the International Gay and Lesbian Aquatics (IGLA) had been officially formed (www.igla.org). Similarly, the Gay Games provided a catalyst for the formation of international gay and lesbian sports bodies and events in soccer, martial arts, bowling, figure skating and wrestling (Symons 2003). These queer sports bodies provide ongoing supportive, affirming and social environments for GLBTQ people. Furthermore, by taking part in gay sport, and especially in an event of the public magnitude of the Gay or EuroGames, a political statement is being made: that of 'coming out' and identifying publicly as gay, lesbian, queer in addition to 'coming in' to the lesbian and gay community. As Hargreaves (2001: 156) observes, this act of identification through gay sport 'ties the individual into a heroic community of resistance'. It is heroic in terms of defining selfhood and community in an affirming manner within a largely hostile and silencing world.

Many of these gay and lesbian sports organisations have also pursued direct political engagement with mainstream sports and government bodies to address issues of homophobic discrimination and harassment. For instance, EGLSF published its research into the discrimination experienced by European gay and lesbian sportspeople in the form of a black book and presented it at a symposium of the Council of Europe dedicated to addressing all forms of societal discrimination (EGLSF 1994). Thus, homophobic resistance within both sport and wider society is explicit and direct here.

Mainstreaming foundations

The founding Gay Games organisers were concerned with normalising gay and lesbian people through the arena of sport and sought legitimacy for the Games in a number of ways. All sports events were strongly encouraged to gain official sanctioning. There were opening and closing ceremonies based on similar traditions to the Olympics. The obvious presence of the drag and leather communities at these early Games was discouraged.[3] Many gay men in the trend-setting San Francisco of the late 1970s and early 1980s celebrated masculine style and this is where the macho clone originated (Segal 1990: 148–50). Negative stereotypes were supposedly discredited through playing sport, especially for gay men. In the promotional brochures of the first Gay Games, Waddell and Schaap (1996: 147) wrote: 'It is an opportunity to expand beyond a falsely tainted image. It is an opportunity to show that gay men and women, like all other responsible citizens of the United States, participate in the same ideal.'

The Co-Director of Sport for the first two Gay Games, Sara Lewinstein, was also concerned with the 'flamboyant' stereotype, particularly of drag queens. The Games for her were 'about people having a go at their sport. They are not a playground for dressing up, dressing weird, undressing' (Lewinstein interview, 1996). For most of these early organisers, displays of sex and gender-bending had no place at their 'healthy and wholesome' sports event. The early Gay Games certainly provided an open and affirming environment for gay and lesbian sports people and, as a result, contested the heterosexual hegemony of sport. However, a transformative sports model that questioned the very heteronormative basis of sport was not on the agenda.

Lesbians playing sport did not challenge any gender stereotypes. However, issues of power and representation within the organisational structure and the sports programme were more significant concerns for the leading women in the organising team of the first Gay Games. Community movers such as Lewinstein and Lindy McKnight were dedicated sportswomen who believed strongly in the liberal feminist ideals of access and equity in sport for women and their right to play any sport at any level (Lewinstein interview 1996; McKnight interview 1996). The Gay Games has provided a much more open and visible sporting environment for lesbians to express and explore their sporting and embodied gender identities and interests. Women with muscles, power, grace and agility who are competitive and/or pleasure seeking in their sporting embodiment are affirmed at the Gay Games. They have been able to enter practically the same number and types of sports as the men. Women have also been relatively well represented within the Boards of Management and the staffing of the Gay Games, and female and male co-chairing of the majority of organisational positions within the Gay Games movement has occurred since the first Games. The participation of women at the Gay Games has also been impressive, with most Games reaching around 40 per cent. The Games held in Amsterdam in 1998 made the most concerted effort to achieve gender parity, with women making up 42 per cent of participants, 41 per cent of the volunteers, 45 per cent of the paid staff and three of the eight principal managers of the Games (Van Leeuwen 1998: 49). However, men have still been the dominant force within the Games organisations, including the international overseeing body, the Federation of Gay Games (FGG), although, in comparison with the significant gender inequality within mainstream sports, this dominance has been muted.

Mainstreaming forces

Most of the founders of the Gay Games and subsequent Games organisers and Federation of Gay Games Directors were from professional, middle class and relatively mainstream political backgrounds. They were not from the radical feminist or gay liberation movements. It was important for them to stage an organisationally efficient Games involving sports competitions that were based on recognised official rules and procedures. Official sanctioning was considered vital in legitimating the event to the sporting lesbians and gay men that were expected to attend the Games.

Having sports competitions that were codified and played in a very similar fashion across the world is a practicality that all national and international multi-sports events have to consider in their programming. Furthermore, sanctioning 'proves that lesbian and gay sports are conducted in strict accordance with the norms of sport' (Pronger 2000: 232). This in turn provides legitimation within the wider society in which the Games are held. Bridges of co-operation and understanding can be built with mainstream civic and sporting authorities and homophobia can be reduced. The city government of San Francisco was a strong and visible backer of the first Gay Games. Republican mayor Rudi Giuliani used his political clout to secure the Yankee stadium for the closing ceremony of Gay Games IV in New York after Games organisers had experienced homophobic treatment from the manager of this famous citadel of sport (Quarto interview 1996). Amsterdam City Council sponsored Gay Games V with over a million US dollars and welcomed Games participants to the 'gay way of Europe' with these words:

> Besides being a great sport and cultural event, the Gay Games 1998 are even more so an opportunity for gays and lesbians from all over the world to make new friends and to be visible, in a world that too often does not want to acknowledge gays and lesbians in their societies. During the Gay Games 1998 you can show the world that gays and lesbians are part of our communities in all countries of the world and that you are here to stay.[4]

Government authorities within Amsterdam and the Netherlands more widely, publicly and financially supported the efforts of these Gay Games to promote the human rights of lesbians and gays and to address homophobia within society.

The success of large multi-sports events like the Gay Games rests on the financial and political backing they receive (Hargreaves 2001: 163). Holding the Gay Games in cities with gay and lesbian communities that have led the world in the securing of gay and lesbian rights have facilitated high levels of visibility and politicisation, which have, in turn, been important in the securing of sanctioning by sports and civic organisations essential to the organisation of the Games. This is all part of playing the mainstream game. The relatively small scale of the first Games made it possible for greater programme innovation but by the 1990s the Games had attracted over 12,000 sports participants from all over the world. Assistance from mainstream sports bodies in the staging of over 28 sports events and the following of globally recognisable competition formats makes practical sense in these circumstances.

The numerous instances of homophobic discrimination faced by organisers of an event specifically for GLBTQ people also encouraged efforts to legitimise the Gay Games. There was an infamous legal battle between the United States Olympic Committee (USOC) and the first Gay Games organisers over the use of the original title Gay Olympic Games. This title was justified by San Francisco Arts and Athletics (SFAA) thus: 'The word Olympic was no doubt chosen to foster a wholesome normal image of homosexuals. Denying SFAA use of the word thwarts that purpose' (SFAA 1986). The USOC under US federal law had monopoly use of this apparently 'sacred' and certainly commercially lucrative word. They chose to exercise this right for the first time when the gay community wanted to stage their Olympics although the USOC had not previously objected to a variety of other events using this term.[5] Gays were deemed an unsuitable group and the USOC feared that their Olympic association could jeopardise the budget of the official Olympics to be held in Los Angeles in 1984 (Primavera 1982). A year before Gay Games III, held in Vancouver in 1990, an extensive and graphically homophobic public scare campaign was launched by Christian fundamentalists based in British Columbia (Vancouver Sun 1989).

In comparison to similar multi-sport and cultural events held in the region, government funding for Gay Games III was also minimal and given reluctantly (Brunt 1990: 4). Organisers of the Sydney Gay Games appear to have experienced similar funding and political difficulties at state and federal government levels. With the exception of Amsterdam, securing major sponsorship has been a significant challenge. Organisers have also experienced barriers to the hiring of sports facilities and lack of co-operation from some mainstream sports bodies. These challenges have added an extra dimension to the already huge and complex feat of staging a large multi-sport and cultural event like the Gay Games. Moreover, the challenges are telling in a more global context considering that the staging of all Gay Games has occurred in cosmopolitan cities renowned for their social tolerance and basic legal protection of gay and lesbian people, indicating that courageous and concerted effort is required to resist or overcome the widespread homophobia and heterosexual hegemony within even these tolerant societies.

Gay Games as an alternative games

Whilst the Gay Games have sought to mainstream the gay and lesbian community, they were also envisaged and organised as a progressive alternative to the hyper-competitive, commercialised and elitist traditions dominant in the most celebrated mainstream sports. Organisers valued sport participation because it gave a focus to people's lives, an opportunity to meet others and form friendships as well as provide validation and an avenue for personal achievement. These early organisers were concerned with breaking down some of the segregations and prejudices alive within the gay and lesbian community of the time. Sport that emphasised inclusiveness and participation instead of winning was considered an excellent medium to achieve this. The nationalism and chauvinism that often accompany major sports events were to be muted at the Gay Games through a number of strategies. Participants were to represent their cities of origin rather than their country. Medal tallies and Games records of athletic feats were not collected or displayed. Medal ceremonies emphasised individual effort rather than national pride and success. The Games organisers recast competition itself. In the following passage, Waddell captures the philosophy of participation and friendly competition that was continually promoted:

> You don't win by beating someone else. We defined winning as doing your very best. That way, everyone is a winner … I don't know that it's possible that this kind of attitude will prevail. It's revolutionary. And it's certainly not what the NFL owners or the United States Olympic Committee wants to hear, where winning is essential.
>
> (Waddell and Schaap 1996: 126)

According to this philosophy, competition and winning is not about the triumph, the 'domination', the beating of one's opponents and exulting in this victory. Emphasis is placed on the 'healthy' challenges and self-fulfilment achievable through sport, where one tries to better oneself and to 'realise their full potential'. The relationship of competitors becomes one of mutual striving in a friendly atmosphere, the performance of one spurring on and enhancing the other. This humanistic approach to sport participation originated within the counter-cultural ferment occurring in California during the 1960s and 1970s. There was a general rejection of the competitive and bureaucratic values of capitalism made by the New Left and the traditional values of competitive sport were also challenged and Waddell referred to his direct experience of this whilst training during the 1970s with Californian radical sports psychologist, sociologist and therapist, Jack Scott (1971).

Diversity, inclusion and challenges to homophobia

The three guiding principles that came out of the first Gay Games, inclusion, participation and doing one's personal best, were brought to life through a number of avenues. The Games were structured to accommodate a number of differences within the diverse gay and lesbian community. This included age-group categories along the line of masters sports events. Outreach committees were active in recruiting participants from minority ethnic and racial groups as well as women. Policies and practices enabling and promoting inclusion were extended at each subsequent Gay Games. Gay Games II, held in San Francisco during the height of the AIDS crisis in 1986, welcomed and enabled the participation of people living with HIV and AIDS. The Executive Director of Gay Games II, Shawn Kelly (1996), saw important opportunities to promote self-esteem and healthy lifestyles (including one of the first safe sex campaigns) through sport and cultural participation. Gary Reese, a Texas-based writer, academic and cyclist at Gay Games III and IV, described the Games as a 'rare chance' to simultaneously celebrate lives and mourn those who had died:

> For once I did not feel the push–pull of trying to do one without the other, as if we have to isolate AIDS and everything it means to us before we can begin to feel good about ourselves and our future.
>
> (Reese 1994: 78–9)

Thus the Games have provided a means to publicly affirm the survival, endurance and multi-faceted nature of their participating communities.

Up until the 1990s the Gay Games had drawn participants primarily from the US, especially California. They had definitely gone global by the New York Gay Games in 1994 and the diversity of the gay, lesbian and queer community was well represented at these Games. Difference politics was a significant force, and groups that played with/transgressed gender norms such as drag queens, radical transfolk and butch dykes were an integral part of the Games week's sport, cultural and political events (Labrecque 1994). A comprehensive policy enabling the participation of differently-abled people within the sport and cultural programmes was operational at these Games. The first transgender participation policy for a major sports event was also in place (Gay Games IV and Cultural Festival 1994: 7–8). The Gender Policy of the Sydney 2002 Gay Games radically defined sex/gender as a social identity, opening the way for indigenous transfolk with different cultural, economic and medical understandings and embodiments of sex/gender to the dominant Western model (Australian National Olympic Committee 2002).

By the Amsterdam Gay Games, policies and practices promoting the inclusion of participants of different ages, genders, sporting and cultural abilities, HIV status, ethnicities, nationalities and so on were very well developed. Furthermore, an extensive Social Issues programme had been developed involving a variety of conferences, workshops and meetings focusing on the sharing of stories, political theories, strategies and community development models that addressed homophobic discrimination, violence and harassment from a global perspective (Gay Games Amsterdam 1998). Many delegates from developing nations and Eastern European countries participated in this programme, their attendance enabled by a targeted and funded Outreach programme (Sydney Gay Games 1998). Thus challenges to homophobia were facilitated and promoted from a local and global perspective.

By the diversity-sensitive 1990s, the centrality of readily recognisable sports, the variety of sports played and the inclusive and participation-based Games spirit allowed for the involvement of diverse sporting communities and cultures. Through archival research, interviews and observation this diversity was investigated and the presence of athletic dedication, traditional masculine sporting cultures and involvement by beginner and recreational sports participants who valued the social and fitness aspects was found (Symons 2003). This research also revealed sports clubs that promoted supportive, inclusive, playful and politically-informed sports cultures; sports events that combined the serious and highly competitive with playful camp culture; lesbian feminist-informed sports cultures; gender conservative and gender transgressive sports performances; sports events highlighting the sensual and sexy along with more traditional sports outcomes, and sports events that resembled any other in the mainstream.

For instance, after five serious days of competition in the pool, swimmers engage in the high camp Pink Flamingo relay. This event started as a drag performance and relay involving the carrying of a tacky pink flamingo as a baton and has become more elaborate with each Gay Games (Symons 2002). Same-sex pairs ice danced together for the first time ever at the unsanctioned figure-skating competition in New York. Sanctioning was not sought because organisers knew that the International Skating Union (ISU) would object strongly to sports performances that did not reinforce heterosexuality (Labrecque 1994). Direct political statements were made by some of these skaters, in particular the male couple dressed in military uniform with black tape across their mouths (Labrecque 1994). Organisers at the Amsterdam Games had their plans of a sanctioned competition destroyed at the last minute when the ISU threatened to ban all licensed skaters from mainstream competition if they participated in the gender and sexually transgressive Gay Games event (Amsterdam Gay Games 1998: 3). The ISU still insisted that pairs should only comprise a man and a woman and that gender-appropriate dress should be worn. The spirit of the Games was well demonstrated at the ensuing exhibition ice-dancing event, where the capacity audience cheered all skaters during their performances and at the mass participatory medal ceremony (Amsterdam Gay Games 1998: 3). Five of the fifteen netball teams participating in the Sydney 2002 Gay Games were composed of transgender women. The heteronormative basis of sport was certainly challenged in all of these examples of sporting cultures and practices at the Gay Games.

From an interview with a member of the London-based Hackney women's soccer team that competed in New York, it became apparent that a variety of sports clubs and cultures made up the large pool of women's soccer teams in this Gay Games tournament (Heather interview 1996). Some teams were very competitive, others were more social and pleasure oriented. Hackney was the first 'out' lesbian soccer team in the local London league. The club was organised on lesbian feminist collective principles. The majority of decisions within the club were made by consensus involving all club members, there were very few appointed positions, and these were mainly in place to satisfy the constitutional and reporting requirements of the 'mainstream' league. These collective principles were expressed in a number of ways, including the spirit of play, the emphasis on encouraging the involvement of women from all skill levels, concentrating on positive achievements rather than denigrating poor performance, emphasising the process and pleasure of the game rather than the outcome, and advocating equal opportunity policies and practices that recognised economic, racial and sexual minority disadvantage within the club as well as the league. There are also similar lesbian sports teams, leagues and events in Australia, North America and Europe where heterosexist sports traditions are directly overturned by lesbian feminist sports cultures and practices.

Chess, bridge and darts were added to the Amsterdam sports programme for the less athletic, as well as those experiencing illness. Many of those interviewed remarked on the encouraging sports environment that they had been part of at the Games. For example, people were cheered whether they were coming first or last in swimming or running events. No official Games records have been kept as benchmarks of achievement. Conversely, as the Games have increased in size and stature, more elite performers and competitive motivations have come to the fore. Gay and lesbian elite athletes can also enjoy an affirming environment, which is quite unique in the sports world. The participation of world champions and the breaking of international masters sport records are valued for increasing Games visibility and promoting credibility. There have been undercurrents of opinion within the FGG expressing support for regional championships and qualifying standards but those involved, especially with the organising of the first two Gay Games, have been directly opposed to any dilution of the 'sport for all' Games philosophy.

Conclusion

Considering the diverse communities participating in the Gay Games, and their different interests and political perspectives especially concerning the organisation and engagement with sport and leisure, tensions and conflicts are endemic and ongoing. To enable this diversity and to mainstream the Gay Games as a legitimate sport and cultural mega-event with mass understanding and appeal, Gay Games organisers and participants have pursued a liberal democratic model of reformist sport. Internationally familiar, codified, officiated and hence sanctioned, sports provide a common language within this arena of international diversity. Some of the most progressive and inclusive policies and practices promote this diverse participation in the sport and cultural programmes of the Gay Games, especially so for people of different sexualities, sex/genders and gender styles. In an intransigent homophobic and heterosexist world, the staging of the Gay Games, the implementation of progressive participation policies, and the development of an extensive international gay and lesbian sports movement are significant achievements. Their inclusiveness, affirmation of GLBTQ sport and culture, public visibility, and mainstream sport and government support make them a significant challenge to entrenched homophobia, at least within the host city and its sports culture.

The Gay Games have also provided an important catalyst for the growth of the international gay and lesbian sports movement and have challenged homophobia at personal and community levels. However this challenge may not be all it seems. Whilst enjoying sport in an open, friendly and supportive environment free of heterosexism and homophobia is vital, the gay and lesbian sports club may be a ghettoised space that creates further barriers between gay and straight people. The latter hardly have to address their own homophobic beliefs and practices unless some form of awareness and integration is also pursued. Notwithstanding this concern, the Gay Games have and continue to challenge homophobia and heterosexism in many important ways.

Notes

1 The Gay Games is the largest international GLBTQ event, and whilst participants come from all corners of the globe, the majority come from North America, Europe and Australia. Most of the research on the experiences of gay and lesbian sports people has come from these Western countries and this chapter will encompass some of this material. The diversity of sexuality and gender systems within the world and their relation to sport requires more research and is beyond the scope of this chapter.

2 The official report was entitled 'A Fair Go': Report of the Special Working Group Investigating Behaviour and Conduct in Australian Women's Cricket to the Australian Women's Cricket Council, 30 April 1995.

3 Such discouragement was evident from in-depth interviews of Gay Games organizers and participants conducted from October to December 1996, and November to December 1997 as part of my doctoral research.
4 This letter was distributed to all participants in their registration 'showbag'.
5 For instance, the Armchair Olympics, Armenian Olympics, Special Olympics, Handicapped Olympics, Police Olympics, Dog Olympics, Xerox Olympics, Diaper Olympics, Rat Olympics and Crab Cooking Olympics, all events held within the US during the 1970s and early 1980s (Waddell and Schaap 1996: 150–1).

References

Amsterdam Gay Games (1998) 'Melting the ice with a hot double axle', *Daily Friendship*, No. 6. Friday 7 August: 3.
Australian National Olympic Committee (2002) *Gender Policy*, Sydney: Australia National Olympic Committee.
Brunt, S. (1990) 'In the gay '90s, the name of the Games is pride', *Globe and Mail*, 4 August.
Bryson, L. (1987) 'Sport and the maintenance of masculine hegemony', *Women's Studies International Forum*, 10, 3: 349–60.
Burroughs, A., Seebohn, S. and Ashburn, L. (1995) '"A leso story": a case study of Australian women's cricket', *Sporting Traditions*, November: 27–46.
Cahn, S. K. (1993) 'From the "Muscle Moll" to the "Butch" ballplayer: mannishness, lesbianism and homophobia in U.S. women's sport', *Feminist Studies*, 19, 2: 348–54.
Canadian AIDS Society (1991) *Homophobia, Heterosexism and AIDS*, Ottowa: Canadian AIDS Society.
Clarke, G. (1999) 'Outlaws in sport and education? Exploring the sporting and education experiences of lesbian physical education teachers', in L. Lawrence, E. Murdoch and S. Parker (eds) *Professional and Development Issues in Leisure, Sport and Education*, Eastbourne: Leisure Studies Association.
Connell, B. (1987) *Gender and Power: Society, the Person and Sexual Politics*, Stanford, CA: Stanford University Press.
Dunning, E. (1986) 'Sport as a male preserve', *Theory, Culture and Society*, 3, 1: 79–90.
Duppert, J. (1979) *A Man's Place: Masculinity in Transition*, Englewood Cliffs, NJ: Prentice Hall.
Ellings, A. (1998) 'Integration through "regular" and "queer" sports: a critical reflection on can the Gay Games "change the world"?', paper presented at Queer Games? Theories, Politics, Sports', Amsterdam, 29–31 July.
ESPN (1998) *The Life of the Gay Athlete*, Television Documentary.
European Gay and Lesbian Sport Federation (1994) *Fair Play, Tolerance and Safety in Sports for Everyone*, Amsterdam: EGLSF.
Freeman, P. (1997) *Ian Roberts, Finding Out*, Australia: Random House.
Gay Games IV and Cultural Festival (1994) *Athlete Registration Book*, New York.
Gay Games Amsterdam (1998) *Sports, Culture, Festivals, Events, Exhibitions*, Official Programme.
Griffin, P. (1998) *Strong Women, Deep Closets: Lesbians and Homophobia in Sport*, Champaign, IL: Human Kinetics.
Hargreaves, J. (1994) *Sporting Females: Critical Issues in the History and Sociology of Women's Sport*, London: Routledge.

Hargreaves, J. (2001) *Heroines of Sport: the Politics of Difference and Identity*, London: Routledge.

Hekma, G. (1994) *Al ze maar niet provoceren. Discriminatie van homoseksuele mannen en lesbische vrouwen in de georganiseerde sport*, Amsterdam: Het Spinhuis.

Hillier, L., Harrison, L. and Dempsey, D. (1999) 'Stories of life on the wild side: same sex attracted young people document their lives', *Journal of the Health Education Association*, Summer: 12–15.

Kell, P. (2000) *Good Sports. Australian Sport and the Myth of the Fair Go*, Annandale, NSW: Pluto Press.

Kolnes, L. (1995) 'Heterosexuality as an organizing principle in women's sport', *International Review for the Sociology of Sport*, 30, 1: 61–80.

Kopay, D. and Young, P. (1977) *The David Kopay Story: An Extraordinary Self-revelation*, New York: Arbor House.

Krane, V. and Barber, H. (2000) 'Social psychological benefits of Gay Games participants: a social identity theory explanation', unpublished paper.

Krane, V. and Barber, H. (2001) *Defining Lesbian Experience in Sport: A Social Identity Perspective*, The Institute for Research on Women and Gender Working Papers No. 52, Michigan: University of Michigan.

Krane, V. and Romont, L. (1997) 'Female athletes' motives and experiences at the Gay Games', *Journal of Gay, Lesbian and Bisexual Identities*, 2, 1: 123–38.

Labrecque, L. (ed.) (1994) *Unity. A Celebration of Gay Games IV and Stonewall*, San Francisco, CA: Labrecque Publishing.

Lenskyj, H. (1991) 'Combating homophobia in sport and physical education', *Sociology of Sport Journal*, 8, 1: 61–9.

Lenskyj, H. (1992) 'Unsafe at home base: women's experiences of sexual harassment in university sport and physical education', *Women in Sport and Physical Activity Journal*, 1, 1: 19–33.

Lenskyj, H. (1995) 'Sport and the threat to gender boundaries', *Sporting Traditions*, 12, 1: 47–61.

Mason, G. and Tomsen, S. (eds) (1997) *Homophobic Violence*, Sydney: Hawkins Press, Australian Institute of Criminology.

McKay, J. (1991) *No Pain, No Gain: Sport and Australian Culture*, Sydney: Prentice Hall.

McKay, J. (1997) *Managing Gender. Affirmative Action and Organisational Power in Australian, Canadian, and New Zealand Sport*, New York: State University of New York Press.

Messner, M. and Sabo, D. (eds) (1990) *Sport, Men and the Gender Order: Critical Feminist Perspectives*, Champaign, IL: Human Kinetics Books.

Messner, M. and Sabo, D. (eds) (1994) *Sex, Violence and Power in Sport*, Freedom, CA: Crossing Press.

Navratilova, M. with Vecsey, G. (1985) *Martina*, New York: Knopf.

Nelson, M. (1994) *The Stronger Women Get, The More Men Love Football: Sexism in the American Culture of Sports*, New York: Harcourt Brace.

Opie, H. (2001) 'Medico-legal issues in sport: the view from the grandstand', *Sydney Law Review*, 23, 3: 375–404.

Primavera, R. (1982) Press Release, SFAA, 'Gay Games Determined to Appeal Federal District Court Decision', 21 August, Archived in San Francisco Public Library, Gay Games Archive, Box 1, Series 1, Gay Games I, Folder 1.

Pronger, B. (1990) *The Arena of Masculinity: Sport, Homosexuality and the Meaning of Sex*, Toronto: University of Toronto Press.

Pronger, B. (2000) 'Homosexuality and sport: who's winning?', in J. McKay, M. Messner and D. Sabo (eds) *Masculinities, Gender Relations and Sport*, London: Sage.

Reese, G. (1994) 'Synchronicity at the Games: athletes, HIV, and disabilities', in L. Labrecque (ed.) *Unity. A Celebration of Gay Games IV and Stonewall*, San Francisco, CA: Labrecque Publishing.

Rienzo, B., Button, J. and Wald, K. (1997) 'School-based programs addressing gay/lesbian/ bisexual youth issues', *Journal of the International Council for Health, Physical Education, Recreation, Sport and Dance*, Winter: 20–5.

Rowe, D. and McKay, J. (1998) 'Sport: still a man's game', *Journal of Interdisciplinary Gender Studies*, 3, 2: 113–28.

San Francisco Arts and Athletics (1986) Petition for Rehearing and Suggestions for Rehearing En Banc, filed 22 March 1986.

Segal, L. (1990) *Slow Motion: Changing Masculinities, Changing Men*, London: Virago Press.

Skirstad, B. (1999) 'Gender verification in competitive sport: turning from research to action', in T. Tannsjo and C. Tamurrini (eds) *Values in Sport. Elitism, Nationalism, Gender Equity and the Scientific Manufacture of Winners*, London: E & FN Spon.

Squires, S. and Sparkes, A. (1996) 'Circles of silence: sexual identity in physical education and sport', *Sport Education and Society*, 1, 1: 77–102.

Sydney Gay Games (1998) *Outreach Report*, presented at the Annual General Meeting of the FGG, Seattle, WA, 17 November 1998.

Symons, C (2002) 'Gay Games: what's the Olympics got to do with them?', paper presented at the International Queer Studies Conference: *Out From the Centre*, Newcastle, Australia, October.

Symons, C. (2003) 'Gay Games: the play of sexuality, sport and community', unpublished doctoral dissertation, Melbourne: Victoria University.

Tent, M. (1996) *Development of Organised Sport for Gays and Lesbians in Europe between 1982 and 1995*, Frankfurt: EGLSF.

Vancouver Sun (1989) 'Time is running out', 5 November.

Van Leeuwen, I. (1998) *Gay Games Amsterdam 1998: Equal Gay and Lesbian Event? The Efforts of the Feminine Politics*, Amsterdam: Gay Games Amsterdam.

Waddell, T. and Schaap, D. (1996) *Gay Olympian: The Life and Death of Dr Tom Waddell*, New York: Alfred Knopf.

Woog, D. (1998) *Jocks: True Stories of America's Gay Male Athletes*, Los Angeles, CA: Alyson Books.

Interviews/conversations

Shawn Kelly, San Francisco, 1996.
Sara Lewenstein, San Francisco, 1996.
Lindy McKnight, San Francisco, 1996.
Roz Quarto, New York, 1996.
Heather, London, 1996.

Index

CPSIA information can be obtained at www.ICGtesting.com
Printed in the USA
LVOW07s0521260713

344298LV00002B/23/P